CRITICAL INSIGHTS

Stephen King

CRITICAL INSIGHTS

Stephen King

Editor
Gary Hoppenstand
Michigan State University

Salem Press
Pasadena, California   Hackensack, New Jersey

Cover photo: Kevin Winter/AP/Wide World Photos

Published by Salem Press

© 2011 by EBSCO Publishing
Editor's text © 2011 by Gary Hoppenstand
"The *Paris Review* Perspective" © 2011 by Nathaniel Rich for *The Paris Review*

∞ The paper used in these volumes conforms to the American National Standard for Permanence of Paper for Printed Library Materials, Z39.48-1992 (R1997).

Library of Congress Cataloging-in-Publication Data
Stephen King / editor, Gary Hoppenstand.
      p. cm. — (Critical insights)
   Includes bibliographical references and index.
   ISBN 978-1-58765-685-9 (vol. 1 : alk. paper)
   1. King, Stephen, 1947- —Criticism and interpretation. I. Hoppenstand, Gary.
   PS3561.I483Z8785 2011
   813'.54—dc22

                                                                    2010030135

PRINTED IN CANADA

Contents_____

Resources

About This Volume

Gary Hoppenstand

Probably more has been published about Stephen King over the past several decades than about any other contemporary best-selling author, a fact that presented something of a challenge for me in preparing the material for this collection. My main concern was how best to present a volume of criticism to an audience that is, no doubt, well aware of King's very public reputation as a renowned author (and many members of which also probably have read King's work more for pleasure than for enlightenment, though there is absolutely nothing wrong with this motivation).

My decisions, then, to include the essays finally selected for this volume were determined by what I considered to be the best balance of criticism written about King's creative efforts. My experience with reading the vast amount of writings published about Stephen King led me to see that this material falls into two main categories. The first of these categories can perhaps best be described as fan criticism, which is understandable because King enjoys a large fan following. The strength of fan writing is its attention to the details of King's work and its enthusiasm in recognizing King's skills as a storyteller. Conversely, the drawback to fan criticism is similar to the problems that many (but not all) types of fan commentary suffer because of their lack of objectivity and their occasional tendency to be blinded by the celebrity of the author himself.

The second category of King criticism that I have read—the scholarly or academic criticism—is somewhat more problematic in that it typically (but not always) presumes that a writer who is both prolific and popular by definition must somehow be artistically inferior. Both approaches, I believe, are wrongheaded and fail to accomplish what good literary criticism should accomplish: the illumination of how a particular writer's fiction works to communicate to an audience and how this audience is rewarded for the time and effort invested in the author.

Thus this volume includes a number of essays that speak, in a balanced way, to King's life and contributions to the field of literature as well as to the cultural and literary influences that inspired King. In addition, the volume features some of the finest articles that have been published in other venues that examine the more sophisticated elements of Stephen King's work. Perhaps you might discover while you read these essays (as I have) that popularity and the ability to entertain are not exclusive of literary quality or of an artist's ability to speak to a reader's soul.

CAREER, LIFE, AND INFLUENCE

On Stephen King_____

Gary Hoppenstand

At the time that Stephen King began his professional writing career, the literary horror genre in America was undergoing an important transformation. Before King, from the 1920s through the 1960s, writers of pulp fiction dominated the horror-story genre. In particular, authors such as H. P. Lovecraft, Clark Ashton Smith, and Robert Bloch, who appeared in pulp magazines such as *Weird Tales*, enjoyed limited popularity with young readers, all the while lingering in a ghetto of hostile literary criticism and enduring the scorn of many critics who viewed the pulp genre as subliterate or adolescent and undeserving of serious attention.

This negative critical reception began to change dramatically in America in the 1950s, 1960s, and early 1970s with the work of five best-selling authors: Shirley Jackson, Ira Levin, Tom Tryon, William Peter Blatty, and Stephen King. What these five writers accomplished was the transmutation of the horror story from the pulp magazine to the national paperback best seller, thus subsequently shifting the demographics of the pulp adolescent readership to an adult readership.

Stephen King's work has been, arguably, the most important bridge between the horror genre and literary respectability from the late 1960s and 1970s up to the present time. Learning his craft by writing for so-called men's magazines such as *Penthouse* and *Cavalier* (which were among some of the better paying short-story markets of the time), he honed a number of his literary skills as a fledgling writing that would later serve him well as he became an internationally known and prolific author of best-selling novels. A number of these early short stories, which were reprinted in the 1978 short-story collection *Night Shift*, drew their inspiration from pulp-magazine sources, but early on King began to develop a voice that was uniquely his own and that would eventually earn him wide notoriety as an award-winning author.

King's breakthrough came with the publication of his novel *Carrie* in 1974. Having been paid a modest advance of twenty-five hundred dollars for the book's hardcover publication, he then received the then-astonishing sum of four hundred thousand dollars for the paperback rights, which gave him the financial freedom that he needed to become a full-time writer. With the 1976 release of director Brian De Palma's film adaptation of the novel, starring Sissy Spacek as the socially inept and persecuted girl who harbors a tremendously destructive telekinetic power, King recruited a widespread readership, previously unheard of for an author of lowly horror fiction. Quickly following the publication of *Carrie* were *'Salem's Lot* in 1975, and *The Shining* in 1977, each novel solidifying and widening King's audience, especially among younger readers.

What made *Carrie* such a popular story was the author's ability to connect with the anxieties and apprehensions of an adolescent in a hostile or indifferent world. King related to young people, especially young people who, like Carrie White, are tormented and persecuted by their peers because they are different; young readers, in turn, responded enthusiastically to King's insight. The young, persecuted protagonist became a staple in a number of King's subsequent short stories and novels, such as *The Shining*, which tells the story of a haunted house (or, in this case, a haunted hotel in Colorado called the Overlook) that attempts to possess a young boy named Danny Torrance and his powerful psychic powers by manipulating his abusive, alcoholic father, Jack, into killing him.

As seen in *The Shining* and in a number of King's other early novels such as *'Salem's Lot*, true evil lies not in the monsters found in the plot but in the human characters, who themselves behave like monsters with each other, exhibiting the worst sort of violent, greedy, or abusive behavior. King employs the supernatural in these stories as a narrative device that allows him to explore the darkest corners of the human condition, and this sophisticated ability to develop and define character quickly differentiated his work from the formulaic thud-and-blunder fare of his pulp-fiction predecessors.

When King's novel *The Stand* was released in 1978, he had begun a new phase of his literary career, one that would elevate his writing to the upper ranks of serious, imaginative fiction. Publishing what was to be the first truly epic horror story, King presented a massive narrative that related an apocalyptic tale of the near destruction of civilization by an artificially created flu virus. The virus all but wipes out humanity, thus setting the stage for a final confrontation between the two groups of survivors, one representing good and the other evil, for the ultimate fate of the world. What King attempted and successfully accomplished was to write the horror-novel equivalent of J. R. R. Tolkien's *The Lord of the Rings*, an expansive adventure featuring numerous and complex characters and enacting the most fundamental conflict between good and evil on the grandest possible scale.

Not satisfied with writing one such epic narrative, King published others, including the 1986 novel *It* (which won the British Fantasy Award in 1987), a coming-of-age story about a group of children who battle a cosmic evil both as adolescents and as adults, and his 2009 novel *Under the Dome*, which has been described by reviewers as King's colossal reworking of William Golding's *Lord of the Flies* (1954).

But Stephen King's greatest achievement as an epic writer of imaginative fiction (even by his own standards) is his *Dark Tower* series. Begun humbly enough as a group of interconnected short stories published between 1977 and 1981 in *The Magazine of Fantasy and Science Fiction*, these tales feature a mysterious gunslinger named Roland who travels the wasteland of a world similar to Earth (but not Earth) in search of a person called "the man in black." From this modest start, King embarked on the construction of a massive seven-volume series, the publication of which spanned several decades, which followed the trials and ordeals of Roland in his quest to locate the Dark Tower. What King produced with this series was a literary achievement of world building that has few, if any, equals in the realm of contemporary speculative fiction.

Yet King's success as a prolific and critically respected writer of genre fiction has not limited his imagination. He has worked extensively in film, writing screenplays, many of which are based on his own fiction, and tried his hand (somewhat unsuccessfully) as a director with the 1986 film *Maximum Overdrive*. He has made cameos in a number of films based on his novels. In addition, the electronic distribution of a selection of his stories has made him a leading supporter of electronic publishing, even as he has supported the publication of his *Dark Tower* books in highly prized limited editions with the small press Donald M. Grant, Publisher.

Among the most prolific of contemporary best-selling authors, King has consistently remained humble about his achievements. Calling himself a "brand-name" author, he often underplays the quality of his work or the extent of his influence on an entire generation of writers, and yet many of today's most popular authors of thrillers and horror fiction owe a great debt to King's contributions both as an artist and as a commercially successful writer who has pressed publishers to develop new methods and modes of publication.

Stephen King remains active and vital today as *the* premier writer of horror fiction, which is fortunate because in the summer of 1999 he was involved in a near-fatal accident in Lovell, Maine, when a driver of a minivan struck him as he was walking on the road. King's physical recovery from this accident was difficult, and at various times he claimed that he was finished with his career as a writer, but eventually he returned to writing, recently publishing some of his best work, including the novels *Cell* in 2006 and *Duma Key* in 2008.

When evaluating Stephen King's larger contributions to literature, the author he most resembles is the nineteenth-century British writer Charles Dickens. Like Dickens, King prefers to write expansive novels featuring large casts of characters who embody a vast and entertaining range of human emotions and expressions. Like Dickens, King is popular with his readership and appeals to a diverse audience, both men and women, and older and younger readers. Finally, like Dickens,

King's appeal supersedes the stifling limitations of genre expectations; he is one of the few well-known writers today who refuses to be pigeonholed by the commercial restrictions of formula fiction, just as Dickens more than a century earlier attracted readers fundamentally interested in good storytelling.

Ultimately, like Dickens, Stephen King is a consummate storyteller, perhaps the best storyteller of our era. A number of high schools and universities in America, for example, now assign stories written by King as an important part of their curriculum in literary studies (stories that are actually read by students), and his many prestigious literary awards, culminating in his 2003 National Book Foundation's Medal for Distinguished Contribution to American Letters, testify to his lasting appeal and our recognition of his immense talent.

Perhaps the best explanation for King's popularity is a relatively simple one. He successfully establishes a personal narrative voice in his stories that communicates directly with his readers. King's strength as a writer is in his character development (more so than in his construction of plot), and his audience responds to these characters, both good and evil, viewing them as intimate friends or enemies that they love or hate. More than any other best-selling author, King often inserts his own notes or commentary in his work, usually explaining the history of a particular tale or the development of a plot idea. He is the consummate storyteller who feels compelled to let us in on his literary secrets. His fiction is confessional (which is why he features so many writers as protagonists in his stories), and he draws us close to hear the tales he must tell. Readers sense a close friendship in his writings.

Biography of Stephen King

Thomas B. Frazier; updated by Gary Hoppenstand

Early Life

Stephen Edwin King was born on September 21, 1947, at Maine General Hospital in Portland, Maine, the second son of Donald Edwin and Nellie Ruth King. His brother, David, had been adopted by the Kings shortly after he was born two years earlier. When King was only two years old, his father, a captain in the merchant marines, deserted the family and never saw them again. This placed hardships on the young family, and they moved often as Nellie looked for work and assistance from her and Donald's families. During these years, they lived in Maine, Massachusetts, Illinois, Wisconsin, and Indiana. Finally, when King was six years old, the family settled in Stratford, Connecticut, where they lived for six years.

King became interested in the horror genre early in life. He listened to suspenseful radio dramas and eventually came under the spell of Robert Louis Stevenson's *Treasure Island* (1883) and *Dr. Jekyll and Mr. Hyde* (1886) and horror films such as *The Creature from the Black Lagoon* (1954). The launch of the Soviet satellite *Sputnik I* also fueled the young King's imagination. King's teachers reported that one of his greatest passions was writing stories of his own, which he began doing at the age of six.

In 1958, when King was eleven years old, his family moved to Durham, Maine. It was here that the future writer discovered that he had something in common with his absent father. In the attic of his aunt and uncle's garage he discovered an old trunk that contained a box of his father's books, including some by New England horror writer H. P. Lovecraft, and some of his father's own early attempts at writing short stories.

King remained interested in writing throughout his early education. After graduating from Lisbon Falls High School, he entered the University of Maine in Orono in 1966. At the University of Maine, he pursued a degree in English; wrote "King's Garbage Truck," a column for the campus newspaper, the *Daily Maine*; and submitted short stories to whatever publications he thought might be interested. In 1967, King made his first sale as an author when *Startling Mystery Stories* purchased his short story "The Glass Floor" for thirty-five dollars. Even with his first sale, King continued his college education and filled empty hours by working campus jobs, writing, protesting local situations, and courting his future wife, fellow University of Maine student and library worker Tabitha Spruce.

King graduated from the university in 1970 and accepted a position as an English teacher at Hampden Academy in Hampden, Maine, in 1971. In the same year, King married the recently graduated Tabitha, who would eventually become a novelist in her own right. The young couple lived in a small mobile home and held additional jobs, King in an industrial laundry and Tabitha in a donut shop, to supplement King's meager teaching salary of $6,400 per year. During this time they began their family: a daughter, Naomi, was born in 1970, and a son, Joseph, was born in 1972. Another son, Owen, would follow in 1977.

Although his early married life proved to be taxing, King did not ignore his drive to write. The small checks his short stories earned were often used to purchase medicine for his children or to finance the repairs of major appliances. When he was not teaching or working in the laundry, King produced several manuscripts, many typed in the furnace room of the Kings' mobile home. He would freely throw away pieces in which he saw no real potential. One such effort, a short story about a telekinetic teenage girl, was saved from the garbage by Tabitha, who saw more than her husband did in the work. She told King she believed there was something of value to be found in the fragment and that he should complete what he had begun. With his wife's encouragement, King finished the manuscript, which was eventually published as *Carrie* (1974). With the sale of *Carrie* to Doubleday for a $2,500 advance (he later sold the paperback rights for $400,000 and saw the novel turned into an award-winning motion picture starring Sissy Spacek), King knew that he could earn his way as a writer and gave up his teaching position to write full-time.

The books that followed *Carrie* were received with varying degrees of acceptance. After King published his modernized vampire tale *'Salem's Lot* (1975) and began work on his third book, *The Shining* (1977), which would be a ghost story, his agent feared that the young writer from Maine would be typecast, but King had no fear that he would fail at his craft or in his chosen genre. His later publication successes proved him correct.

In 1981, King published *Danse Macabre*, an exploration of the horror genre, to illuminate his fascination with both motion pictures and literature that investigate humanity's darker emotional and psychological sides. In producing his own works of horror, King soon found that the clearest way for him to begin a new story would be to ask himself, "What if?" From early on, this question has been central to each of King's works: *The Stand* (1978) asks how people act following an almost total annihilation of humanity, *Misery* (1987) asks how an obsessed fan might act if she met her favorite author, *The Tommyknockers* (1987) asks what effect extraterrestrial visitors might have on a community, and the six-part *The Green Mile* (1996) asks how various people might respond to capital punishment.

In addition to his many novels, King has also written numerous successful short stories, many of which have eventually appeared in collections, including "The Body" (*Different Seasons*, 1982), "The Woman in the Room" (*Night Shift*, 1978), and "Word Processor of the Gods" (*Skeleton Crew*, 1985). In addition, he has produced seven novels under the pen name "Richard Bachman," which he created in order to publish works he felt did not quite fit the Stephen King persona and to circumvent his publisher's refusal to bring out more than one King book per year. The true identity of Bachman was revealed in 1985, thanks to the curiosity and research of a bookstore clerk, after five novels had been published: *Rage* (1977), *The Long Walk* (1979), *Roadwork*

(1981), *The Running Man* (1982), and *Thinner* (1984). *The Regulators* (1996) and *Blaze* (2007) were later also published under Bachman's name.

King's audience grew even larger as film and television versions of his works and original screenplays and teleplays by King caught the attention of viewing audiences. Many of these versions have been called weak at best; however, some have received rave reviews as well as major awards. The motion pictures with King ties that are generally considered the best are *Carrie* (1976), *The Dead Zone* (1983), "The Body" spinoff *Stand by Me* (1986), *The Shining* (1980), and *Misery* (1990). Among the King television movies and miniseries are *'Salem's Lot* (1979 and 2004), *It* (1990), *The Tommyknockers* (1993), *The Stand* (1994), and *The Shining* (1997).

The name of Stephen King has become familiar even to those who have never read any of his works. Though he tries to maintain a degree of privacy for himself and his family, the author does have a high public profile. In 1985, King made television spots for American Express, and he has also made spots for a national publicity drive for library usage. He has made appearances on many top network talk shows and has twice appeared as a contestant on the game show *Jeopardy*. He gained particular attention in 1994 when he set out on a cross-country motorcycle trip during which he touted both his new novel *Insomnia* and independent bookstores.

King was again in the news in 1999 when he was struck by a van while out for his daily walk and suffered near-fatal injuries. He was in the midst of a memoir at the time, *On Writing* (2000), and included the incident in the book. Two years after its publication, King announced that he would be retiring, though by all appearances he has no such plans. He has published six novels since then, and though he finished what he claimed would be the last volume of his *Dark Tower* series in 2004, in 2009 he hinted that another book would be forthcoming.

Because of his vast audience and his high public profile, Stephen King has become more than merely an author who writes scary stories.

Even though King maintains that his books contain disturbing acts and characters because the world contains evil and it must be confronted, some critics, fearing that he may adversely influence children and teenagers, have sought to ban his works from public school libraries. In 1989 and again in 1996 and 1997, King was drawn into legal proceedings when high school students brought guns into their schools and acted out scenarios that were eerily similar to the one depicted in *Rage*. The level of some readers' devotion to King has also placed the author in a unique (and sometimes unwanted) position. More than a few fans have traveled to Bangor, Maine, to take pictures of the author's house. In 1991, King's home was invaded by a distraught and mentally unbalanced man from Texas who threatened to destroy the house, and in 1992 another man appeared in Bangor with signs blaming King for John Lennon's murder.

The greatest contentious confrontations have come, however, when critics and reviewers have debated the significance and quality of King's fiction. Many critics have simply dismissed King as just an author who caters to the prurient curiosity of the reading masses. In contrast, others have compared King to Charles Dickens and Edgar Allan Poe and have considered him to be among the best of modern storytellers. Perhaps the most significant validation of King's work came in 2003, when the National Book Foundation honored King with its Medal for Distinguished Contribution to American Letters, citing his storytelling abilities and his generous support of new writers, libraries, and schools.

Throughout his career, King has approached his work with all seriousness, writing almost every day of the year. He also realizes that he has been much more fortunate than most and has sought out ways to share his good fortune with others. The philanthropic efforts of King and his wife have benefited such diverse causes as the Bangor, Maine, recreation program; various educational institutions, most noticeably the University of Maine; library rebuilding programs such as one in Old Town, Maine; and needy students.

In addition to their separate writing careers and their philanthropic gestures, King and his wife put most of their efforts into rearing their three children. As in King's fiction, one of the driving impulses in King's life has been to ensure that his children have a normal, loving family life.

Bibliography

Beahm, George W. *The Stephen King Story*. Kansas City, Mo.: Andrews McMeel, 1992. A good, updated biography of King. Includes bibliographical references and an index.

_____, ed. *Stephen King from A to Z: An Encyclopedia of His Life and Work*. Kansas City, Mo.: Andrews McMeel, 1998. Encyclopedic compendium of entries on every aspect of the author's fiction and biography.

Bloom, Harold, ed. *Stephen King*. Modern Critical Views. Philadelphia: Chelsea House, 1998. One of the best single collections of essays about King, many collected from other sources listed here, but including previously unreprinted pieces from journals or non-King-specific books. High-quality pieces cover a range of themes and King's works through *Needful Things*. Good chronology, bibliography, and index.

Collings, Michael R. *Scaring Us to Death: The Impact of Stephen King on Popular Culture*. 2d rev. ed. San Bernardino, Calif.: Borgo Press, 1997. Examines King's influence on the rise of horror fiction in the United States.

_____. *The Work of Stephen King: An Annotated Bibliography and Guide*. San Bernardino, Calif.: Borgo Press, 1996. Provides both a good chronology and useful descriptions of some of King's hard-to-find works as well as a copious annotated list of secondary sources.

Docherty, Brian, ed. *American Horror Fiction: From Brockden Brown to Stephen King*. New York: St. Martin's Press, 1990. This collection of essays places King's works in context with those of other American horror writers.

Herron, Don, ed. *Reign of Fear: Fiction and Film of Stephen King*. Los Angeles: Underwood-Miller, 1988. The essays in this collection discuss the significance of film in the development of King's reputation.

Hohne, Karen A. "The Power of the Spoken Word in the Works of Stephen King." *Journal of Popular Culture* 28 (Fall 1994): 93-103. Discusses the tension in King's work between slang speech, which codifies a knowledge rejected by those in power, and monologic orality, which embodies that power; claims his works illustrate the tension between official and unofficial languages and ideologies that exists not only in literature but also throughout society.

Hoppenstand, Gary, and Ray B. Browne, eds. *The Gothic World of Stephen King: Landscape of Nightmare*. Bowling Green, Ohio: Popular Press, 1987. This collection of academic criticism of King includes an introduction by Hoppenstand and essays on themes ("Adolescent Revolt," "Love and Death in the American Car"), characters ("Mad Dogs and Firestarters," "The Vampire"), genres (King's "Gothic Western," technohorror), technique ("Allegory"), and individual works.

King, Stephen. *Bare Bones: Conversations on Terror with Stephen King*. Ed. Tim Underwood and Chuck Miller. New York: McGraw-Hill, 1988. Though many of the interviews collected in this volume become somewhat repetitive, they provide a good sense, in King's own words, of what he is trying to do in his fiction and why he does it. The interviews were held between 1979 and 1987; the opening transcript of a talk King gave at the Billerica Public Library is most useful.

_____. *Danse Macabre*. New York: Everest House, 1981. King researched and wrote this critical work on horror fiction and film at the instigation of his editor. He focuses on works since the 1940s and discusses novels, B-films, and horror comics to support his thesis that monsters such as Godzilla are a way of making tangible people's fears about such things as nuclear war.

Magistrale, Tony. *Stephen King: The Second Decade, "Danse Macabre" to "The Dark Half."* New York: Twayne, 1992. Discusses King's work in the 1980s, including his nonfictional analysis of the horror genre in *Danse Macabre*, his Richard Bachman books, *Misery*, and the novellas of the *Dark Tower* saga. Also includes a 1989 interview in which King discusses fairy-tale references in his work as well as his treatment of sexuality, masculinity, and race; discusses critical and popular reaction to his fiction.

_____, ed. *The Dark Descent: Essays Defining Stephen King's Horror-scape*. Westport, Conn.: Greenwood Press, 1992. This academic collection of interpretive essays covers subjects such as homophobia, treatment of female characters, and dialogic narratives in King's work; the sixteen pieces examine most of King's novels and some short fiction.

_____, ed. *Landscape of Fear: Stephen King's American Gothic*. Bowling Green, Ohio: Popular Press, 1988. Placing King in an American gothic tradition with Edgar Allan Poe, Nathaniel Hawthorne, Herman Melville, and William Faulkner, this study treats sociopolitical themes such as "The Betrayal of Technology," individual accountability, innocence betrayed, and survival in the novels through *It*. The text is supplemented by a bibliography of scholarship from 1980 to 1987.

Power, Brenda Miller, Jeffrey D. Wilhelm, and Kelly Chandler, eds. *Reading Stephen King: Issues of Censorship, Student Choice, and Popular Literature*. Urbana, Ill.: National Council of Teachers of English, 1997. Examines issues at the heart of horror fiction. Includes bibliographical references and an index.

Reino, Joseph. *Stephen King: The First Decade, "Carrie" to "Pet Sematary."* Boston: Twayne, 1988. This book-by-book analysis attempts to show King's literary merits, stressing subtle characterization and nuances of symbolism and allusion. The text is supplemented by a chronology, notes, and primary and secondary bibliographies.

Russell, Sharon. *Revisiting Stephen King*. Westport, Conn.: Greenwood Press, 2002. Provides analyses of King's later works, from *The Green Mile* through *Dreamcatcher*.

Spignesi, Stephen J. *The Complete Stephen King Encyclopedia: The Definitive Guide to the Works of America's Master of Horror*. Chicago: Contemporary Books, 1991. First published with the title *The Shape Under the Sheet*, this is an important guide for all students of King. Includes bibliographical references and indexes.

_____. *The Essential Stephen King: The Greatest Novels, Short Stories, Movies, and Other Creations of the World's Most Popular Writer*. Franklin Lakes, N.J.: New Page, 2001. A useful discussion of the horror writer's works by a King enthusiast.

Underwood, Tim, and Chuck Miller, eds. *Fear Itself: The Horror Fiction of Stephen King, 1976-1982*. San Francisco: Underwood-Miller, 1982. Articles in this collection on King's work vary in quality, with Ben Indick's "King and the Literary Tradition of Horror" providing a good introduction to the history of the horror genre. Douglas E. Winter's essay "The Night Journeys of Stephen King" discusses several of the short stories. Includes a bibliography.

Vincent, Ben. *The Road to the Dark Tower: Exploring Stephen King's Magnum Opus*. New York: NAL Trade, 2004. In-depth study of King's seven-volume masterwork, which revolves around the mystery of the tower from which the series takes its name.

Wiater, Stanley, Christopher Golden, and Hank Wagner. *The Stephen King Universe: A Guide to the Worlds of the King of Horror*. Los Angeles: Renaissance Books, 2001. A critical feast of all things King. The authors explore the common themes, places, and characters that run through King's novels. Resources include a biographical chronology, a bibliography, and an index.

Winter, Douglas E. *The Art of Darkness: The Life and Fiction of the Master of the Macabre, Stephen King*. Rev. Ed. New York: New American Library, 1989. Provides a perceptive critical overview of King's work, with long articles on each novel up to *The Talisman* and a chapter on the short stories in *Night Shift* and *Skeleton Crew*. Also includes summaries of King's short stories, a short biography of King, and extensive bibliographies both of King's work and of books and articles written about him.

the PARIS
REVIEW

The *Paris Review* Perspective_____

Nathaniel Rich for *The Paris Review*

When I was between the ages of nine and fourteen, my formative reading years—and perhaps the most important years of my intellectual development—all the books I read outside school were written by the same author: Stephen King. It all started when I spotted, on the top rung of my parents' bookshelf, a thick gray Signet edition of *Firestarter*. On the cover there was a picture of a young girl, roughly my own age. Flames engulfed her head. I asked my mother about it. No way, she said. Too scary. You'll have nightmares. As soon as she left the room, I scaled the bookshelf.

The novel is full of government conspiracies, religious zealots, and graphic violence, much of it caused by a pretty blond girl named Charlie who can start bonfires with her brain. Before King, I had never read anything scarier than the Hardy Boys; it had not occurred to me that a book could deeply upset me. As a child I did not have much use for the emotions that adult literature sought to engender—melancholy, longing, or regret—but every child understands fear. And I was terrified. *Firestarter* was the book that made me love fiction. It showed me that a story could burrow deep inside you and make the world feel like a much larger place than you had ever imagined.

When I interviewed King in 2006 for *The Paris Review*'s Writers at Work interview series, I told him (in the most casual tone I could manage) about my experience with *Firestarter*. He laughed—the same exact thing had happened to him. He had grown up in Durham, a small town in Maine. There was no library, but every few weeks the state sent a green van called the bookmobile to town. Children were allowed to borrow any three books—and they didn't have to be children's books. King picked out three Ed McBain 87th Precinct novels, and his life was changed forever: "In the one I read first, the cops go up to question a woman in this tenement apartment and she is standing there in her slip. The cops tell her to put some clothes on, and she grabs her breast through her slip and squeezes it at them and says, 'In your eye, cop!' And I went, Shit! Immediately something clicked in my head. I thought, That's real, that could really happen. That was the end of the Hardy Boys. That was the end of all juvenile fiction for me. It was like, See ya!"

For most of King's career, book critics treated his books like juvenile fiction—denigrated, if regarded at all, and often in correlation to the mushrooming size of his readership (to this date he has sold more than 300 million books). A sampling of reviews that appeared in the *New York Times*: "*Thinner* . . . is very bad"; "*The Tommyknockers* . . . is impressively bad"; "[*It*] tries too hard; it reaches for too much; it's too damn complicated"; "He is a writer of fairly engaging and preposterous claptrap. . . . [*The Shining*] is slapdash, unfocused and eventually preposterous."

But something has changed in the last decade, in part because the critical establishment that scorned the young horror writer has been put out to pasture by a new generation of readers and critics. As King himself put it, "People who have grown up reading you become part of the literary establishment. They take you as part of the landscape that was there when they came along. In some ways you get a squarer shake." In 1997 he received the Writers for Writers Award from *Poets & Writers* magazine for his devoted efforts to support and promote the work of other authors, and in 2003 he won the Medal for Distinguished Contribution to American Letters from the National Book Foundation. Along the way he has forced a culture to reexamine the vigilantly patrolled border between popular and literary fiction.

To understand the power of King's work, it is crucial to understand that the source of any great horror story is not some external spook—an apparition, a plague, or an invasion of hobgoblins with bloody eyes and shovels for hands. The fear comes from within. "What I do is like a crack in the mirror," said King. "If you go back over the books from *Carrie* on up, what you see is an observation of ordinary middle-class American life as it's lived at the time that particular book was written. In every life you get to a point where you have to deal with something that's inexplicable to you, whether it's the doctor saying you have cancer or a prank phone call. . . . What that shows about our character and our interactions with others and the society we live in interests me a lot more than monsters and vampires and ghouls and ghosts."

King is the master of the cracked mirror: his world is just like ours, only more crooked and refracted, a place where the familiar—a pet dog, a beat-up Plymouth Fury, a clown—turns strange, and the most frightening things—a spaceship buried in the backyard that exerts powers of mind control, a dense mist that suffocates an entire village, a dead child brought back, against his will, from the grave—begin to seem disturbingly familiar. Even if you're only nine years old.

Bibliography

King, Stephen. "The Art of Fiction No. 189: Stephen King." Interview by Christopher Lehmann-Haupt and Nathaniel Rich. *The Paris Review* 178 (Fall 2006).

_____. *Danse Macabre.* New York: Everest House, 1981.

_____. *On Writing: A Memoir of the Craft.* New York: Charles Scribner's Sons, 2000.

Leonard, John. "King of High and Low." *New York Review of Books* 14 Feb. 2002.

Spignesi, Stephen. *The Essential Stephen King.* Franklin Lakes, NJ: New Page Books, 2001.

CRITICAL
CONTEXTS

The Popularity Problem:
Stephen King's Cultural Context_____
Amy Palko

In his introduction to *The Best American Short Stories 2007*, Stephen King describes his search among a chain bookstore's "Wall of Magazines" for the new issues of *Tin House* and *Zoetrope: All-Story*:

> I stare at the racks of magazines, and the racks of magazines stare eagerly back. Celebrities in gowns and tuxes, models in lo-rise jeans, luxy stereo equipment, talk-show hosts with can't-miss diet plans—they all scream *Buy me, buy me! Take me home and I'll change your life! I'll light it up!* (xiv; emphasis in original)

Finally, he spots them on the bottom shelf, beneath *The New Yorker* and *Harper's*, and crouches on the floor "like a school janitor trying to scrape a particularly stubborn wad of gum off the gym floor" (xiv).

The visual image of a "Wall of Magazines" (xiv), which is structured as a physical embodiment of the hierarchical literary field, illustrates the gulf between texts that are economically successful and those that enjoy literary credibility. The prominent positions of the ephemeral celebrations of the rich and famous signify, as King writes, "fiction's out-migration from the eye-level shelves" (xv) to the "lowest shelf, where neatness alone suggests few ever go. . . . Britney Spears has become a cultural icon, available at every checkout, while an American talent like William Gay labors in relative obscurity" (xv).

However, as King recognizes, his own work is not shelved in the recesses of the bookstore; instead, it appears on a "table filled with best-selling hardcover fiction at prices ranging from 20 to 40 percent off. James Patterson is represented, as is Danielle Steel" (xiv). These books, he says, are "the moneymakers and rent payers; these are the glamour ponies" (xiv). The rise of "glamour pony" fiction and its multimillionaire authors was one of the defining characteristics of the twentieth-century publishing industry, and it still persists into the twenty-first. The result has been, as King's "Wall of Magazines" demonstrates, a differentiation between popular, best-selling fiction and serious, credible literature.

To understand the rather complex reasons for why this differentiation exists within contemporary American literary production, we need to take into account the process of sacralization. According to Lawrence W. Levine in *Highbrow/Lowbrow: The Emergence of Cultural Hierarchy in America* (1988), sacralization results from a cultural shift in which art becomes less shared across the culture, less the purview of all members of a culture, and instead is elevated in such a way that only elite audiences are considered to have the knowledge and means to access it. These audiences, in turn, "approach the matters and . . . works" of serious cultural producers, such as classical orchestras, "with proper respect and proper seriousness, for aesthetic and spiritual elevation rather than mere entertainment" (146). As Levine argues, beginning at the end of the nineteenth century and reaching a zenith during the modernist period of the early 1900s, American society became increasingly bifurcated along the lines of "low" and "high" culture.

An exploration of the roots of this bifurcation in the publishing industry and its effects on authors and their literary output during the American Renaissance can be found in William Charvat's *The Profession of Authorship in America, 1800-1870* (1968). In this posthumously published collection of papers, Charvat discusses the case of Herman Melville, whose authorial career serves to illustrate sacralization as it became a defining characteristic of cultural production. Melville's first two novels, *Typee* and *Omoo*, were instant popular successes, but his next few novels were not so, and as the author entered the middle of his career, he became torn between his financial difficulties and his conviction that he needed to produce original literature capable of shaping a national literary identity. After writing two successful potboilers, *Redburn* and *White-Jacket*, he began working on the more serious *Moby Dick* with the encouragement of Nathaniel Hawthorne. Yet as a June 1, 1851, letter Melville wrote to Nathaniel Hawthorne demonstrates, the author was still anxious about the incompatibility between artistic and financial success. He complained, "Dollars damn me. . . . What I feel most moved to write, that is banned,—it will not pay. Yet, altogether, write the other way I cannot. So the product is a final hash, and all my books are botches" (191). The fortunes of the novel seemed to prove Melville right: though Hawthorne praised it, other critics savaged it, and it sold poorly. It was not until decades later that critics rediscovered it and established it as the classic it is today. As Charvat proclaims, *Moby Dick* is "Herman Melville's one unquestionably great full-length book" that was "the work of a writer who was in a state of creative tension" and a product "of the author's wish [to] express himself and yet be bought and read and taken seriously" (240-41).

Though Melville did not achieve the success he hoped for in his lifetime, in the early twentieth century he was adopted by the modernists. As Paul Lauter explains in "Melville Climbs the Canon" (1994), Melville was "deployed [by the modernists] as a lone and powerful artistic beacon against the dangers presented by the masses" (6); he was celebrated for his role "not as a transparently approachable chronicler of sea tales, but as a densely allusive composer whose most precious treasures would be yielded up, as with other modernist texts, only to learned initiates" (18). This view of Melville's work complements the view of modern art set out by José Ortega y Gasset in *The Dehumanization of Art* (1925), which John Carey summarizes in *The Intellectuals and the Masses*: "It is the essential function of modern art to divide the public into two classes—those who can understand it and those who cannot. Modern art is not so much unpopular, he argues, as anti-popular" (17). In this sense, Lauter states, "Melville's difficulties appear not as problems to be overcome but as virtues which place him in the camp of modernist poets" (15).

King, born in the mid-twentieth century, arrived in an era in which the cultural producers were inevitably embroiled in an agonistic struggle with their predecessors, the modernists, and in which the divide between the serious and the popular was deeply entrenched. Indeed, King's first experience with literary production reflects this state of affairs, as he recalls in *On Writing* (2000). He writes that after watching a film adaptation of Edgar Allan Poe's "The Pit and the Pendulum" as a child, he decided that he would novelize the film, print copies at home, and sell them to his classmates. He remembers, "My thoughts were focused almost entirely on how much money I might make if my story was a hit at school" (37). The plagiarized editions sold even better than he anticipated—King calls it his "first best-seller" (37). Yet, upon discovering one, his teacher, Miss Hisler, exclaimed, "What I don't understand, Stevie . . . is why you'd write junk like this in the first place. You're talented. Why do you want to waste your abilities?" (45).

Even though he had successfully produced a work of fiction that covered his costs of production and gave him a sizable profit, King identifies this experience as the point at which he became "ashamed about what I write" (46). Though he would continue writing and profitably selling stories to his classmates—his next effort was an original short story, "The Invasion of the Star Creatures," of which he "sold all but four or five" (46) of a print run of four dozen—his teacher's comments stayed with him. As he explains, "I won in the end, at least in a financial sense. But in my heart I stayed ashamed. I kept hearing Miss Hisler asking why I wanted to waste my talent, why I wanted to waste my time, why I wanted to write junk" (46).

Whether shame is the most appropriate term for what King says he felt is less important here than the fact that he chose to include this incident in his memoir among the other "assorted snapshots" that together form "a kind of *curriculum vitae*" of his writing life (4). This articulation of shame is rooted in the attribution of literary worth to the ability to attract what Pierre Bourdieu calls symbolic capital, a kind of capital available only to "those who can *recognize* the specific demands of this universe and who, by concealing from themselves and others the interests at stake in their practice, obtain the means of deriving profits from disinterestedness" (75). Bourdieu, a French sociologist whose theories pertain to the structuration of society and the way in which these societal structures inform and are informed by those operating within them, provides a dynamic, interpretive model for understanding cultural production and the sociology of texts.

He posits that society functions according to fields: hierarchical strata that construct and are constructed by the various agents participating in a specific area of society, such as the field of cultural production and, more specifically, the literary field. Bourdieu recognizes that the literary "field is at all times the site of a struggle between the two principles of hierarchization: the heteronomous principle . . . and the autonomous principle" (40). Authors who produce according to the "heteronomous" principle, Bourdieu argues, "dominate the field economically and politically" (40), while those who produce according to the "autonomous" principle "identify with degree of independence from the economy, seeing temporal failure as a sign of election and success a sign of compromise" (40). One can see the tension that exists between these two principles in the aforementioned example of Herman Melville as he struggled to attract both economic and symbolic capital and as his work was co-opted for a modernist agenda. However, the immediacy of King's economic success, as intimated by his memories of these early commercial ventures, automatically precludes him from "deriving profits from disinterestedness." His ability to generate income through his literary production signifies a fundamental incompatibility between King's literary production and the distribution of symbolic capital.

On Writing charts the development of a best-selling novelist, and its narrative is one in which the financial realities of a poverty-stricken childhood and early adulthood loom large. This narrative of economic impoverishment not only informs King's work but also serves as a justification for the type of fiction he produced. In the early and mid-1970s, King published a handful of short stories—"Graveyard Shift" (1970), "Battleground" (1972), "Trucks" (1973), and "Strawberry Spring" (1975)—in men's magazines such as *Cavalier.* The money generated from these publications was, as King states, "just enough to create a rough sliding margin between us and the welfare office" (72). He recalls in particular the five-hundred-dollar check he received for "Sometimes They Come Back" (1974), a "long story that [he] hadn't believed would sell anywhere" (74) that gave him the money he needed to take his sick daughter to the doctor and to buy her medication. Thus King's literary production, then as now, is a consciously commercial concern.

Yet by working so hard to justify his commerciality, King reveals that it is not an aspect of his work with which he feels particularly comfortable. He is extremely keen that his short stories be acknowledged as not primarily commercial but as having a degree of intrinsic literary worth. In the how-to section of *On Writing*, King describes the journey of a composite early-career writer, Frank, whose first published short story earns him twenty-five dollars. As King states, "Twenty-five bucks won't pay the rent, won't even buy a week's worth of groceries for Frank and his wife, but it's a validation of his ambition, and that— any newly published writer would agree, I think—is priceless" (291-92). Applying this insight to King's own early career, we can see that, though the money King's stories earned kept him and his young family afloat during their lean years, he did not perceive it as solely a component of his economic strategy. Rather, it was also a "validation of his ambition."

This art/money dialectic is explored further in King's foreword to *Skeleton Crew* (1985), in which he discusses the financial details regarding one of his short stories, "Word Processor of the Gods" (1983). He relates a conversation he had with a friend, who argued that, while King's novels "were making very good money . . . the short stories were actually losers" (1). His friend reasoned that—after agent fees of 10 percent, business management fees of 5 percent, and taxes of 50 percent, with an additional 10 percent of that tax bill paid to the state of Maine—King had earned the same amount of money during the week it took to write "Word Processor of the Gods" as a New York plumber would have earned for a week's work. After recounting his friend's calculations, King rejoins by contrasting them with his own, taking into account the story's inclusion in his second collection of short fiction. Later, he writes in a note to his friend, "My total take on 'Word Processor of the Gods'—net—is now just over twenty-three hundred dollars, not even counting the $769.50 you hee-hawed so over at my house at the lake" (3).

However, after all these calculations, King proceeds to state, "You don't do it for the money, or you're a monkey. You don't think of the bottom line, or you're a monkey. You don't think of it in terms of hourly wage, yearly wage, even lifetime wage, or you're a monkey" (4). This matches his response in *On Writing* to the question, "Do you do it for the money, honey?" (301): "No. Don't now and never did. Yes, I've made a great deal of dough from my fiction, but I never set a single word down on paper with the thought of being paid for it" (301). This same refusal is reiterated during his 2003 acceptance speech for his National Book Foundation's Medal for Distinguished Contribution to American Letters:

> Now, there are lots of people who will tell you that anyone who writes genre fiction or any kind of fiction that tells a story is in it for the money and nothing else. It's a lie. . . . I never in my life wrote a single word for money. From those early days to this gala black tie night, I never once sat down at my desk thinking today I'm going to make a hundred grand.

This rebuttal follows the criticism he received for accepting the award from both critics and academics, including Harold Bloom, who stated, "By awarding [the Medal for Distinguished Contribution] to King they recognize nothing but the commercial value of his books, which sell in the millions but do little more for humanity than keep the publishing world afloat."

King's continued reiterations that he does not write "for money" can be seen as stemming from an anxiety arising from the stated beliefs of cultural custodians—or "gatekeepers" as Bourdieu classifies them—

like Bloom, that any piece of popular fiction's artistry is compromised by its economic success. By stating again and again in his forewords, speeches, nonfiction, and interviews that he is not writing for money, King is attempting to claim a level of "disinterestedness" and thus position himself as an author deserving of symbolic capital.

Despite King's supposed disinterestedness, however, his interest in the economic realities of not only his literary production but also his role as literary producer is rendered explicit in his discussions of marketing and the critical attention given to him. For example, during a 1984 interview with Stanley Wiater and Roger Anker in which he discusses his decision to participate in an American Express commercial and his decision to turn down a part in a Miller Lite commercial, King explains:

> The other day these people called me up from some other agency: "Saw your American Express ad. Loved it! You wanna do a Miller Lite ad?"
>
> And I went, "Jesus, yeah, I *do* want to do a Miller Lite ad—those are really cool!" Then I thought to myself: "You know, you're a *writer*. You do about three more of these things and you can go on Hollywood Squares, for all the reputation that you've got." Not that I've got much of a reputation anyway. But there has to be a point when, before you sell, you say, "I'm not a huckster, a commercial object." (*Bare Bones* 242)

King clearly appreciates that his literary reputation is inextricably bound to his commercial objectification: if he were to participate in commercials that advertise products such as alcoholic beverages and credit cards, he would risk irreparable damage to his potential to attract symbolic capital. The large advances that he has accepted in the past have already contributed toward his texts' incompatibility with the attraction of symbolic capital—a fact King recognized in a 1982 interview with Bob Spitz when he stated, "You can always tell a bad review coming, because it will be a review of my check-book and my contractual agreements" (*Bare Bones* 257). He continued by saying that a "review like that will start out saying, 'This is the third book in Stephen King's multi-million-dollar contract for New American Library,' and then you know, well . . . the trouble's going to start" (257). King recognizes a direct correlation between his economic success and the critical reception of his work: a correlation that emphasizes his literary production as arising from the heteronomous rather than autonomous principle.

At no time was this more apparent than in 1976, when *'Salem's Lot* topped the *New York Times* best-seller list. The following month, the *Times* featured an article by King in which he attempted to establish his text's literary worth, regardless of the amount of money its publication generated. This article, "Not Guilty: The Guest Word" (1976), relates a "bizarre coincidence" in which, after reading an article about novelist David Madden's earnings from *Bijou* (1975), King received a phone call informing him that *'Salem's Lot* was expected to take the top slot on paperback best-seller list within the space of a few hours. This coincidence led King to reflect, "Madden worked on *Bijou* for six years and made $15,000. I worked on *'Salem's Lot* for about eight months . . . and stand to make nearly half a million dollars, if all falls together" (para. 2). King asked himself:

> How does the contrast make me feel? In a word, guilty. But in another two words, not guilty. The two feelings are perfectly joined at hip and shoulder like Siamese twins, and I'm going to try to cut them apart before your very eyes. (para. 3)

The way in which he attempts to perform this excision is to present the possibility of there being an "art to accessibility." Though *Bijou* may be more artful and "a better book," the accessibility of a book like *'Salem's Lot* is rooted in an art "of a more humble sort than that which belongs to the artist who will not hew his peg to fit accessibility's hole" (para. 6). By emphasizing the accessibility of his literature, King confirms his role as a producer of heteronomous art. Madden, by contrast, is portrayed as a disinterested writer: one who writes autonomously in his production of "art for art's sake," art that succeeds through "temporal failure." By admitting to writing a text that is "easy to slip into, pleasant to stroke around in for the next 400-odd pages" (para. 5), King makes it clear that he produces with his market in mind, which enables him to make considerably more money than a writer like Madden.

Another point at which King's dissatisfaction with the correlation of literary worth with disinterestedness can be discerned is in his derision of university creative writing classes. This issue is raised briefly in *On Writing*, where he admits that while attending a class as part of his undergraduate degree, he preferred his future wife's poem "A Gradual Canticle for Augustine" over the other students' poems. As he explains, "There was a view among the student writers I knew at that time that good writing came spontaneously, in an uprush of feeling that had to be caught at once" (62) in which "there *were* no mechanics, only that seminal spurt of feeling" (63). In Tabitha's poem, however, there was "a work-ethic" that "had as much in common with sweeping the floor as with mythy moments of revelation" (65).

This "work-ethic" and its connection to profitable literature is explored fictively in King's epic horror novel *It* (1986). One of the novel's protagonists, Bill Denbrough, is a hugely successful popular novelist who recalls his own dissatisfaction with university creative writing classes. He voices his frustration during one such class in which the students have spent the last seventy minutes discussing "a sallow young woman's vignette about a cow's examination of a discarded engine block in a deserted field," which is supposed to be "a socio-political statement in the manner of the early Orwell" (132-33). Bill asks the class, "Can't you guys just let a story be a *story*?" to which his instructor responds, "Do you believe William Faulkner was just telling *stories*? Do you believe Shakespeare was just interested in making a *buck*?" (133). Bill counters, "I think that's pretty close to the truth" (133), leading the instructor and the rest of the class to deride him publicly for holding such a belief. Bill receives an F on his next story, along with the damning comments "PULP" and "CRAP" (134). Yet King's description of Bill's actual process of "the business of writing this story" (133) furthers his own connection between "work-ethic" and literary production: it is as though Bill "is not so much *telling* the story as he is allowing the story to *flow through* him" (133), although not as the "seminal spurt of feeling" King accuses his writing class peers of producing. Instead, Bill feels:

> After ten years of trying he has suddenly found the starter button on the vast dead bulldozer taking up so much space inside his head. It has started up. It is revving, revving. It is nothing pretty, this big machine. It was not made for taking pretty girls to proms. It is not a status symbol. It means business. It can knock things down. If he isn't careful, it will knock *him* down. (134)

This mechanized literary production, which has nothing in common with the "uprush of feeling" (62) King's fellow students believed in, is simultaneously incapable of garnering critical validation and deserving of financial recompense. For the story, Bill receives two hundred dollars from *White Tie*, a men's magazine similar to those in which King published during his fledgling career, and he promptly decides to drop his creative writing class, with which his incompatibility had been painfully obvious. Stapling his drop card to the editor's congratulatory note and pinning them to the department notice board earns him an overall F for the course and a comment from his instructor: "Do you think money proves anything about anything, Denbrough?" (135). Bill's response is, "Well, actually, yes" (135), although it is his text's actualized potential to gain economic rather than symbolic capital that later prevents him from being appreciated as a writer of serious, autonomous literature by critics and the academy—a fate shared by his creator, Stephen King.

This theme of economic influence on literary credibility is also articulated in one of King's early novels and in its film adaptation. *The*

Shining, King informs us in "On Becoming a Brand Name" (1982), was his "first hardcover best-seller; it went to Number 8 on the *Times* list . . . to Number 7 on the *Publishers Weekly* list, to Number 6 on the *Time Magazine* list" (41). King also found himself "a popcorn celebrity one week in *People* magazine—a two-page spread sandwiched in between Bjorn Borg and Larry Flynt" (41). After already seeing a dramatic increase in sales of *Carrie* following Brian De Palma's film adaptation, King knew that he could expect a similar success following Stanley Kubrick's film *The Shining* (1980). This economic success, however, further consolidated his position as a writer of popular fiction and adversely affected his potential to attract symbolic capital. This, along with the condemnatory remarks made by film critics, influential academics, and Kubrick himself regarding the literary worth of his novel, exacerbated King's anxiety concerning the commerciality of his fiction and his need to be appreciated as a serious writer. As King states in "Brand Name," "I have written seriously since I was twelve, and to me that means that I always wrote in order to make money" (16); yet being a serious writer also means that one has received cultural consecration, the lack of which King felt and still feels keenly.

The fallout from the publication of the novel and the release of Kubrick's film has long haunted King. He once wondered, in a 1985 interview with Charles L. Grant, if he would end up feeling the same way about Kubrick's *The Shining* as he presumed Robert Bloch, the author of *Psycho*, must have felt about Alfred Hitchcock's adaptation of his novel (1960). He wondered how

> Bob Bloch . . . has been able to cope with people asking, "How did you like *Psycho*?"—for twenty-some years. He must be a little bit tired of that question. I'm getting tired of *The Shining* question. . . . I hope people aren't asking me that question in twenty years. (*Bare Bones* 117)

However, over the more than twenty years since that interview, the press has continued to ask King that question. During a 1983 interview with Eric Norden for *Playboy*, King confessed that, while he admired Brian De Palma's version of *Carrie* (1976), Stanley Kubrick's adaptation of *The Shining* left him feeling "profoundly ambivalent" (*Bare Bones* 47). In 2006, during an interview for *The Paris Review*, the subject of Kubrick's version was raised again, and King admitted that it is "certainly beautiful to look at: gorgeous sets, all those Steadicam shots. I used to call it a Cadillac with no engine in it. You can't do anything with it except admire it as sculpture" ("Art" 79).

Kubrick, on the other hand, consciously distanced his version of *The Shining* from its origins in a 1984 interview with Michel Ciment, dismissing the novel as "by no means a serious literary work" (181). Kubrick's derision of King's original is palpable in his discussion of the adaptation process:

> It is in the pruning down phase that the undoing of great novels usually occurs because so much of what is good about them has to do with the fineness of the writing, the insight of the author and often the density of the story. But *The Shining* was a different matter. Its virtues lay almost entirely in the plot, and it didn't prove to be very much of a problem to adapt it into the screenplay form. (185)

Kubrick suggests here that the original did not contain "fineness of writing," authorial insight, or "density of . . . story" and was therefore a straightforward text upon which to leave his own directorial mark. However, as Kian Bergstrom points out, Kubrick's choice of novel was more than just a question of adaptational convenience:

> Starting with *The Shining*, his films would become increasingly concerned with the differences between "popular" taste and "high culture," between sensationalism and intellectualism, internalizing this dialectic within the themes and actions of the works, even as Kubrick wrestled with it externally, in terms of marketing, casting, and *choice of material*. (para. 1; emphasis added)

This dialectic that Kubrick was exploring in his work and struggling with as a cultural producer at "the beginning of his increasing interest in definitions and analyses of popular culture and the end of his definitive standing as a critical darling" (para. 4) accounts for his decision to adapt a popular novel while simultaneously distancing himself from its best-selling author.

It should not be assumed, however, that this dialectic remains foreign to the novel and was only imposed upon it through its cinematic adaptation. Rather, the relationship between high and low, popular and serious, economic and symbolic is, I want to suggest, central to the original narrative, and it may have been these dialectics that appealed to Kubrick over and above his belief that the novel could easily be adapted to his own purposes. The anxiety King reveals in his comment about Kubrick's critically revered version did not stem from the film critics' damning indictment of his novel but was actually present prior to his production of the text and, indeed, is an integral part of his narrative about the Torrance family's nightmarish incarceration in the Overlook Hotel.

Jack Torrance, who is conspicuously one of King's least successful author-protagonists in the struggle to attract either symbolic or economic capital, demonstrates the prominence of this aspect of the narrative, and it is through him that King dramatizes issues pertaining to the hierarchical structure of the field of literary production, the distribution of both economic and symbolic capital, and the relationship of literary production to labor, alienated or otherwise. It is a text that directly engages in the art/money dialectic, and, as such, it invites us to consider the role of the cultural producer in the late capitalist era: an invitation duly accepted by Stanley Kubrick.

Underlying Jack's character is the trope of the *poète maudit*, a gifted writer who has been cast out of society for the unsettling truths he tells; however, that King uses the trope does not mean that he is endorsing the reversal of economic success that the stereotype is invested with effecting. The image of the *poète maudit*, Bourdieu determines, is informed by "an upside down economy where the artist could win in the symbolic arena only by losing in the economic one" (201); however, according to Bourdieu, this failure within the economic "arena" is only a "short term" (201) failure, as financial success is effectively deferred rather than refused. King makes Jack Torrance's investment in the image of the *poète maudit* appear ineffectual in that it does not bring him either symbolic or deferred economic capital. Instead, Jack fears that he has "failed as a teacher, a writer, a husband and a father" (365); he fears that failure has tainted every part of his life, including his literary production. According to Bourdieu's logic, failure in his literary efforts could ultimately lead to cultural consecration and the economic benefits that status would bring; however, Jack, the sole author-protagonist within King's fiction to pursue this path toward literary legitimacy, never makes it to this point. Through Jack, King dramatizes his belief that the *poète maudit* has no place within contemporary American economics, thus exposing the *poète maudit* to be a "false face" (468), merely a mask to disguise the hidden economic intentions of those aiming for cultural consecration. Jack is condemned as a writer who pursues a fundamentally flawed strategy, one which, according to King, offers no hope of success in any arena. In essence, *The Shining*'s narrative is one in which the image of the *poète maudit* is stripped of its power to attract symbolic capital; its status as no more than a redundant, reified image is confirmed. It is configured as a simulacrum: an image operating at the level of the hyperreal with its foundations in counterfeit. This in itself does not strip the image of its power, but, by exposing its function within a flawed economic strategy, King hopes to assert his own literary strategy, in which the attraction of economic and symbolic capital are not mutually exclusive.

In this way, King signaled early on in his career the intention he rendered explicit in his National Book Foundation award speech as he championed the cause of bridge building between "the popular and the literary" (para. 33). It is impossible to say whether his many attempts to bring the two together have been successful; only time will tell. What can be said, however, is that King is still determined to subvert the structures that separate the "so-called literary" and "the so-called popular" (para. 27). Not only is his resolve evident in his early fiction, but also its presence persists undiminished in the fiction he still publishes today, thus demonstrating his ongoing commitment to build a bridge between the popular and the serious, between economic success and literary credibility.

Works Cited

Bergstrom, Kian. "'I Am Sorry to *Differ* with You, Sir': Thoughts on Reading Kubrick's *The Shining*." The Kubrick Site, 2000. 29 Jan. 2010. http://www.visual-memory.co.uk/amk/doc/0089.html.

Bloom, Harold. "Dumbing Down American Readers." *Boston Globe* 24 Sept. 2003. 29 Jan. 2010. http://www.boston.com/news/globe/editorial_opinion/oped/articles/2003/09/24/dumbing_down_american_readers/.

Bourdieu, Pierre. *The Field of Cultural Production: Essays on Art and Literature*. Ed. Randal Johnson. Cambridge: Polity Press, 1993.

Carey, John. *The Intellectuals and the Masses: Pride and Prejudice Among the Literary Intelligentsia, 1880-1939.* 1992. Chicago: Academy Chicago, 2002.

Carrie. Dir. Brian De Palma. Screenplay by Lawrence D. Cohen. Perf. Sissy Spacek, Piper Laurie, and Amy Irving. United Artists Corporation, Redbank Films, 1976.

Charvat, William. *The Profession of Authorship in America, 1800-1870*. Columbus: Ohio State UP, 1968.

Ciment, Michel. *Kubrick: The Definitive Edition*. Trans. Gilbert Adair and Robert Bononno. New York: Holt, Rinehart and Winston, 1984.

King, Stephen. "The Art of Fiction No. 189: Stephen King." Interview by Christopher Lehmann-Haupt and Nathaniel Rich. *The Paris Review* 178 (Fall 2006).

_____. *Bare Bones: Conversations on Terror with Stephen King*. 1988. Ed. Tim Underwood and Chuck Miller. London: New English Library, 1990.

_____. "Battleground." *Night Shift*. London: New English Library, 1978. 129-37.

_____. "Graveyard Shift." *Night Shift*. London: New English Library, 1978. 56-70.

_____. *It*. 1986. London: New English Library, 1987.

_____. National Book Award acceptance speech. National Book Foundation. 19 Nov. 2003. 29 Jan. 2010. http://www.nationalbook.org/nbaacceptspeech_sking.html.

_____. "Not Guilty: The Guest Word." *New York Times* 24 Oct. 1976.

_____. "On Becoming a Brand Name." *Fear Itself*. Ed. Tim Underwood and Chuck Miller. San Francisco: Underwood Miller, 1982. 15-42.

_____. *On Writing*. 2000. London: New English Library, 2001.

_____. *'Salem's Lot*. 1975. London: New English Library, 1977.

_____. *The Shining*. 1977. London: New English Library, 1978.

_____. *Skeleton Crew*. 1985. London: Warner Books, 1993.

_____. "Sometimes They Come Back." *Night Shift*. London: New English Library, 1978. 153-77.

_____. "Strawberry Spring." *Night Shift*. London: New English Library, 1978. 178-86.

_____. "Trucks." *Night Shift*. London: New English Library, 1978. 138-52.

_____. "Word Processor of the Gods." *Skeleton Crew*. London: Warner Books, 1993. 319-39.

_____, ed. *The Best American Short Stories 2007*. Boston: Houghton Mifflin, 2007.

Levine, Lawrence W. *Highbrow/Lowbrow: The Emergence of Cultural Hierarchy in America*. Cambridge, MA: Harvard UP, 1988.

Madden, David. *Bijou*. London: Avon, 1980.

Melville, Herman. "Letter to Nathaniel Hawthorne" 1 June 1851. *Correspondence: The Writings of Herman Melville*. Vol 14. Ed. Lynn Horth. Evanston, IL: Northwestern UP, 1993. 188-94.

Poe, Edgar Allan. "The Pit and the Pendulum." *The Complete Tales and Poems of Edgar Allan Poe*. London: Penguin, 1982.

The Shining. Dir. Stanley Kubrick. Screenplay by Stanley Kubrick and Diane Johnson. Perf. Jack Nicholson, Shelley Duvall, and Danny Lloyd. Warner Bros., Hawk Films, 1980.

Stephen King's Critical Reception_____

Philip L. Simpson

Stephen King is one of the most well-known and financially successful writers of all time, having published hundreds of novels, novellas, novelettes, poems, and short stories since his novelistic debut in 1973 with the horror thriller *Carrie*. Over the past four decades, his novels have consistently reached best-seller lists and been translated into many languages. Many of his books and short stories have been turned into financially successful movies. Through his use of contemporary vernacular language and realistic everyday settings, pointed cultural critique, sharp moral sensibility, and strongly imagistic writing, he has succeeded in attracting a loyal readership. As one of the most prolific writers working today, his track record has made him a brand name virtually synonymous with the horror, science fiction, and fantasy genres in which the majority of his work can be categorized.

His work is so popular and so identified with the horror genre, as a matter of fact, that he has long suffered from the dismissal or outright contempt of those literary critics who shun genre writing or equate market success with artistic failure. It is no exaggeration to state that many establishment and literary critics consider King to be a purveyor of cultural garbage—a writer of cheap horror thrillers, a trafficker in the supernatural, a panderer to the lowest common denominators in public taste, a hack incapable of writing a complex character or even of mastering the technical skills of his trade. This is why it was such a shock to those critics to learn one day in 2003 that the National Book Foundation, as part of its annual awards, had conferred upon King its prestigious lifetime achievement award: the Medal for Distinguished Contribution to American Letters. Now, certainly there had been warning signs for years that King was creeping slowly into literary respectability. After all, as George Beahm points out, King's writing had been appearing regularly in *The New Yorker*, and his story "The Man in the Black Suit" had won the coveted O. Henry Award in 1996, a notable landmark in King's journey to legitimacy because this fantasy story beat out other eligible stories by more "literary" writers (31). King had won many other awards over the years—including numerous Bram Stoker Awards, British Fantasy Awards, and Horror Guild Awards—but the O. Henry Award and the Medal for Distinguished Contribution were different. The National Book Foundation award in particular marks the moment at which King stepped forward from the ranks of popular genre writers and into the kind of serious literary respectability enjoyed by previous Distinguished Contribution winners—Eudora Welty, Gwendolyn Brooks, Toni Morrison, John Updike, Arthur Miller, and Philip Roth. It was a legitimation that had long eluded him in spite (or maybe because) of his possession of one of the most enviable sales records in American publishing history.

Most prominent (and outspoken) among the critics who were dismayed by the National Book Foundation's decision was Harold Bloom, Sterling Professor of the Humanities and English at Yale University and author of not only the weighty tome *The Western Canon* (1994) but also numerous scholarly books on authors as diverse as William Shakespeare, William Blake, and Wallace Stevens. An outraged Bloom, speaking for many of his fellow literary gatekeepers, wrote in a September 24, 2003, op-ed piece for the *Boston Globe* that the decision to give the award to King was "extraordinary, another low in the shocking process of dumbing down our cultural life. I've described King in the past as a writer of penny dreadfuls, but perhaps even that is too kind. He shares nothing with Edgar Allan Poe. What he is is an immensely inadequate writer on a sentence-by-sentence, paragraph-by-paragraph, book-by-book basis." For his part, King responded to his vocal detractors in his acceptance speech for the award:

> There are some people who have spoken out passionately about giving me this medal. There are some people who think it's an extraordinarily bad idea. . . . I salute the National Book Foundation Board, who took a huge risk in giving this award to a man many people see as a rich hack. For far

too long the so-called popular writers of this country and the so-called literary writers have stared at each other with animosity and a willful lack of
understanding. . . . But giving an award like this to a guy like me suggests
that in the future things don't have to be the way they've always been.
Bridges can be built between the so-called popular fiction and the so-called
literary fiction.

King's words explicitly acknowledge the schism between literary fiction and popular fiction but, at the same time, challenge both camps to
erase this distinction as arbitrary at best. It is also hard to miss the fact
that, in what should be a moment of personal and professional vindica-
tion, he is still making a defensive plea for acceptance from the literary
community that, for the most part, shuns him as a symbol of the death
of reading in America.

The irony of King's positioning vis-à-vis American literary history
could not be sharper. He is dismissed or even reviled because he, arguably more than any other living American popular writer, understands
and practices the ancient art of storytelling in a gripping, entertaining
manner. More than most (if not all) of the "literary" writers one could
name, his work directly touches the lives of many millions of people on
a regular basis, year after year. He confronts pressing topical issues and
social concerns through his fiction in an immediate way that leads
those same millions of readers to consider their own perspectives on
these issues even while they are entertained by a thrilling story. Finally,
and most significant, King is one of a handful of popular authors (J. K.
Rowling being another) who still cause vast numbers of people to read
rather than sit in front of their televisions or go to movies.

King's lengthy career (which, in spite of his frequent announce-
ments that he is retiring from writing, shows no signs of flagging) in its
most reductive sense can be characterized by two words: "prolific" and
"successful." Since 1973, he has published more than sixty novels
(several under the pseudonym Richard Bachman) and hundreds of
short stories. He has collaborated with writers such as Peter Straub. His

books have sold somewhere north of 350 million copies. Nearly eighty movies and television miniseries based on his work have been produced. He has written or cowritten more than forty screenplays for both television and film, and he has branched out into e-books and graphic novels. While most famous for his work in the horror genre, the versatile King has written science fiction (*The Tommyknockers*, 1987), epic fantasy (the seven-volume *Dark Tower* series, 1982-2004), apocalyptic fantasy (*The Stand*, 1978; expanded and revised, 1990), captivity narrative (*Misery*, 1987), mystery (*Dolores Claiborne*, 1992), hardboiled fiction (*The Colorado Kid*, 2005), literary criticism (*Danse Macabre*, 1981), nonfiction (*Faithful: Two Diehard Boston Red Sox Fans Chronicle the Historic 2004 Season*, 2004; with Stewart O'Nan), and writing primer/memoir (*On Writing*, 2000). Beginning with the four novellas contained in *Different Seasons* (1982), King moved away from the kind of supernatural horror tales that marked the beginning of his career into more realistic fiction, albeit fiction that contains horrific elements. He has also moved toward writing the kind of more intimate, personal dramas favored by many critics and away from the large-scale, crowd-pleasing epics that marked his early career.

Through sheer volume alone, King's career is a testament to the productive power of a year-round, disciplined writing schedule. While it is uncertain how much wealth King has accumulated during this massive multiple-decade output, there is absolutely no doubt that he is a millionaire many times over. *Forbes* magazine reported that in 2008 alone, for example, he made $45 million. In terms of output and commercial success, it is no exaggeration to label King a publishing industry or franchise unto himself—and hence the problem with his critical reception. Few critics trust a so-called franchise when it comes to judging artistic merit.

One of the biggest obstacles King faces in the critical evaluation of his legacy is his reputation as America's premier writer of supernatural horror. This convenient genre label dominates the popular media coverage of his work, and it is the label by which his status as celebrity writer is understood by most people. Yet the horror genre is regarded with deep suspicion by many social commentators and critics who proclaim themselves to be guardians of the public morality. The links between the violence depicted in horror fiction and cinema and the violence committed by real-life criminals have been debated without any clear resolution for decades; the concern over the morality of horror fiction historically goes back even further. King devotes an entire chapter in his critical study *Danse Macabre* to an examination of the morality of horror and the question of whether he shares any culpability for real-life instances of violent behavior that are seemingly inspired by horror movies or books, including his own. He finds that the horror tale is, at its core, actually quite conservative in its reaffirmation of "the virtues of the norm by showing us what awful things happen to people who venture into taboo lands" (395). He concludes by saying, "If the horror story is our rehearsal for death, then its strict moralities make it also a reaffirmation of life and good will and simple imagination—just one more pipeline to the infinite" (409). It is a valiant intellectual and moral attempt to defend horror as a story type against its detractors. Nevertheless, King's indelible association with a genre often considered disreputable by so-called serious literary critics serves, from the perspective of some, to automatically disqualify him from consideration as a literary writer—this in spite of the many stories and novels King has written that may contain horrific elements but do not actually fall within the horror genre.

Of course, King did not help his own case much when he described his fiction back in 1982 as "the literary equivalent of a Big Mac and fries," a phrase that has since been widely quoted. This charmingly self-deprecating remark, by which King likely intended to throw off his detractors by partially agreeing with their appraisals of his work, only gave critics more leverage to hoist King by his own petard. Starting with the publication of *Carrie* in 1974 and continuing ever since, the literary elite have tended to aggressively deny King admittance into the "club," while King has continued to both deny his need to be validated by critical acceptance and work hard to gain it. At times King has made plaintive admissions that he does crave acceptance from the literary establishment, as when he told *New York Times* book reviewer Bill Goldstein, "I'd like to win the National Book Award, the Pulitzer Prize, the Nobel Prize. . . . But it's not going to happen" (8). King's public persona is paradoxical in this regard. He is a study in contradictions. He eschews intellectualism and has made many acidic remarks both verbally and in his writing about the pretensions endemic to the academic study of literature, but, as a former English teacher, he quite clearly knows literary tradition and history and can readily discuss how his own work fits within them and which canonical writers have influenced him. *Danse Macabre* can even be counted as a work of literary criticism. He favors an unpretentious, blue-collar, Joe Six-Pack look and vernacular language but is a multimillionaire many times over. He is grateful for his celebrity, but he can also be derisive about the endless inane questions adoring fans ask him. At times he seems to fear what some of his more unbalanced fans might be capable of doing. (King's darkest fears about his readership can be found encapsulated in his novel *Misery*, in which a writer of popular romance fiction is held captive and tortured by his "Number One Fan.") In spite of his sometime prickly attitude toward critics, he has no trouble garnering plenty of blurbs from favorable reviews for the covers of his paperback best sellers. But true validation from the literary establishment eluded him until his Medal for Distinguished Contribution. Meanwhile, indifferent to the critical tussle over King's literary legacy, King's readership maintains its enthusiastic embrace of his work, catapulting each newly published book to the top of best-seller lists.

Another irony inherent to the conflicted critical reception of King's work is just how many scholars over the years have written about him and, of these, how many have forcefully advocated for his inclusion in the pantheon of great American writers. During the 1970s and early 1980s, very little published King criticism existed, and only then did it seem credible to claim that scholars were somehow ignoring King. But beginning with pioneering works such as Tim Underwood and Chuck Miller's edited volume *Fear Itself: The Horror Fiction of Stephen King* (1982) and Douglas E. Winter's *Stephen King: The Art of Darkness* (1984), which were directed at niche markets, many dozens more monographs, journal articles, and edited volumes on the so-called meaning of King's fiction have been published. The market for King scholarship has exponentially increased. As one of the earliest critical advocates for King and a self-acknowledged fan, Winter writes that *The Art of Darkness* "is best described as a critical appreciation; it is an intermingling of biography, literary analysis, and unabashed enthusiasm" (xiii). Tony Magistrale, another critic and enthusiast, has claimed that King's best work is reminiscent of Shakespeare. (One can practically hear Bloom, author of the hagiographic *Shakespeare: Invention of the Human* [1998], gasp in horror at this comparison.) But for sheer adoration, no one matches Jonathan P. Davis, who embarked on "a research project centered around traveling to [King's] home base, Maine, where I would study his life and read the volumes of his work he has donated to his alma mater, the University of Maine at Orono" (4).

In the conclusion to his introduction of the resulting *Stephen King's America*, Davis waxes rhapsodic:

> Stephen King trips some live wire deep in the hearts of his reading public in a way that cannot be compared to other popular artists. He calls to us, he speaks our language, he shares our problems. He understands who we are. (5)

If the sheer volume of published critical analyses of a writer's work and the ardor of the writer's champions are indicators of whether said writer is so-called legitimate, then King obviously clears the threshold.

But of course quantity and enthusiasm of criticism do not necessarily equate to admission into the canon of American literature. Don Herron, while acknowledging the breadth of the secondary "King criticism" industry, argues that most of this criticism comes from "fantasy-horror" fans and not "major mainstream critics and working professors." Thus, Herron says, much of the extant King scholarship is flawed by the reverence in which the writers hold King and the absolute authority they grant to his frequent public statements about the meaning of his own fiction. Of King's work itself, Herron says he has "never read fiction as ready made for critical explication as King's. He has taught English at both high school and college levels, and he loads his work with themes, recurring motifs, cross-references." According to Herron, King wants his work to be taken seriously by critics and toward that end fills his novels with what King calls in *Danse Macabre* "subtext," which Herron defines as "important adult concerns about politics, relationships, or economics which invest an otherwise popular novel or film with serious intent" (21). Herron's unequivocal claim that working professors do not publish scholarly work on King is demonstrably erroneous, as the scholarly output of professor and King critic Tony Magistrale alone attests, but Herron's point about King's intent to be recognized as both a popular and a literary writer is spot on.

Clearly, beneath the fictional horror, King constructs his novels to be about something—the real-life horrors of loneliness, cancer, disease, spousal abuse, child neglect. For King, this nod toward literarily treating serious social ills legitimates the horror genre and, most important, his fiction. How well he manages this balancing act between social realism and horror fantasy is at the heart of the critical debate about King.

The tension between critics who embrace or at least appreciate King's aesthetic and those who deplore it is readily apparent in any examination of the critical response. Of the latter, Harold Bloom undoubtedly has the highest profile. As a major literary critic by anyone's definition, Bloom has made it something of a personal crusade to point out not so much what he considers to be the obvious deficiencies in King's fiction but what King's success signifies about the general state of American literacy. Bloom readily concedes his own fight to be hopeless in the face of King's enduring popularity (he even agrees that

King seems to be a decent enough fellow), and he does acknowledge that his writing possesses undeniable imagistic strength. But for Bloom, King's weaknesses far outweigh his strengths. In his introduction to the King volume in his Modern Critical Views series, Bloom states:

> The triumph of the genial King is a large emblem of the failures of American education. . . . I cannot locate any aesthetic dignity in King's writing: his public could not sustain it, nor could he. There is a palpable sincerity to everything that he has done: that testifies to his decency, and to his social benignity. Art unfortunately is rarely the fruit of earnestness, and King will be remembered as a sociological phenomenon, an image of the death of the Literate Reader. (2-3)

The "death of the Literate Reader" motif looms large in Bloom's writings about popular writers, most of whom he has even less use for than he does King. To Bloom, King's ascendancy augurs what seems to be nothing less dire than the decline of Western literature. He charges that King emerges from the "subliterary" tradition of Edgar Allan Poe and H. P. Lovecraft and constitutes a cultural nadir of sorts, in which visual storytelling and the World Wide Web dethrone reading. According to Bloom, King as an imagistic writer creates "visually oriented scenarios" that "tend to improve when filmed" (BioCritiques 2). This visual tendency in King's work is perhaps Bloom's most urgent complaint about him: King is not so much a writer of literature as a presenter of information in the virtual era.

Of King's detractors, Bloom makes the most sweeping case against acceptance of King into the American literature canon. Bloom rarely breaks his indictment down into its particulars; however, many other critics from both the mainstream and academia are all too happy to articulate their charges against King in granular detail. A range of complaints are summarized thusly by Herron: King's characters are flat, he "borrows" all his ideas, he is too sentimental or naive to be considered a "great" writer, he does not have technical mastery over his material, and his narratives display frequent logical lapses (24-36). Magistrale writes that King is frequently criticized for "the fact that his writing tries to do too much. He often employs sentence fragments and awkward metaphors, and sometimes his prose gets so caught up with the emotion of the moment that it veers out of control" ("Stephen King" 854). Other critics take issue with King's signature themes and concerns. Michael R. Collings argues that King's fiction often displays an alarming amount of homophobia—as exemplified in the scene at the beginning of *It* (1986) in which a homosexual young man is beaten and thrown into a canal by a group of men—and that King himself shares this homophobia (*Phenomenon* 23).

King also comes under criticism for racism in his work, particularly for his use of what are sometimes called "magical Negro" characters: black characters, such as John Coffey (whose initials significantly are J. C.) in *The Green Mile*, who possess supernatural or otherworldly powers and sacrifice themselves to save white characters. King himself concedes that his black characters, including Dick Hallorann in *The Shining* and Mother Abagail in *The Stand*, "are cardboard caricatures of superblack heroes, viewed through rose-tinted glasses of white-liberal guilt" (*Bare Bones* 47). But the charge most often leveled against King is sexism or phallocentrism, which began with Chelsea Quinn Yarbro in 1982 when she wrote, "It is disheartening when a writer with so much talent and strength and vision is not able to develop a believable woman character between the ages of seventeen and sixty" (65). Mary Pharr observes, "King's women are reflective of American stereotypes" (21). Kathleen Margaret Lant goes beyond even King's fiction to charge that the author, in his frequent addresses to readers in his introductions, constructs himself as a powerfully masculine seducer and his audience as pliantly feminine. Lant finds the dynamic between King and his audience to be disturbingly similar to that of a rape: "For [King's] penis is linked very strongly to his creativity, and his creativity is most clearly a weapon by means of which, when as an audience we behave properly, he pleases, but by means of which, when we transcend the bounds of appropriate behavior, he punishes. His greatest moments of creative joy seem to come when he can reduce us to the submissive position of female audience to his masculine creator" (163). Responding directly to these kinds of accusations, in the early 1990s King embarked on a period in which he wrote what are often called his domestic novels: *Gerald's Game* (1992); *Dolores Claiborne* (1993); and *Rose Madder* (1995). These stories center on abused women who empower themselves against the threat posed by cruel or repressive men. Though doubt remained as to King's credentials as a feminist writer, his forays into female-centered stories, as well as nonsupernatural-themed fiction such as *Misery*, began to shift "the critical tide," as Karin Coddon notes, "in favor of King" (24).

The critics who find value in King's work tend to focus on his ability to anchor his more fantastic imaginings to social realism. As Edwin F. Casebeer observes, King infuses his narratives with enough subtext to craft elaborate allegories that address the corruption inherent in everyday life and institutions, a thematic agenda that eventually expands to pathological heterosexual relationships in works such as *Gerald's Game*. However, even while exploring such volatile territory, King manages to avoid polemic, for the most part. In fact, Casebeer argues, King's "chief artistic talent—the talent that has kept all his work in print throughout his career and is likely to keep it in print—is his ability to balance opposing realities. The reader must resolve the issues." King's thematic ambiguity, in fact, is often cited as the strongest aspect of his writing. Others, such as Tony Magistrale, laud King for carrying forth the gothic vision of nineteenth-century writers such as Edgar Allan Poe and Nathaniel Hawthorne into contemporary America. King has also been called the literary heir to William Shakespeare and Charles Dickens, both of whom wrote crowd-pleasing "popular" works and have also been canonized among the greats of Western literature. Critics further note that King's ability to create believable characters has also improved during his career, moving from the precocious children and adolescents of his early fiction to rounded, mature adults—both male and female—in his later work. But as both King's critics and general readers might agree, one of the main reasons for valuing King's contribution to American culture is his ability to tell a riveting story populated by believable characters.

So much critical commentary has been published on King's fiction that readers hoping to utilize this material to gain a better understanding of King's signature themes and his place within American letters may find it quite daunting to sort through. Space limitations here make it impossible to provide any kind of comprehensive listing or summary of all the published critical responses to King. What is possible is to identify the categories of critical responses and examine a few representative examples of each. The categories include concordances and readers' guides, biographical works, essay collections, and book-length studies, both those of a general nature and those of more specialized interests.

Through his enormous output of writing, King's imaginative world has grown so large, his story lines so interrelated, and his number of characters so vast that the casual reader can be quickly overwhelmed. A little more than a decade after King's first novel was published, it became clear that a reference guide was needed to provide a compass to help readers navigate the topography of King's fictional landscapes. Toward that end, Michael R. Collings's *The Stephen King Concordance* (1985) was published. As prolific as King is, however, a relatively steady need exists for new concordances and reference guides. Stephen J. Spignesi's *The Shape Under the Sheet: The Complete Stephen King Encyclopedia* (1991), later revised as *The Essential Stephen King: A Ranking of the Greatest Novels, Short Stories, Movies, and Other Creations of the World's Most Popular Writer* (2001), is a comprehensive reference guide, covering characters and place-names in all of King's works to date. Spignesi is also the author of *The Lost Work of Stephen King* (1998), which catalogs unpublished work, alternative versions to published work, and the like. George Beahm's *Stephen King from A to Z* (1998) is quite accessible to the general reader, containing hundreds of entries on all aspects of King's life, career, and critical reception.

The most recent such reference work is Stanley Wiater, Christopher Golden, and Hank Wagner's *The Complete Stephen King Universe* (2006). As the authors note in the book's introduction, King's universe is "an incredible place of grotesque terror, dark magic, and fearsome wonder, a great multiverse conjured from one individual's imagination. It is a vast and still growing kingdom, and its many pathways can veer off into the darkest regions, where it's all too easy to get lost without guidance" (xv). *The Complete Stephen King Universe* is the most up-to-date reference work available to cover the gamut of King's short fiction, novels, films, screenplays, and miniseries, although, as the authors note, the book is not so much a concordance or encyclopedia as a guidebook. Including a chronology of King's life and fiction, the book is divided into sections, each dealing with a significant "corner" of King's multiverse, such as the worlds of the *Dark Tower* series and *The Stand*; the fictional cities of Derry, Castle Rock, and Jerusalem's Lot and the state of Maine itself; the sinister supersecret governmental agency The Shop; and the novels of King's alter ego Richard Bachman.

While *The Complete Stephen King Universe* provides a comprehensive overview of King's work, it does not do justice to the complexity of King's magnum opus fantasy series *The Dark Tower. The Dark Tower* is the collective title of a series of books (numbering seven volumes as of 2010) totaling thousands of pages in length and extending over the breadth of King's career. The fantasy epic, begun in 1970, has evolved into the fundamental fictional universe upon which the rest of King's fiction is built. The "Tower" of the title is the bolt or "nexus" that holds all of King's fictional worlds together: as the epic unfolds, the world of the Dark Tower and King's other parallel realities frequently overlap. Just to give a few examples, the villainous Randall Flagg of *The Stand* plays a pivotal role in the *Dark Tower* series. Father

Callahan, fallen from grace after his encounter with the king vampire Barlow in *'Salem's Lot* (1975), reappears. King himself even appears as a character. In collaboration with Stephen King, Robin Furth published volume 1 of *Stephen King's "The Dark Tower": A Concordance* in 2003, with the second volume following in 2005 and the complete concordance in 2006. King states in the introduction to volume 1 that the concordance was not intended for publication but rather as a writer's tool to keep straight all of his place-names, characters, plot twists, and so on, as he worked on the later novels in the series. However, as he acknowledges, the concordance is also valuable to King's "Constant Reader," hence its publication (x). With *The Complete Stephen King Universe* and *Stephen King's "The Dark Tower": The Complete Concordance*, King's readership now has access to two indispensable guidebooks.

Biographical material on Stephen King is readily available, but typically as a chapter in a book-length critical study or a mass-media article. For example, Douglas E. Winter's *Stephen King: The Art of Darkness*, contains one of the first published biographical chapters on King. King himself reveals many autobiographical details in the interviews contained in *Bare Bones: Conversations on Terror with Stephen King* (1988), edited by Tim Underwood and Chuck Miller. The same editors followed up this volume with *Feast of Fear: Conversations with Stephen King* (1989, 1992). *The Stephen King Story* (1991) by George Beahm is a relatively early book-length biography and critical analysis of the first phase of King's career, but the book tends to suffer from Beahm's uncritical view of King. Beahm's second biography of King, *Stephen King: America's Best Loved Boogeyman* (1998), is equally reverent, if not more so, but it contains a wealth of biographical detail and a slightly more in-depth analysis of King's influences. *Haunted Heart: The Life and Times of Stephen King* (2008), a recent unauthorized biography by Lisa Rogak, is well researched and quite detailed. Rogak's work includes not only the customary ruminations on the possible linkages between biographical circumstance and King's preoccupation with horror but also insightful accounts of King's troubled family relationships, struggles with alcohol and drug addiction, and painful recovery from his near-fatal 1999 accident, when he was struck by a van while taking his daily walk. Rogak's work is recommended for the reader interested in learning more about King's life in relation to his art.

Many collections of critical essays on King have also been published. The first, the aforementioned *Fear Itself*, contains an eclectic mix of essays written by, among others, traditional scholars; best-selling novelists such as Peter Straub, Fritz Leiber, Charles Grant, and Chelsea Quinn Yarbro; film archivist Bill Warren; columnist and bookstore owner Deborah L. Notkin and filmmaker George R. Romero. The result is uneven. King himself pinpoints a flaw in the book: "I think a lot of the essays in it are kind of sophomoric. They're sort of like essay questions on a junior-level college English exam" (*Bare Bones* 151). *Reign of Fear: Fiction and Film of Stephen King* (1988), edited by Don Herron, shares something of the same hodgepodge feel, in that it contains essays by genre writers such as Frank Belknap Long, a physician, and actress Whoopi Goldberg, among others. But in short order, other collections, consisting of essays from a more traditional and rigorous scholarly perspective, were published, including *Discovering Stephen King* (1985), edited by Darrell Schweitzer, and *Kingdom of Fear: The World of Stephen King* (1986), edited by Tim Underwood and Chuck Miller. The former book contains essays by Randall D. Larson and Michael R. Collings; the latter is striking for Underwood's comment in his essay "The Skull Beneath the Skin" that King's fiction "probably won't last" (255). An important early volume is *The Gothic World of Stephen King: Landscape of Nightmares* (1987), a collection of essays edited by Gary Hoppenstand and Ray B. Browne. In the introduction, the editors posit that King's success in defiance of the critics is attributable to his storytelling ability and the broad appeal of his Horatio Alger-like rise from rags to riches (2). The volume includes essays by writers soon to become integral to the scholarly study of King, including Magistrale and Pharr. Another important volume, *The Dark Descent: Essays Defining Stephen King's Horrorscape* (1992), edited by Tony Magistrale, marks one of the first sustained scholarly attempts to make a serious case for King's inclusion in the canon of American literature. Magistrale also edited two King casebooks focused on a single work: *"The Shining" Reader* (1991), later republished as *Discovering Stephen King's "The Shining"* (1991), and *A Casebook on "The Stand"* (1992). However, one of the largest hurdles King faces in his bid for literary respectability is the frequent accusation of sexism that is leveled against him. From this perspective, the essays contained in *Imagining the Worst: Stephen King and the Representation of Women* (1998), edited by Kathleen Margaret Lant and Theresa Thompson, directly confront what is for many the problematic gender construction and gender politics of King's fiction. Harold Bloom, in the course of his introduction to the Stephen King volume of his Modern Critical Views series, presents the most negative critical assessment of King, saying that his popularity represents the failure of American education and reading (2).

In the 2000s, compilations of King criticism continue to flourish. Bloom's BioCritiques volume *Stephen King* (2002), edited by Harold Bloom, contains the customary dismissive opening by Bloom, but then moves into notable essays by Michael R. Collings and Tony Magistrale, among others. *Readings on Stephen King* (2004), edited by Karin Coddon and published by Greenhaven Press as part of its series of literary companions to contemporary authors, contains essays by King stalwarts George Beahm, Michael R. Collings, and Douglas E. Winter, among others. Bloom returns to the fray once more with a 2007 update to his Modern Critical Views volume on King, which includes essays on subjects as diverse as masculinity, the gothic tradition, homophobia, political consciousness, naturalism, and sexuality in King's work. Finally, there is *The Films of Stephen King: From "Carrie" to "Secret Window"* (2008), edited by Tony Magistrale. It contains scholarly analyses of, among others, the film adaptations of *Apt Pupil*, *Pet*

Sematary, Christine, The Shining, Misery, The Green Mile, The Dead Zone, Needful Things, and *Secret Window.*

Many book-length analyses also have been published in the expanding field of King studies. Clearly, King's literary reputation underwent something of a small but noticeable tectonic shift during the mid-1980s and on through the 1990s, and, as Greg Smith notes, the rehabilitation of King's reputation owes a great deal to books written by Tony Magistrale and Michael R. Collings. Both of these critics argue that King is not a schlockmeister, that he indeed transcends the horror genre in which he began, and that he is a social critic or even satirist whose supernatural monsters stand in for the real demons confronting Americans: a corrupt political system, alcoholism, religious extremism, disintegrating family structures, prescriptive gender roles, and the like. In *Landscape of Fear: Stephen King's American Gothic* (1988), Magistrale states unequivocally that his intent is "to enhance the literary reputation—which, as we have seen, is often at odds with a popular one—of Stephen King's fiction by giving it the type of analysis it justly deserves, and for too long has failed to enjoy" (12). Magistrale goes even further in *The Moral Voyages of Stephen King* (1989), writing that King is "the rightful heir to a literary tradition that includes Poe and Hawthorne, Dickens and Stoker" (iv) and hectoring the critical establishment to embrace King before he is consigned to obscurity as just another popular writer. It is this kind of zealous defense that characterizes Magistrale's King scholarship. For Magistrale, King is the heir to the modern American gothic tradition, a critical stance Magistrale returns to repeatedly. Other books authored by Magistrale include *Stephen King: The Second Decade, "Danse Macabre" to "The Dark Half"* (1992) and *Hollywood's Stephen King* (2003). The former examines the sheer diversity of literary genres in which King is adept, while the latter makes a strong case that, in spite of some highly publicized "flops," the screen adaptations of King's work are a proven commodity both commercially and critically and, like King's published work, require more extensive scholarly examination.

Collings's attitude toward King is slightly more circumspect than Magistrale's, but his enthusiasm can be inferred from a statement such as this, from the foreword to his *Many Facets of Stephen King*: "[King's] forms and themes intertwine, reflecting each other, glittering like the continuous movement of light around a brilliantly set gemstone" (3). Collings is notable not only for the academic quality but also the sheer quantity of scholarly studies on King that he published with Starmont House in a few short years, including *The Shorter Works of Stephen King* (1985), *The Many Facets of Stephen King* (1985), *Stephen King as Richard Bachman* (1985), *The Films of Stephen King* (1986), *The Annotated Guide to Stephen King: A Primary and Secondary Bibliography of the Works of America's Premier Horror Writer* (1986), and *The Stephen King Phenomenon* (1987). Collings writes of his own work for Starmont that the "volumes are not specifically academic; they are, instead, intended for serious readers of King who might benefit from discussions, backgrounds, and generalized analysis" (77-78); as such, these books constitute an important bridge between an academic and general readership—an endeavor King himself would undoubtedly endorse. Collings's latest King book is the exhaustive *Horror Plum'd: An International Stephen King Bibliography and Guide, 1960-2000* (2003), which covers everything written by and about King for forty years. For the general reader or the serious scholar, this reference work is invaluable.

Other notable book-length studies include Joseph Reino's *Stephen King: The First Decade, from "Carrie" to "Pet Sematary"* (1988); Tyson Blue's *The Unseen King* (1989), a valuable exploration of King's student writing, poetry, and screenplays; Carroll F. Terrell's *Stephen King: Man and Artist* (1990); James Van Hise's *Stephen King and Clive Barker* (1990), in which Van Hise determines that King's belief in good stands in stark contrast to Barker's more amoral fictional universe and may account for King's greater popularity; Jonathan P. Davis's *Stephen King's America* (1994), which explores the many uniquely American subtexts in King's fiction; Linda Badley's *Writing*

Horror and the Body: The Fiction of Stephen King, Clive Barker, and Anne Rice, in which Badley contrasts King's norm-affirming ethos against the "carnival of the perverse" (xii) embodied by Clive Barker and Anne Rice; Sharon A. Russell's *Revisiting Stephen King: A Critical Companion* (2002), which provides in-depth readings of selected novels and makes the case that, as King changed publishers with *Bag of Bones* in 1998 and began experimenting with narrative form, "some people sensed a new seriousness in his fiction" (16); Heidi Strengell's *Dissecting Stephen King: From the Gothic to Literary Naturalism* (2005), which rests on the central belief that "King (when he is not Richard Bachman, the naturalistic pseudonym) is a traditionalist writer in our post-traditional world, . . . whose multiverse presents the moral message that dedication, determination, and will power may sometimes overcome seemingly impossible odds" (17); and Patrick McAleer's *Inside the "Dark Tower" Series* (2009), which constitutes the first genuine scholarly study of *The Dark Tower*, notwithstanding Bev Vincent's more general work *The Road to the Dark Tower: Exploring Stephen King's Magnum Opus* (2004).

As this wealth of secondary material illustrates, the field of King studies is not only alive but also thriving. As King himself continues to push beyond the boundaries of genre in his experiments with narrative form and contemporary social allegory, so too does his status as "America's foremost writer of supernatural horror" continue to evolve. By combining genres and playing the kind of metatextual narrative games (such as writing himself as a character into his own narrative) associated with postmodernism, King has worked diligently to keep himself relevant to the critics as well as the public. Perhaps swayed by his much-debated turn to so-called feminist and nonsupernatural writing in the 1990s, by the fervor of his early critical champions, or by the sheer magnitude of the impact he has had upon the culture, many of the mainstream critics and literary scholars who once dismissed King as a hack writer have come to reevaluate his work. Indeed, the National Book Foundation rewarded King as much for his charitable work, his advocacy for beginning or lesser-known writers, and the number of his books adapted for the screen as it did for the artistry of his work. King's work has been turned into films and television episodes, series, and miniseries, thus creating a secondary industry that, in its reach and financial power, rivals or even exceeds King's own formidable written output. Additionally, King's cultural influence is apparent in the number of allusions to him and his work that appear in film, television, music, and novels. King's literary output shows no sign of dissipating: his latest novel, *Under the Dome* (2009), clocks in as one of his longest works yet. So it is certain that King's career will continue to evolve, and that he will continue to please audiences, rile his detractors, marshal his champions, and generate critical commentary for a long time to come.

Works Cited

Badley, Linda. *Writing Horror and the Body: The Fiction of Stephen King, Clive Barker, and Anne Rice*. Westport, CT: Greenwood Press, 1996.

Beahm, George. *Stephen King: America's Best Loved Boogeyman*. Kansas City, MO: Andrews McMeel, 1998.

_____. "Stephen King: Celebrity Writer or Modern Master?" *Readings on Stephen King*. Ed. Karin Coddon. San Diego, CA: Greenhaven Press, 2004. 29-33.

_____. *Stephen King from A to Z: An Encyclopedia of His Life and Work*. Kansas City, MO: Andrews McMeel, 1998.

_____. *The Stephen King Story: A Literary Profile*. 1991. Boston: Little, Brown, 1993.

Bloom, Harold. "Dumbing Down American Readers." *Boston Globe* 24 Sept. 2003. 29 Jan. 2010. http://www.boston.com/news/globe/editorial_opinion/oped/articles/2003/09/24/dumbing_down_american_readers/.

_____. "Introduction." *Stephen King*. Ed. Harold Bloom. Bloom's BioCritiques. Philadelphia: Chelsea House, 2002. 1-2.

_____. "Introduction." *Stephen King*. Updated ed. Ed. Harold Bloom. Bloom's Modern Critical Views. Philadelphia: Chelsea House, 2007. 1-3.

_____. *Shakespeare: The Invention of the Human*. New York: Riverhead Books, 1998.

_____. *The Western Canon: The Books and School of the Ages*. New York: Harcourt Brace, 1994.

_____, ed. *Stephen King*. Bloom's BioCritiques. Philadelphia: Chelsea House, 2002.

_____, ed. *Stephen King*. Updated ed. Bloom's Modern Critical Views. Philadelphia: Chelsea House, 2007.

Blue, Tyson. *The Unseen King*. Mercer Island, WA: Starmont House, 1989.

Casebeer, Edwin F. "The Art of Balance: Stephen King's Canon." *A Dark Night's Dreaming: Contemporary American Horror Fiction*. Ed. Tony Magistrale and Michael A. Morrison. Columbia: University of South Carolina Press, 1996. 42-54.

Coddon, Karin. "Stephen King: A Biography." *Readings on Stephen King*. Ed. Karin Coddon. San Diego, CA: Greenhaven Press, 2004. 16-27.

_____, ed. *Readings on Stephen King*. San Diego, CA: Greenhaven Press, 2004.

Collings, Michael R. *The Annotated Guide to Stephen King: A Primary and Secondary Bibliography of the Works of America's Premier Horror Writer*. Mercer Island, WA: Starmont House, 1986.

_____. *The Films of Stephen King*. Mercer Island, WA: Starmont House, 1986.

_____. *The Many Facets of Stephen King*. Mercer Island, WA: Starmont House, 1985.

_____. *Stephen King as Richard Bachman*. Mercer Island, WA: Starmont House, 1985.

_____. *The Stephen King Concordance*. Mercer Island, WA: Starmont House, 1985.

_____. *The Stephen King Phenomenon*. Mercer Island, WA: Starmont House, 1987.

Collings, Michael R., and David Engebretson. *The Shorter Works of Stephen King*. Mercer Island, WA: Starmont House, 1985.

Davis, Jonathan P. *Stephen King's America*. Bowling Green, OH: Bowling Green State University Popular Press, 1994.

Furth, Robin. *Stephen King's "The Dark Tower": A Concordance*. 2 vols. New York: Charles Scribner's Sons, 2003-2005.

_____. *Stephen King's "The Dark Tower": The Complete Concordance*. New York: Charles Scribner's Sons, 2006.

Goldstein, Bill. "King of Horror." *Publishers Weekly* 24 Jan. 1991: 6-9.

Herron, Don. "Stephen King: The Good, the Bad, and the Academic." *Stephen King*. Updated ed. Ed. Harold Bloom. Bloom's Modern Critical Views. Philadelphia: Chelsea House, 2007. 17-40.

_____, ed. *Reign of Fear: Fiction and Film of Stephen King*. Los Angeles: Underwood- Miller, 1988.

Hoppenstand, Gary, and Ray B. Browne, eds. *The Gothic World of Stephen King: Landscape of Nightmares*. Bowling Green, OH: Bowling Green State University Popular Press, 1987.

King, Stephen. *Bare Bones: Conversations on Terror with Stephen King*. Eds. Tim Underwood and Chuck Miller. 1988. New York: Warner, 1989.

_____. *Danse Macabre*. 1981. New York: Berkley Books, 1983.

_____. National Book Award acceptance speech. National Book Founda-

tion. 19 Nov. 2003. 29 Jan. 2010. http://www.nationalbook.org/nbaacceptspeech
_sking.html.

Lant, Kathleen Margaret. "The Rape of Constant Reader: Stephen King's Con-
struction of the Female Reader and Violation of the Female Body in *Misery*."
Stephen King. Updated ed. Ed. Harold Bloom. Bloom's Modern Critical Views.
Philadelphia: Chelsea House, 2007. 141-66.

Lant, Kathleen Margaret, and Theresa Thompson, eds. *Imagining the Worst: Stephen
King and the Representation of Women*. Westport, CT: Greenwood Press, 1998.

McAleer, Patrick. *Inside the "Dark Tower" Series: Art, Evil, and Intertextuality in
the Stephen King Novels*. Jefferson, NC: McFarland, 2009.

Magistrale, Tony. *Hollywood's Stephen King*. New York: Palgrave Macmillan,
2003.

_____. *The Moral Voyages of Stephen King*. Mercer Island, WA:
Starmont House, 1989.

_____. "Stephen King." *Popular Contemporary Writers*. Vol. 6. Ed. Mi-
chael D. Sharp. New York: Marshall Cavendish Reference, 2006.

_____. *Stephen King: The Second Decade, "Danse Macabre" to "The
Dark Half."* New York: Twayne, 1992.

_____, ed. *A Casebook on "The Stand."* Mercer Island, WA: Starmont
House, 1992.

_____, ed. *The Dark Descent: Essays Defining Stephen King's Horror-
scape*. Westport, CT: Greenwood Press, 1992.

_____, ed. *Discovering Stephen King's "The Shining."* San Bernardino,
CA: Borgo Press, 1998.

_____, ed. *The Films of Stephen King: From "Carrie" to "Secret Win-
dow."* New York: Palgrave Macmillan, 2008.

_____, ed. *"The Shining" Reader*. Mercer Island, WA: Starmont House,
1991.

Pharr, Mary. "Partners in the *Danse*: Women in Stephen King's Fiction." *The Dark
Descent: Essays Defining Stephen King's Horrorscape*. Ed. Tony Magistrale.
Westport, CT: Greenwood Press, 1992. 19-32.

Reino, Joseph. *Stephen King: The First Decade, from "Carrie" to "Pet Sematary."*
Boston: Twayne, 1988.

Rogak, Lisa. *Haunted Heart: The Life and Times of Stephen King*. New York:
Thomas Dunne Books, 2008.

Russell, Sharon A. *Revisiting Stephen King: A Critical Companion*. Westport, CT:
Greenwood Press, 2002.

Schweitzer, Darrell, ed. *Discovering Stephen King*. Mercer Island, WA: Starmont
House, 1985.

Smith, Greg. "The Literary Equivalent of a Big Mac and Fries? Academics, Moral-
ists, and the Stephen King Phenomenon." *Midwest Quarterly* 43.4 (Summer
2002): 329-45.

Spignesi, Stephen J. *The Essential Stephen King: A Ranking of the Greatest Novels,
Short Stories, Movies, and Other Creations of the World's Most Popular
Writer*. Franklin Lakes, NJ: New Page, 2001.

_____. *The Lost Work of Stephen King: A Guide to Unpublished Manuscripts, Story Fragments, Alternative Versions, and Oddities*. Secaucus, NJ: Birch Lane Press, 1998.

_____. *The Shape Under the Sheet: The Stephen King Encyclopedia*. Ann Arbor, MI: Popular Culture Ink, 1991.

Strengell, Heidi. *Dissecting Stephen King: From the Gothic to Literary Naturalism*. Madison: U of Wisconsin P, 2005.

Terrell, Carroll F. *Stephen King: Man and Artist*. Orono, ME: Northern Lights, 1990.

Underwood, Tim. "The Skull Beneath the Skin." *Kingdom of Fear: The World of Stephen King*. Ed. Tim Underwood and Chuck Miller. New York: New American Library, 1986. 255-67.

Underwood, Tim, and Chuck Miller, eds. *Fear Itself: The Horror Fiction of Stephen King*. 1982. New York: Signet, 1985.

_____, eds. *Feast of Fear: Conversations with Stephen King*. 1989. New York: Carroll & Graf, 1992.

_____, eds. *Kingdom of Fear: The World of Stephen King*. New York: New American Library, 1986.

Van Hise, James. *Stephen King and Clive Barker: The Illustrated Masters of the Macabre*. Las Vegas: Pioneer Books, 1990.

Vincent, Bev. *The Road to the Dark Tower: Exploring Stephen King's Magnum Opus*. New York: New American Library, 2004.

Wiater, Stanley, Christopher Golden, and Hank Wagner. *The Complete Stephen King Universe: A Guide to the Worlds of Stephen King*. New York: St. Martin's Griffin, 2006.

Winter, Douglas E. *Stephen King: The Art of Darkness*. 1984. New York: Signet, 1986.

Yarbro, Chelsea Quinn. "Cinderella's Revenge: Twists on Fairy Tale and Mythic Themes in the Work of Stephen King." *Fear Itself: The Horror Fiction of Stephen King*. 1982. Ed. Tim Underwood and Chuck Miller. New York: Signet, 1985. 61-71.

Writers and Metafiction in Three Stephen King Texts_____

Dominick Grace

Few things fascinate Stephen King more than the process of writing itself. He has written two books on the process of composition: *On Writing: A Memoir of the Craft*, and *Secret Windows: Essays and Fiction on the Craft of Writing*, both published in 2000. The title of the second of these echoes that of his novella *Secret Window, Secret Garden*, to be discussed below. He has also written his own idiosyncratic study of and commentary on horror as a genre, *Danse Macabre* (1981). Furthermore, he has also repeatedly used writers as major characters in his work. While at times their writerly craft is relatively unimportant (the fact that Ben Mears, the protagonist of King's second novel, *'Salem's Lot* [1975], is a writer, for instance, is not a central plot element, and the writer character of *Lisey's Story* [2006], Scott Landon, is dead before the novel begins), the status of the writer *as* writer is often central. One of the best-known examples, perhaps, is Jack Torrance, protagonist of *The Shining*, whose descent into insanity is directly linked to his writer's block—an idea King revisited years later in *Bag of Bones* (1998), though with a happier result for that novel's protagonist, Mike Noonan.

However, three of King's works stand out as especially concerned with the writing process and its dangers. These are *Misery*, *The Dark Half*, and the novella *Secret Window, Secret Garden*, published in *Four Past Midnight*. King himself links these works as a kind of unofficial trilogy in his prefatory note to *Secret Window, Secret Garden*:

> A few years ago [1987], I published a novel called *Misery* which tried, at least in part, to illustrate the powerful hold fiction can achieve over the reader. Last year [1989] I published *The Dark Half*, where I tried to explore the converse: the powerful hold fiction can have over the writer. While that book was between drafts, I started to think that there might be a way to tell

both stories at the same time by approaching some of the plot elements of *The Dark Half* from a different angle. Writing, it seems to me, is a secret act—as secret as dreaming—and that was one aspect of this strange and dangerous craft I had never thought about much. ("Two Past Midnight" 238)

The result was *Secret Window, Secret Garden*, which King thought at the time would be his "last story about writers and writing and the strange no man's land which exists between what's real and what's make-believe" (237-38). Though this proved not to be true, King clearly sees these three works in particular as thematically linked. In them, King engages in a self-conscious exploration of fiction through the medium of fiction. That is, he writes metafiction.

"*Metafiction*," writes Patricia Waugh, "is a term given to fictional writing which self-consciously and systematically draws attention to its status as an artefact in order to pose questions about the relationship between fiction and reality. In providing a critique of their own methods of construction, such writings not only examine the fundamental structures of narrative fiction, they also explore the possible fictionality of the world outside the literary fictional text" (2). *Misery*, *The Dark Half*, and *Secret Window, Secret Garden*, all focus on a writer as a protagonist; all comment self-consciously on their status as fictional artifacts, especially in relation to generic form; all include embedded fragments of narratives within narratives; all therefore lay bare "the construction of a fictional illusion" (6); and all express ambivalence about the creative process, including the mental balance of those who engage in it, notably through the invocation of the motif of the doppelgänger. In short, these stories are as much about fiction making as they are about anything else, and they function as horror texts primarily by rendering writing itself problematic, if not monstrous.

Misery is arguably the most complex of the three works but also the one ultimately most complacent about the problematic nature of writing. All three works deal with writing as a compulsion, but *Misery* distances this aspect of writing by fully externalizing the compulsive force in the person of Annie Wilkes. By contrast, George Stark in *The Dark Half* and John Shooter in *Secret Window, Secret Garden* are literal manifestations of the psyches, or aspects of the psyches, of Thad Beaumont and Mort Rainey. Neither offers a particularly comforting image of writerly sanity. Indeed, King has himself suggested that he writes what he does to maintain his own sanity, exorcising his nightmares onto the page ("Novelist Sounds Off" 80). In *Misery*, however, insanity is displaced into a crazed fan, rather than resident in the writer himself (or, more accurately, the novel downplays the writer's own imbalances by playing up those of the fan). Novelist Paul Sheldon suffers a car accident in a remote area and rather implausibly finds himself in the custody of Annie Wilkes, who is not only a trained nurse and a huge Paul Sheldon fan but also a crazed serial killer who will go to any lengths to force Paul to resurrect his romance heroine, Misery Chastain, whom he has killed off in the latest (and presumably last) book in the series. Paul suffers misery to resurrect Misery and write *Misery's Return* for Annie; as Clare Hanson suggests, "The text thus explores the relation between 'misery' as a common noun (defined by King as 'pain, usually lengthy and often pointless') and the generation of texts, stories. The access to misery must be there, King seems to suggest, in order for the text to be" (149).

Misery Chastain is Paul Sheldon's bane, in his opinion. He conceives of himself as a writer of two kinds of books, "good ones and best-sellers" (*Misery* 7), setting up an opposition between popularity and literary quality, or, to put it another way, between the demands of the marketplace and the demands of art. Misery is Paul's sop to the marketplace, the heroine of his best-selling series but also the basis of his reputation as a popular hack and consequently a creation he resents, even hates. Though the narrative denies that he deliberately murdered her in the final book, arguing that the story simply followed its natural course, Sheldon had already brutalized Misery in an earlier private chapbook meant for his friends only, in which Misery has sex with a dog, and when she does die, his reaction is "cheerful capering" (35).

Therefore, despite the surface assertions that Misery's death was the natural outcome of the story, Annie's counterargument that Paul murdered her is not so easy to dismiss: *"Characters in stories DO NOT just slip away! God takes us when He thinks it's time and a writer is God to the people in a story, he made them up just like God made US up"* (35-36; emphasis in original).

And clearly as Misery was to Paul, so in many respects is Paul to Annie. Just as romance fiction depends on implausible coincidences and extreme behavior, so have implausible coincidences placed Paul in extreme circumstances. In effect, he has become like a character in one of his own books, but whereas his heroine is a passive female victim, Paul has become a passive male victim of a horrifying mirror image of Misery—a literalizer of Misery's name, for him. The book is most overtly metafictional in its frequent reflections on how Paul's current circumstances are akin to the world of fiction. Early in his recovery process, before Annie's full madness is revealed (before she has read the book in which Misery dies, in effect), Paul reflects, "It was as if he was a character in a story or a play, a character whose history is not recounted like history but created like fiction" (11), and such self-reflexive comments recur throughout the book. Such a narrative strategy serves superficially as a way to encourage the reader to accept the fiction as real, precisely because the fiction contrasts itself with fiction. However, the novel involves more complex and extensive metafictional commentaries that problematize this strategy's use merely as a realistic device.

The frequent comparisons of the action to other works of fiction, for instance, serve not only as a kind of source for the new Misery novel Paul writes but also as devices to contextualize Paul's own experiences in terms of fiction. For instance, Paul wonders if Annie "had John Fowles's first novel on her shelves" (163); that novel, *The Collector*, is about a madman who kidnaps and imprisons a woman to make her over into his ideal, and as such is a kind of mirror image precursor text to *Misery*. King also quotes from it for the epigraph to part 3 of the novel. Such references remind us that the novel we are reading has novelistic antecedents, despite its claims to be reality, not a book. Similarly, Paul invokes H. Rider Haggard, author of such classic adventure novels as *King Solomon's Mines* and *She* (both mentioned by King), early in the novel. The plot of *Misery's Return*, with its exotic African setting and quest narrative among strange lost peoples, is highly reminiscent of Haggard's characteristic plots and devices, but in fact the first invocation of Haggard is in relation to Annie, whom Paul imagines as a figure akin to "the graven images worshipped by superstitious African tribes in the novels of H. Rider Haggard" (7). This likening of Annie to an idol, and not merely an actual idol but to an idol from a fictional world, contributes to the blurring of the line between reality and fiction in the novel. Though the novel (characteristically for King) is set in a resolutely realistic environment, we are invited to see shadowed beneath its prosaic surface the contours of more overtly constructed fictions. Since we watch Paul construct *Misery Returns* to Annie's specifications, we are inescapably aware of how our preconceptions about reality are shaped by fiction.

Annie insists, for instance, that fiction requires a sort of provisional reality. Though she has already noted that the fiction writer is God to his creations and therefore presumably capable to doing literally whatever he wants, she nevertheless expects fiction to conform to reality in at least acceptably plausible ways. In a key passage in the book, she rejects Paul's first attempt at the new novel out of hand because he has simply ignored the ending of the previous book and resurrected Misery without explanation or logic. The example she provides is of old movie serials that end with a cliff-hanger one week only to open the subsequent week with a "cheat" that opens up the narrative corner into which the protagonist had been painted. Paul recognizes that Annie is objecting to the hoary device of the deus ex machina, a standby of fiction that, as Paul Sheldon notes, "*finally went out of vogue around the year 1700. Except, of course, for such arena as the Rocket Man serials and the Nancy Drew books*" (108; emphasis in original). Furthermore, he recognizes that she has caught him trying to use a simple narrative trick to resolve his problem, and she's having none of it. Misery was dead and buried at the end of the previous novel, and that's where he has to start: Annie "would not allow him to kill Misery . . . but neither would she allow him to cheat Misery back to life" (107). And Paul in fact agrees with her: "The real stuff would make the crap he had given Annie to read last night, the crap it had taken him three days and false starts without number to write, look like a dog turd sitting next to a silver platter. Hadn't he known it was all wrong?" (114) Consequently, the process of how an author goes about finding his way out of an apparently impossible narrative predicament becomes a major element in the next movement of the novel. The irony is that the novelist is also in an apparently inescapable predicament himself, and his hope for escaping his own death depends on him finding a way to resurrect Misery.

He does so, of course, but, tellingly, the germ of the idea of how he does so comes from Annie, not his own subconscious (which is imaged repeatedly in the novel as "the guys in the sweatshops," whose work is sending up flares, which represent ideas). As Hanson notes, "Annie acts . . . as Paul's hellish muse" (151), not only by literally forcing him to write but also by providing the narrative kernel that not only explains Misery's apparent death but also serves as the basis of the entire plot of the novel, when she suggests that Misery's deathlike coma was caused by a bee sting (149). She thereby becomes a sort of collaborator with Paul, a role reflected graphically in one of King's favorite strategies, playing with the physical appearance of the text (which appears in both *The Dark Half* and *Secret Window, Secret Garden* as well). King renders the physical reality of writing graphically by having Annie provide Paul with a typewriter that drops its *n*, leaving a blank space where the letter should appear. (It begins to drop other letters later, and Paul is finally reduced to completing the manuscript in longhand—several pages of *Misery Returns* appear in the book in handwritten form.) Annie's collaborative role is reflected by the fact that Paul has her fill in the missing *n*'s (at least initially), though it is probably not fair to say that the *n*'s justify her meanness.

In fact, as becomes clear, despite the brutal conditions and the literal compulsion to write—write or die—Paul recognizes that *Misery Returns* is easily the best of the Misery books. Even when he first begins to write the "real" novel, rather than the hackwork he initially tried to pass off, Annie's role as taskmaster is amusingly inverted, as when she tells Paul he should knock off for the night and he asks "for another fifteen minutes" (122), much like a child eager to stay up just until the next commercial break. Paradoxically, Annie might force Paul to create the book, but his own writerly nature forces him truly to devote himself to the task. And what Annie does to him helps make the book what it is; as Anthony Magistrale notes, she "makes him write the best *Misery* novel of his career because this time he is able to invest his heroine with the reality of his own suffering" (275).

The relationship between them, therefore, is not quite as clear-cut as it might appear, and as clear-cut as the text, on one level, wants it to be, given that Annie's monstrosity is repeatedly stressed. "There could hardly be a clearer image . . . of the feminine as monstrous," Hanson argues (150), but though this may be true, and though Paul and, arguably, the book aim ultimately to destroy and deny the monster, neither can fully efface her. Paul comes increasingly to understand Annie not simply through experience but by coming to recognize some kinship with her. He is able to deduce why she chose her earlier murder victims, for instance: "The Annie in him knew" (192). He's like Annie in his own narrative desire—"Some part of him that was as addicted to the chapter plays as Annie had been as a child had decided he could not die until he saw how it all came out" (241)—which he realizes as he struggles to give birth to *Misery's Return* (a metaphor in fact employed in the novel). He even begins to adopt Annie's vocabulary, such as "cockadoodie" and "brats," in his internal monologues, tellingly when he is thinking of the critics who did not recognize his "good" books as having merit: "*Don't you DARE turn away from me! Don't you DARE, you cockadoodie brats!*" (286). And ultimately Paul does to Annie what she would have done to him: he kills her in a scene with overtones of rape, overtones that echo her saving of him in the novel's opening pages, when her mouth to mouth resuscitation is imaged as her forcing her breath into him "the way a man might force a part of himself into an unwilling woman" (5). To inspire is, literally, to breathe life into, so this early image can hardly be an accident.

As Lauri Berkenkamp notes, the relationship between Paul and Annie is "both antagonistic and eerily complementary" (209), with Paul becoming a sort of conduit for Annie as author: "Their roles as writer and reader blur, at times even becoming indistinguishable" (204). Paul even confuses them in terms that explicitly blur their roles, as when he "dreamed that Annie Wilkes was Scheherazade. . . . But of course it wasn't *Annie* that was Scheherazade. *He* was" (66). Scheherazade, the narrator of the *The Thousand and One Nights* (commonly called *The Thousand and One Arabian Nights*), is able to live only by telling stories so interesting that her husband keeps her alive to finish them. In this analogy, Annie is akin to the sultan who spares the tale-weaving wife (note the gender inversion, by the way), but that Annie is a kind of author, too, is an essential point in the book. Her narrative senses may be derived from "best-sellers"—bad books rather than good ones—but she shows an ability to plot comparable to Paul's. Her strategy to test whether Paul has been out of his room, by leaving strands of hair to see whether they become displaced, is right out of thriller fiction, as Paul recognizes, and her elaborate scenario for deferring suspicion when the police arrive is another example of her narrativity. While Michael Arnzen's suggestion that "Annie, ostensibly, is the monster that Sheldon has created, a Frankensteinian creation which threatens to take its master's place" (244) may be a bit extreme (though we'll revisit this idea shortly), Annie clearly is presented as a kind of novelist herself, rewriting the world to her own muse.

The point is literalized when Paul finds Annie's book, a scrapbook of her career as a serial killer and the real-life analogue to the books she is making him write. Just as Paul has a concordance in his usual life as a writer—"a loose-leaf binder where I have all my *Misery* stuff . . . characters and places, but cross-indexed three or four different ways. Time lines. Historical stuff" (62)—so too does Annie have her carefully ordered record of her own history. Paul's is the invented history he must keep track of to keep the Misery books internally consistent; Annie's is the real history of her life and murders, but it reads to Paul as compellingly as a novel: "He bent over the book again. In a weird way it was just too good to put down. It was a like a novel so disgusting you just have to finish it" (194). Here Paul becomes Annie's reader, as she has been his, compelled, as this passage suggests, by a comparably perverse dynamic of attraction and repulsion. His own writerly nature reasserts itself as he attempts to interpret Annie's book, to read between the lines and deduce what has happened, such as when he discovers, through a careful parsing of word order, that Annie's husband left her (195). Later, he compares the imaginative power he uses to create fiction with the imaginative power Annie uses to reshape her world: "She was playing Can You? in real life. *Maybe*, he thought, *that's why she doesn't write books. She doesn't have to*" (275).

Such passages suggest that Paul and Annie have much in common despite the polar opposition between them on the level of plot. These similarities offer unsettling suggestions about the power of the imaginative force on which writers rely. When the line between reality and fiction blurs, the result, *Misery* suggests, becomes destructive rather than creative. Even when Paul merely falls in a creative fervor as he writes, Annie sees a fearsome power in him: "It was as if she was a little frightened to come any closer—as if she thought something in him might burn her" (148). Allen Pangborn has a similar response to Thad Beaumont in *The Dark Half*. In *Misery*, however, the dark and unsettling subtexts suggested by the metafictional elements of the book are pushed aside. Their fruits are allowed to thrive, as *Misery's Return* survives and is published and Annie is literally killed (ironically a victim of the instrument of writing, when the typewriter becomes the chief weapon used against her) and relegated to the shadowy realms of imagination and nightmare. The figure of the mad writer is elided.

The Dark Half, by contrast, narrows the gap between the writer and the monstrous other. Like Paul Sheldon, Thad Beaumont is a novelist with a dual career, one under his own name as a critically respected but unpopular novelist, another under the pseudonym George Stark as the author of a series of extremely popular but critically dismissed crime novels—a split comparable to the one in *Misery* between being the author of good books and best sellers. The Stark pseudonym has not only generated more popular success and more money than Beaumont, but also more actual books: Thad's literary career has stalled after two books, and the Stark books have become the only ongoing outlet for his creativity. However, George Stark proves to be more than just a pen name. Even before George Stark is retired—by being metaphorically killed and buried in a mock grave—Thad seems almost like another person when working on a Stark book. As his wife, Liz, reports, "'When he was writing as George Stark—and, in particular, when he was writing about Alexis Machine—Thad wasn't the same. When he—opened the door is maybe the best way to put it—when he did that and invited Stark in, he'd become distant. . . . There was no big personality change . . . but he wasn't the same'" (206-07). So much so, in fact, that despite this characterization of the differences as relatively minor, Liz also asserts, "'Not only was George Stark not a very nice guy, he was in fact a *horrible* guy. He made me more nervous with each of the four books he wrote, and when Thad finally decided to kill him, I went upstairs to our bedroom and cried with relief'" (198).

Though only a mask, a pseudonym, Stark also seems to Thad and Liz to have some degree of independent reality, despite his fictionality. As Thad says, "I don't have the slightest idea when he became a . . . a separate person. He seemed real to me when I was writing as him, but only in the way all the stories I write seem real to me when I'm writing them. Which is to say, I take them seriously but I don't believe them . . . except I do . . . then . . ." (206). He is, in effect, a manifestation of an aspect of Thad—Thad's dark half, as the title suggests. The idea of the double, or the doppelgänger, is central to the novel. The doppelgänger is an ancient concept, with roots in many myths. Cain and Abel, for instance, can be seen as opposites sides of the same coin, though also clearly separate characters. And as this example attests, as do other famous ones such as Jekyll and Hyde, or Poe's William Wilson (indeed, one of Thad's twin infants is named William), or Dorian Gray and his portrait, or Frankenstein and his monster, the double usually functions symbolically as a representation of the monstrosity that lurks beneath the surface of an apparently good person. It "is transgressive and exposes an uncontrollable and unpleasurable side of the individual often concealed behind the facade of cohesive selfhood and social and literary convention" (Slethaug 19). It may be a fully separate figure functioning purely symbolically as a manifestation of the dark half, or it may be a single person literally divided, as it is in the case of Jekyll and Hyde, and as it arguably is in the case of Thad Beaumont. The man who discovers Thad's use of a pseudonym refers to Thad's "divided mind" (120), for instance, and Thad himself shows some anxiety about the coherency of his own identity as a writer even before Stark's nature becomes clear:

> He sometimes believed that the compulsion to make fiction was no more than a bulwark against confusion, maybe even insanity. It was a desperate imposition of order by people able to find that precious stuff only in their minds . . . never in their hearts.
>
> Inside him a voice whispered for the first time: *Who* are *you when you write, Thad? Who are you* then?
>
> And for that voice he had no answer. (128-29)

Here the common metaphor of the self as internally split, able to talk and debate with itself, serves as the basis not only of Thad's anxiety about his own sanity but also the genesis of the novel's supernatural monster.

Though writing here may seem to be the anchor to sanity—as the bringer of order—it is also the root of a profound sense of doubt about the coherency of the self, as in Thad's sudden anxiety about his identity when he writes. As Stephen Bruhm suggests, "King's postmodern Gothic documents the fear of doubleness and self-splitting that is the result of documentation, of the act of writing and of representing the self" (58). George Stark is "the projection of Thad's own fear: fear of writing as an addiction, and as something that will take over our lives, fragment us, and alienate us from our families/and ourselves" (57-58). Bruhm goes on to make the Frankenstein comparison that was arguably somewhat unsuitable in the case of *Misery* but which fits well here, since George Stark is indeed a monster of Thad's creation: "Horror is the result of a *chain* of signifiers, a veritable lexis machine; Frankenstein's monster is the written word" (58) made flesh. Bruhm's reference to a "lexis machine" puns on the name Alexis Machine, a recurring Stark character, the basis for Stark's personality, and "a fiction within a fiction" (164) doubly removed from reality (it is perhaps worth noting, too, that King borrowed the name from the work of another novelist, thus further fictionalizing his fictional fiction). A "lexis machine" would be a word machine, and Stark is in some respect a creature made literally of words, able to exist because of writing and able to continue to exist only through writing.

However, he is not merely the manifestation of Thad's imagination. He is also on some level a revenant, the ghost of the twin brother Thad absorbed in the womb—a doppelgänger. At the age of eleven, just when he discovered writing, Thad began suffering from headaches, hallucinations, and seizures brought on by a growth in his brain. This growth, however, turned out not to be cancer—or not a conventional cancer, anyway. The brain surgeon opens Thad's skull and sees "protruding from the smooth surface of the dura . . . a single blind and malformed human eye" (9). Also removed from Thad's brain are "part of a nostril, three fingernails, and two teeth" (9), which, for reasons unknown, began to grow in Thad's brain after lying dormant since Thad's womb war with the vanished brother. The novel suggests strongly that the revivification of this tissue coincides with Thad's discovery of writing, and that Thad's creation of the George Stark pseudonym constitutes another such originary moment; Stark becomes real, literally, as a manifestation of Thad's imagination, but Stark is also on some level literally Thad's twin, or double. He does not look like Thad but instead like what Thad imagined George Stark would look like. Still, Stark shares Thad's blood type and fingerprints, and Liz actually recognizes their shared identity despite their apparent differences: "They looked nothing whatever alike. . . . Thad was slim and darkish, Stark broad-shouldered and fair in spite of his tan. . . . Yet they were mirror images, just the same" (426). Even the infant twins recognize their daddy in Stark. King blurs the line between self and other in the book, allowing an explanation (such as it is) for Stark that rationalizes him as an intruder, an externally existing manifestation of the horrific other, much like Annie.

However, even as other, Stark is intimately linked with Thad as his double or twin, and Thad's absorption of his brother in the womb, as natural an occurrence as this may be, also suggests Thad's own monstrosity. Stark is *both* other *and* self, one might argue, an attempt to project the horrific aspects of the self out of the self that fails. It's clear, for instance, that Stark is darkly appealing to Thad; Michael J. Meyer points out that "despite Thad's alleged aversion to the type of writing Stark produces, his attraction to Stark is depicted as similar to alcohol or drug addiction" (111). Part of Thad does want to be George Stark because part of him *is*. And the final threat Thad faces in the novel is that he will become Stark—or that Stark will become him. Just as Thad absorbed the infant in the womb, Stark hopes to absorb Thad through the medium of writing. The novel suggests that if Stark succeeds in learning to write from Thad, then Thad will disappear and only Stark will be left. In order for Thad to write, the novel pessimistically suggests, Thad needs Stark; he must become Stark. His choice is stark. He must become his dark half, or surrender his gift: "He wanted to write stories . . .

but more than that, more than he wanted the lovely visions that third eye sometimes presented, he wanted to be free" (447). But freedom from Stark is very different from freedom from Annie. Whereas Paul is able to return to his career as a writer, even turning his horrific experience into a successful novel, Thad is left bereft. There is no indication that his writer's block is broken. Indeed, the epigraph of the epilogue comes not from the new book Thad is evidently still unable to write but from one of his earlier novels, and it's an epigraph that recounts lovers parting and that denies the viability of happy endings. In *The Dark Half* writing is so dangerous that the writing itself becomes the horrific, destructive other. Losing the dark half of the self means losing the ability to write.

Secret Window, Secret Garden pushes this idea even further. Like Paul and Thad, Mort Rainey is a novelist and, like Thad, one suffering from writer's block. He, too, is confronted by a terrifying figure, John Shooter, who wants to force him to write. But while Annie forces Paul to return to Misery's world, and George Stark tries to force Thad back into the blood-soaked world of popular crime fiction, the threat John Shooter presents is somewhat different. He turns up accusing Mort of stealing a story he wrote and demands that Mort write him a new story in its place. Not until relatively late in the novella is it made clear that, like Stark, Shooter is a manifestation of Mort. This is hinted at in various ways in the early chapters, though, most notably when Mort thinks he has Shooter trapped in the bathroom and attacks him with a poker: "Mort brought the poker down in a whistling overhand blow and he had just time enough to realize that Shooter was also swinging a poker, and to realize that Shooter was not wearing his round-crowned black hat, and to realize it wasn't Shooter at all, to realize it was *him*, the madman was *him*, and then the poker shattered the mirror over the washbasin" (313). This realization is truer than Mort realizes at the time; he really is the madman, the writer so absorbed in his love that he literally rewrites his reality.

Elana Gomel argues that in the novella, "The relationship between the writer and the author is figured in terms of demonic possession, with the added ironic twist that Mort Rainey's 'ideal self' is not even his own creation. He is the phantom of recycled texts and worn-out formulae, which are Rainey's stock in trade" (90). Shooter, she argues, is the construction of literary clichés and formulae; Rainey's dark half, his demonic possessor, is a purely fictional construct. This is true enough, but the assertion that Shooter is not Rainey's creation is perhaps misleading. Shooter's *only* source is Mort's mind; he may be constructed from scraps and fragments Mort has picked up in various places—e.g., Shooter's hat is actually an old hat of Mort's, his hometown is a place Mort invented in an earlier book, and so on—but he is assembled in Mort's mind and eventually takes it over. Like Thad, Mort creates an alter ego, but, unlike Thad, he is subsumed by his. As his ex-wife, Amy, observes, "'He was two men. . . . He was himself . . . and he became a character he created'" (377-78). He loses his mind, literally. And so powerful was its imagination that, like George Stark, John Shooter acquires a degree of reality. After the climactic revelation that Mort in fact *is* Shooter, the epilogue provides counterevidence of Shooter's manifestation in an account of a ghostlike presence seen in dialogue with Mort, and in the form of a letter received from "Shooter" after Mort's death, reporting that Shooter has finally received his story. (Dare we speculate that Shooter's story is the very one we are reading?) Amy concludes, "'I think there *was* a John Shooter. . . . I think he was Mort's greatest creation—a character so vivid that he actually *did* become real'" (381). And if so, he is writer as madman.

King's metafictional conceits in these stories explore in a fantasy context the problematic relationship authors have with their art. *Misery* is in some respects the most complex and successful of the stories, but it is also the most reassuring in the conclusions it draws. While it acknowledges that writing itself is dualistic and the cause of considerable anxiety, it displaces any serious concerns about the dangers of writing on to readers by making Annie into an unrepresentative extreme of the fan. *The Dark Half* internalizes the madness manifested in Annie

Wilkes but ultimately exorcises it as well. Though the novel's conclusion is not optimistic, it also allows for escape from the mental stresses of writing, and in subsequent King novels Thad Beaumont's unhappy fate is reported briefly. *Secret Window, Secret Garden*, the shortest and most straightforward of King's most overt metafictions, is also the most unsettling. It ultimately denies the writer any escape from his imagination, dissolving the line between the real and the imagined and rendering the writer the insane God feared in *Misery's Return*: "His ideas about God had changed. . . . He had discovered that there was not one God but many, and some were more than cruel—they were insane, and that changed all. Cruelty, after all, was understandable. With insanity, however, there was no arguing" (310).

Works Cited

Arnzen, Michael. "The *Misery* of Influence." *Paradoxa* 4.10 (1998): 237-52.

Berkenkamp, Lauri. "Reading, Writing, and Interpreting: Stephen King's *Misery*." *The Dark Descent: Essays Defining Stephen King's Horrorscape*. Ed. Tony Magistrale. Westport, CT: Greenwood Press, 1992. 203-11.

Bruhm, Stephen. "On Stephen King's Phallus; Or, the Postmodern Gothic." *Narrative* 4.1 (Jan. 1996): 55-73.

Gomel, Elana. "Oscar Wilde, *The Picture of Dorian Gray*, and the (Un)death of the Author." *Narrative* 12.1 (Jan. 2004): 74-92.

Hanson, Clare. "Stephen King: Powers of Horror." *American Horror Fiction: From Brockden Brown to Stephen King*. Ed. Brian Docherty. Houndmills: Macmillan, 1990. 135-54.

King, Stephen. *Danse Macabre*. New York: Everest House, 1981.

_____. *The Dark Half*. 1989. New York: Signet, 1990.

_____. *Misery*. 1987. New York: Signet, 1988.

_____. "The Novelist Sounds Off." *Time* 6 Oct. 1986: 80.

_____. *On Writing: A Memoir of the Craft*. New York: Charles Scribner's Sons, 2000.

_____. *Secret Window, Secret Garden*. *Four Past Midnight*. 1990. New York: Signet, 1991. 241-381.

_____. *Secret Windows: Essays and Fiction on the Craft of Writing*. New York: Quality Paperback Book Club, 2000.

_____. "Two Past Midnight: A Note on *Secret Window, Secret Garden*." *Four Past Midnight*. 1990. New York: Signet, 1991. 237-39.

Magistrale, Anthony. "Art Versus Madness in Stephen King's *Misery*." *The Cele-*

bration of the Fantastic: Selected Papers from the Tenth Anniversary International Conference on the Fantastic in the Arts. Ed. Donald E. Morse, Marshall B. Tymn, and Csilla Bertha. Westport, CT: Greenwood Press, 1992. 271-78.

Meyer, Michael J. "Stephen King's Writers: The Critical Politics of Literary Quality in *Misery* and *The Dark Half*." *Literature and the Writer.* Ed. Michael J. Meyer. Amsterdam: Rodopi, 2004. 97-117.

Slethaug, Gordon E. *The Play of the Double in Postmodern American Fiction.* Carbondale: Southern Illinois UP, 1993.

Waugh, Patricia. *Metafiction: The Theory and Practice of Self-Conscious Fiction.* New York: Routledge, 1984.

The Dark Tower:
Stephen King's Revision
of Browning and Eliot_____

Matthew J. Bolton

Stephen King's monumental *Dark Tower* novels take as their point of departure Robert Browning's brief, elliptical 1855 poem "Childe Roland to the Dark Tower Came." Browning's and King's protagonists share a name and a backstory as well as a destination: a menacing tower where they will confront an unspecified enemy. King is quite explicit about his debt to Browning. In his afterword to *The Gunslinger*, the first volume in the series, King recalls being assigned the "gorgeous and rich and inexplicable" poem in a college English course on romantic poetry (311). While most of the other poems he studied soon faded from his memory, "Childe Roland" remained. King "played with the idea of trying a long romantic novel embodying the feel, if not the exact sense, of the Browning poem" (311). It may be the fragmentary, "inexplicable" quality of "Childe Roland" that set King thinking about the poem as a writer rather than as a reader. Browning's poem is deliberately unfinished, breaking off just as Roland reaches the goal of his quest, and it may have been this lack of closure that spurred King to expand and transform the poem. And while Browning's poem may be the first inspiration for King's novel, a second canonical poem looms over the Gunslinger's world: T. S. Eliot's *The Waste Land*. King simply cannot write about a blighted desert without channeling Eliot's vision of a cultural and spiritual wasteland. *The Gunslinger* begins with Browning's title and situation, but ends with a scene that echoes the conclusion of Eliot's poem, with Roland sitting on the shore with the desert at his back. Comparing *The Gunslinger* with Browning's "Childe Roland to the Dark Tower Came" and Eliot's *The Waste Land* therefore makes for a fascinating study in the dynamics of appropriation, adaptation, and popularization. King reworks the wasteland motif of these two poems, turning what is for Browning and Eliot a metaphorical landscape into a concrete and objective one. Understanding the process by which King objectifies the wasteland makes clear a connection between the Victorian and modernist trope of the spiritual and cultural desert and the late twentieth-century trope of the postapocalyptic desert. King's novel lights the way from Tennyson to *The Terminator*, from modernism to *Mad Max*.

"Childe Roland to the Dark Tower Came" is narrated in the first person by its questing protagonist. Never having come to Hamlet's realization that "There is nothing either good or bad, but thinking makes it so" (II.ii.250), Roland's description of his journey through a grotesque wasteland reveals as much about his inner life as it does about his outer surroundings. The poem's first line establishes both Roland's fatalistic bent and his unreliability as a narrator: "My first thought was, he lied in every word" (1). Logically speaking, Roland would refer to a *first* thought only if he has subsequently had a second one. In other words, his first thought—his very instinct—was wrong. Roland's initial misapprehension of the "hateful cripple" who gives him directions to the Dark Tower therefore casts doubt on his subsequent judgments (44). He suspects the stranger to be an agent of some larger, malevolent force intent on frustrating his quest, asking, "What else should he be set for?" (7). This is a suspicion that borders on paranoia. Roland accepts the stranger's counsel, not out of "hope" but out of "gladness that some end might be" (18). Last of a band of knights who rode in quest of the Dark Tower, Roland no longer hopes to succeed but only to "fail as they" (41):

> Thus, I had so long suffered in this quest,
> Heard failure prophesied so oft, been writ
> So many times among 'the Band'—to wit,
> The knights who to the Dark Tower's search addressed
> Their steps—that just to fail as they, seemed best,
> And all the doubt was now—should I be fit?
>
> (37-42)

Roland, whose title "childe" indicates that he is a knight in training rather than a full-fledged knight, was part of a noble order. Like Arthur's Knights of the Round Table, who were broken by their oath to find the Holy Grail, this brotherhood of knights has been destroyed by a monomaniacal quest. Memory, too, has therefore become a wasteland for Roland. He tries to call up "one draught of earlier, happier sights," but finds that he can only remember his friends' fall: the "one night's disgrace" of Cuthbert and the hanging of the traitorous Giles (87, 95). He resolves to think of the past no more, saying, "Better this present than a past like that" (103). Yet these brief glimpses into Roland's past create for him a rich and compelling background, locating him in a chivalric tradition like that of the Arthurian cycle.

Roland's fatalism is most clearly revealed through his metaphors and similes. He compares himself to "a sick man very near to death" (25). Of the landscape around him he notes: "As for the grass, it grew as scant as hair/ In leprosy; thin dry blades pricked the mud/ Which underneath looked kneaded up with blood" (73-74). Death and decay are never far from his mind. Indeed, Roland's preoccupation with death compromises his credibility as a narrator, for one suspects that the horrors which he describes are projected onto his surroundings rather than inherent to them. Why, for example, does he say of the "old stiff blind horse" that he passes: "I never saw a brute I hated so;/ He must be wicked to deserve such pain" (83)? There is nothing about the animal that would justify Roland's disgust. By the same token, the "gray plain" across which he travels could be a quite ordinary, if desolate, landscape. It may be Roland's gaze, and not the land through which he travels, that is jaundiced.

Oscar Wilde once quipped about the Victorian novelist George Meredith, "Meredith is a prose-Browning, and so is Browning. He used poetry as a medium for writing in prose" (qtd. in Litzinger and Smalley 526). There is indeed a prosaic quality to Browning's dramatic monologues: they mimic the spontaneity and rhythmic variety of extemporaneous spoken English. Only a masterful poet could create this illusion of immediacy, however. In the hands of a lesser stylist, the rhyme scheme of the sestets in "Childe Roland" (which would be represented as *abbabb*) would produce stilted and monotonous verse. Browning, however, uses enjambment to soften his sestets' relentless rhyming. Consider the poem's final stanza:

> There they stood, ranged along the hill-sides, met
> To view the last of me, a living frame
> For one more picture! in a sheet of flame
> I saw them and I knew them all. And yet
> Dauntless the slug-horn to my lips I set,
> And blew. *"Childe Roland to the Dark Tower came."*
>
> (199-204)

The phrases and sentences of this stanza tend to spill across two lines, ending with and giving weight to unrhymed medial words rather than to the rhymed ones with which the lines end. "Picture," "all," "blew," and "came" are emphasized, while rhymes such as "met" and "yet" and "set" are effectively muffled. The stanza, like the poem as a whole, is in an exceedingly regular meter, yet the sense and dramatic weight of the stanza follows an order that is at odds with that meter. Were these lines written as a paragraph, many readers would not notice the rhymes imbedded in them.

It is easy to see why this particular Browning poem, with its novelistic qualities and haunting story line, would have appealed to the young King. Browning is using poetic form in the way that Homer, Mallory, or Shakespeare did: to tell a dramatic story. As such, the dramatic verse of "Childe Roland" may have more in common with a modern novel than with lyric poetry.

It is surprising that King was assigned the poem in a course on romanticism. Few would consider Browning a romantic. By the 1830s, when Browning started writing verse, Shelley, Byron, and Keats had all been dead for more than a decade. Browning, like his contemporaries Alfred, Lord Tennyson and Matthew Arnold, inherited from his romantic predecessors a lyric form in which the poet speaks directly to his audience—think of Wordsworth's "Lines Composed upon Westminster Bridge" or Shelley's "Mont Blanc." But Victorian poets such as Browning and Tennyson changed the dynamics of this form by speaking from behind masks; their poems are narrated by dramatic personae who are quite distinct from the poets themselves and whose accounts therefore may be unreliable. Tennyson used this dramatic monologue form in poems such as "Ulysses" and in his Arthurian cycle *The Idylls of the King* (one book of which centers on a journey through a desert wasteland, incidentally). Browning wrote monologues narrated by madmen, murderers, lusty bishops, vengeful monks, and a whole rogues' gallery of narcissistic narrators. Some critics see Roland, last of a band of fallen knights, as a stand-in for Browning, who might have thought of himself as the last of a fallen line of romantic poets. Yet Browning's use of the poetic forms he inherited departs radically from the example his predecessors set.

The poem that haunted King is therefore not an example of romantic verse but rather an example of the Victorian dramatic monologue. Yet King's transformation of the poem into a novel in turn transforms the story's point of view: rather than a first-person monologue, it becomes third-person narrative. This is a tremendously important decision, for it moves Roland out of the privileged position of being his story's narrator. Much of the dramatic tension and ambiguity in Browning's poem comes from the balance between the reader's acceptance of Roland's account and his or her suspicion that his account is not to be believed. We see the blighted wasteland through Roland's eyes, and yet at the same time we suspect that blight may in fact be a projection of Roland's own fatalistic state of mind. To use a formulation that many Browning critics have discussed, our feelings toward the monologue's narrator are a mixture of sympathy and judgment.

By writing in the third person, King accepts Roland's account of the blighted wasteland at face value, erasing the ambiguity of Browning's poem. The first two paragraphs make Roland's subjective description wholly objective:

> The man in black fled across the desert, and the gunslinger followed.
>
> The desert was the apotheosis of all deserts, huge, standing to the sky for what might have been parsecs in all directions. White; blinding; waterless; without feature save for the faint, cloudy haze of the mountains which sketched themselves on the horizon. (11)

It is an impartial narrator rather than the fatalistic Roland who gives us an account of this landscape, making it seem as if Roland was right all along. He had described the wasteland as a "grey plain all round:/ Nothing but plain to the horizon's bound" (52-53). King's description accepts and amplifies Roland's account; by shifting the narrative voice from the first person to the third, King objectifies this blighted wasteland, rendering it a concrete and assailable reality. As a result, the hero's relationship to the land and to the reader changes: there is no longer any doubt as to Roland's reliability and to the reality of the horrors he faces. Whereas Browning's protagonist shapes the blighted world around him, King's protagonist is shaped by that world. This smoothing over of narrative ambiguity moves King's story into a more heroic vein, for the psychological and moral crisis that Browning's Roland faced has become physical and externalized.

Because the burden of narration has shifted from Roland himself to an omniscient narrator, the hero can become laconic and internal in a way Browning's knight could not. It is fitting, therefore, that King has reinterpreted the knight errant as a gunslinger. King's Roland owes much to Browning but also much to the Western movie. With two guns strapped across his hips, he is the iconic American hero of the Wild West, an inheritor of John Wayne's wanderer from *The Searchers* and of Clint Eastwood's Man with No Name. Unlike that other great American archetype, the private detective, the cowboy does not speak for himself. Sam Spade's voice-over threads its way through *The Maltese*

Falcon, for example, and the great detective novels of Raymond Chandler, Dashiell Hammett, Robert B. Parker, and Lawrence Block are told in the first person. Not so with the cowboy. The camera or the third-person narrator cause him to be rigorously externalized. A first-person narrative similar to Browning's poem would undercut this laconic and stoic silence, and so King assumes a narrative voice that renders Roland an object rather than a subject. In so doing, the wasteland, too, is objectified. Were we able somehow to enter the world of Browning's poem, we might find ourselves standing in a perfectly ordinary field, devoid of menace, beside a raving and delusional Roland. In King's novel, on the other hand, there can be no doubt that the world itself is strange and menacing and that Roland possesses the sort of fatalistic toughness necessary to cope with such a world. His conflict is externalized in a way that that of Browning's knight is not.

It is fitting that Roland's first encounter at the edge of the desert is not with the "hoary cripple" of Browning's poem but with a young man named Brown. A farmer scraping out a living from his barren field, Brown welcomes Roland to his house and hearth. Roland is as distrustful as his avatar in the poem, worrying, as he fills his waterskins at the bottom of Brown's well, that the settler might "drop a rock on him, break his head, and steal everything on him" (21). Later he thinks Brown may have drugged him, may be lying to him, may have put a spell on him, or may be the man in black himself. Yet, like the guide in "Childe Roland," Brown's advice regarding Roland's quest is good. King's choice of names for this settler associates him with Browning himself, and Roland's encounter with Brown reads like a negotiation between King and Browning as authors. Sitting in the hut after dinner, Roland tells Brown his own story, one that takes up almost the first hundred pages of the novel. It is as if Roland, a stand-in for King, must show Brown, a stand-in for Browning, that he has what it takes to venture out on the gray plain of "Childe Roland to the Dark Tower Came." Brown stands sentinel at the edge of the wasteland that Browning created. In telling of his pursuit of the man in black and of the trap that he escaped in the doomed town of Tull, Roland proves that he has the fatalistic stoicism of his poetic avatar, while King proves that he has the storytelling chops necessary to take up Browning's mantle. King, in essence, asks for and receives Browning's blessing before setting his own version of Roland on a path through the wasteland to the Dark Tower.

In its opening passages and in the basic arch of its story, King's novel hews closely to Browning's poem. Yet the novel is an expansive form, whereas the poem is a compressed one, and so, almost from the start, King must add to or depart from Browning's elliptical poem. The negotiation in Brown's hut, for example, feels like an amplification and drawing out of Roland's encounter with the stranger who guides him to the edge of the plain. Yet the embedded narrative of Roland's time in Tull has no precedent in Browning's poem. The same could be said for most of the other episodes in the novel: finding Jake at the way station, defeating the oracle that inhabits the foothills, and fighting the mutants in the tunnel under the mountains. "Childe Roland" may be King's source of inspiration, but it does not provide him with enough dramatic incidents to fill out a whole novel, much less a series of novels. Browning states a theme or motif upon which King must improvise variations.

Part of the challenge King faces in his process of adaptation lies in Browning's poem being at once fragmentary and self-contained. The poem starts in medias res, with Browning already in the midst of his quest, and ends just as he reaches the tower. The final line finds Roland not yet fighting or even seeing his enemy but rather announcing himself at the tower: "Dauntless the slughorn to my lips I set:/ and blew: *Childe Roland to the Dark Tower Came.*" On the one hand, the poem seems to have broken off just before the confrontation that should be its climax. Yet by announcing himself with the words that are the title of his narrative, Roland creates a narrative loop: the poem's last words become its first. The reader finds himself back where he began, with Roland encountering the "hateful cripple" and setting out across the gray plain. The poem is therefore both a jagged fragment and a perfect round, and by possessing both qualities it creates the illusion of a self-contained narrative world of which the reader has only been allowed a brief glimpse.

King cannot simply expand each part of Browning's poem to create a novel that mirrors the proportions of "Childe Roland." Instead, he must, as he wrote in his afterword, capture the "feel, if not the exact sense" of the poem. In one regard, Browning has already demonstrated how to do this; his own poem is inspired by lines that Edgar sings in Shakespeare's *King Lear*: "Childe Rowland to the dark tower came,/ His word was still, 'Fie, foh, and fum,'/ I smell the blood of a British man'" (III.iv.182-4). Browning acknowledges his source in a legend carried between the title and the first line: "See Edgar's song in *Lear*." These three lines set a mood and state a theme, but Browning obviously will need to depart from them if he is to write a poem of substance. Much as Browning drew on Shakespeare for the germ of a story and a setting, King will draw on Browning. He does this admirably, for the character of Roland, the desert across which he travels, the memory of his fallen companions, and the mysterious quality of the tower itself all resonate with the fatalism and haunting lyricism of Browning's poem. But a "feel" and a mood are not enough to structure a novel, and midway through *The Gunslinger* King begins to reach for heavier machinery with which to move Roland's story forward. Browning's poem ends with Roland finding the Tower, nestled in a hollow surrounded by hills on the far side of the plain. King's hero, too, finds himself approaching the end of the plain. Yet the narrator has long established that the man in black whom Roland seeks is only a signpost on the way to the Tower itself; Roland's journey is far from over. As he crosses the desert with the boy Jake in tow, the gunslinger draws closer to a great range of mountains, lit up at night with lightning. Beyond these will lie the sea and the man in black, who will tell Roland's future by dealing from a deck of tarot cards. In passing beyond the plain, Roland and King alike are passing beyond the domain of Browning's elliptical poem. King's novel enters a new phase as the author draws on the geography, imagery, and structuring principles not of Browning's poem but of T. S. Eliot's *The Waste Land*. Eliot's poem juxtaposes a series of distinctive landscapes, each with its own symbolic resonance and import. King ignores the real-world settings that have no bearing on his novel—the modern city of London, the banks of the Thames, a pub, a dressing room, and the Hofgarten in Munich—but he borrows from Eliot's poem its three most universal landscapes: the desert, the mountains, and the seashore. The desert King's protagonist crosses, for example, initially seems indebted to Browning's vision of "a gray plain," with King's "devil grass" a version of Browning's "grass, [that] grew as scant as hairy in leprosy." This is not so much a sandy desert as a scrubland or savanna. By the time Roland reaches the way station of the second chapter, however, the terrain has changed. Dying of thirst, he walks through true desert: "Out here even the devil-grass has grown stunted and yellow. The hardpan had disintegrated in places to mere rubble" (99). The landscape owes more to Eliot now than to Browning, for Roland is passing through Eliot's universal desert that undergirds modern life:

> What are the roots that clutch, what branches grow
> Out of this stony rubbish? Son of man,
> You cannot say, or guess, for you know only
> A heap of broken images, where the sun beats,
> And the dead tree gives no shelter, the cricket no relief,
> And the dry stone no sound of water.
>
> (19-24)

For Eliot, the desert is a metaphor or symbol for spiritual and cultural sterility. Yet like any good metaphor, his desert functions on both a literal level and an allegorical one. His poem's most distinctive and fully realized characters do not actually wander this stony desert—instead they commute to work, prepare themselves for evenings out, and gossip in pubs. The wasteland is not a physical space they inhabit but rather a reflection of their empty lives. But the wasteland motif works precisely because the landscape itself is convincingly drawn; the place feels real, even if its relation to most of the poems' characters is a metaphorical one. King's interest in *The Waste Land* centers entirely on its metaphorical or symbolic elements. In reworking Browning's poem, King eliminated the ambiguous nature of Roland's first-person narrative, taking as literal Roland's highly subjective description of the landscape through which he walks, and he adopts a similar technique with his borrowings from Eliot's poem. He externalizes the metaphorical elements of *The Waste Land*, such that the desert and the mountains beyond it become an actual landscape for Roland to explore.

Upon reaching the edge of the desert, Roland and Jake make their way through foothills and mountains. The peaks are lit up by lightning, and by day and night they hear "the thick mouth of the perpetual thunder" (167). This is Eliot country, for King's description echoes Eliot's "dead mountain mouth of carious teeth" that gives voice to "dry sterile thunder without rain." Yet this terrain is a relief after the stony desert, and the man and boy might agree with Eliot's Marie that "in the mountains, there you feel free." Nestled in the mountains of Eliot's wasteland is a deserted chapel, where an anonymous quester has an epiphany:

> In this decayed hole among the mountains
> In the faint moonlight, the grass is singing
> Over the tumbled graves, about the chapel
> There is the empty chapel, only the wind's home.
>
> (386-89)

Roland, too, encounters a holy or demonic site in the mountains: an abandoned altar haunted by an oracle. Like Eliot's grail knight, King's Roland will learn of his quest's end here, in this forgotten shrine in the mountains.

King's novel ends with Roland having passed through the mountains and come to the sea: "He sat on a beach which stretched left and right forever, deserted. The waves beat endlessly against the shore. . . . there the gunslinger sat, his face turned up into the fading light" (304). This scene is familiar to readers of *The Waste Land*, for in the poem's final passage Eliot's questing knight, too, has passed through the desert and come to the sea: "I sat upon the shore/ Fishing, with the arid plain behind me." King has borrowed Eliot's geographic structure, having Roland move from desert, to mountains, to sea. There is a long tradition of ending a story with the protagonist reaching the water's edge. Think of the powerful conclusion of François Truffaut's film *The 400 Blows*, for example, which features one long shot in which the protagonist runs to the ocean. Cormac McCarthy's novel *The Road*, too, finds a father and son making their way toward the ultimate goal of the ocean. The land's end and the story's end become one and the same.

King concludes the novel with a final nod to Browning: sitting on the beach, Roland "dreamed his long dreams of the Dark Tower, to which he would some day come at dusk and approach, winding his horn, to do some unimaginable final battle" (304). Yet, in having Roland pass beyond the plain without finding the Tower, King has already moved beyond his source material. Eliot's poem offers him a deep structure that can take the place of "Childe Roland"'s elliptical one. Roland and the Tower may still be Browning's creations, but Browning can no longer serve as a guide to King. Instead, he borrows from Eliot, adopting not only the geographic progression of *The Waste Land* but also the poem's trope of a tarot card reading. In poem and novel alike, the dealing of the cards serves to structure the events and episodes that will come.

Even before his counsel with the man in black, Roland finds himself thinking about the tarot: "All chips on the table. Every card up but one. The boy dangled, a living Tarot card, the hanged man, the Phoenician sailor, innocent lost and barely above the wave of a stygian sea" (268).

The man in black will later produce an actual set of cards, saying, "These are tarot cards . . . a mixture of the standard deck and a selection of my own development" (279). He does a reading for the gunslinger, turning over seven cards that will predict his fate: the Hanged Man, the Sailor, the Prisoner, the Lady of Shadows, Death, the Tower, and Life. The reading looks back and looks ahead, mapping out some of the major developments in King's series of novels. In its most immediate sense, the tarot reading prepares Roland and his reader for the events of the next novel, *The Drawing of the Three*, in which the gunslinger will be joined by three companions whose characters and fates are prefigured in the cards.

All this is familiar to a reader of *The Waste Land*; indeed, King goes out of his way to acknowledge that this scene is inspired by Eliot's poem. Roland's reference to "the Phoenician sailor," for example, could not be more deliberate an homage to *The Waste Land*. King has appropriated wholesale Eliot's idea of using the tarot cards to create a narrative structure. In *The Waste Land* and *The Gunslinger* alike, the reading of the tarot is also a reading of the text. Eliot's Madame Sosostris draws a series of cards that prefigure characters, episodes, and whole sections of *The Waste Land*:

> Here, said she,
> Is your card, the drowned Phoenician Sailor,
> (Those are pearls that were his eyes. Look!)
> Here is Belladonna, the Lady of the Rocks,
> The lady of situations.
> Here is the man with three staves, and here the Wheel,
> And here is the one-eyed merchant, and this card,
> Which is blank, is something he carries on his back,
> Which I am forbidden to see. I do not find
> The Hanged Man. Fear death by water.
>
>   (46-55)

In his footnotes to the poem, Eliot elaborates on some of the structural connotations of this tarot reading. The Phoenician sailor, for example, will appear later in the poem, while "Death by Water" will constitute the fourth part of the poem. Like the cards dealt by the man in black, Eliot's deck is eccentric; he writes in his footnote: "I am not familiar with the exact constitution of the Tarot pack of cards, from which I have obviously departed to suit my own convenience" (51). Ironically, Madame Sosostris thinks of herself as a shyster and does not understand that the cards she reads for profit do in fact hold prophetic power. Unwittingly, she deals a hand that lays out the overall structure of Eliot's poem.

Much as Brown, the settler on the edge of the desert, was a stand-in for Robert Browning, the card-dealing man in black becomes a stand-in for T. S. Eliot. Like Eliot, he works from a pack of cards that mixes the traditional tarot deck with cards of his own design. One might be tempted to read this deck of cards as a manifestation of Eliot's concept of "Tradition and the Individual Talent," in which the living writer works within a tradition by bending it to his own ends. Eliot claims:

> What happens when a new work of art is created is something that happens simultaneously to all the works of art which preceded it. The existing monuments form an ideal order among themselves, which is modified by the introduction of the new (the really new) work of art among them. (5)

If Roland gains from the tarot reading a sense of his own fate, King gains from it a deep structure and a logical principle for ordering his magnum opus. He borrows Eliot's tarot trope in order to create for himself a narrative and thematic structure that can take the place of Browning's journey across the plain.

Therefore, King's debt to Eliot may go beyond an appropriation of *The Waste Land*'s geography and of its tarot-reading trope. *The Gunslinger* grew out of King's fascination with Browning's poem, but it is sustained by an Eliotic logic in which the new writer is licensed to adapt and reorder all of the traditions that he has inherited. This is the organizing principle behind *The Waste Land*, the final lines of which contain the pronouncement: "These fragments I have shored against my ruins." Eliot gathers in his great poem the lines and sequences from literature that are most important to him. In the textual landscape of *The Waste Land*, he creates a new order through the juxtaposition and arrangement of these shored fragments.

The postapocalyptic world of Roland works according to a similar logic. Much of Western culture has been swept away, but some fragments remain: a half dozen Beatles songs, snatches of the Bible, beer and hamburgers, guns and ammo, the occasional working electric light, and an order of knights who subscribe to a higher moral code. Like Eliot, King has selected and shored these fragments in the midst of ruins. This process of selection can be particularly idiosyncratic because the Gunslinger's world does not offer itself as a likely future or as a logical extrapolation of current trends. In King's postapocalyptic novel *The Stand*, as a point of comparison, America has been decimated by an artificially engineered virus. The reader sees the world as it is now, sees its devastation, and sees the new postapocalyptic order that arises in the wake of the plague. The setting has a plausible, cause-and-effect relationship with the everyday world: it is our world in the aftermath of a single cataclysm. The world of *The Gunslinger* thwarts such logic. "The world has moved on," say Roland and many of the people he meets on his journey, and this laconic explanation is the only one we will get. Roland's world is the product not of a single catastrophe but of a less-particularized entropy; it is a world that has faded and become senile. Toward the end of the novel, Roland and the man in black have a vision of their world as an insignificant, subatomic particle. "Could it be that everything we can perceive . . . is contained in one blade of grass?" ponders the man in black. "What if that blade should be cut off with a scythe? When it began to die, would the rot seep into our own universe and our own lives, turning everything yellow and brown and desiccated?" (293). Because it is a metaphysical desiccation rather than a physical catastrophe that has produced Roland's world, King gives himself free rein to select and recombine those elements of our own culture that will remain.

In *The Waste Land*, Eliot licenses a form of creative destruction. His own domain is the Western canon, which he both demolishes and saves by building his own poem from its remnants. A similar mode of creative destruction marks not only King's setting in *The Gunslinger* but also the postapocalyptic setting as a whole. The ravished world has become a twentieth-century inversion of Arcadia, a shared dystopian landscape that any number of writers and filmmakers may choose to inhabit. Films such as *Planet of the Apes*, *Mad Max*, *The Terminator*, *I Am Legend*, and *Wall-E*, as well as books such as King's *The Stand* and *The Gunslinger*, Jonathan Christopher's *The Tripods* and *The Burning Lands*, Margaret Atwood's *Oryx and Crake*, and McCarthy's *The Road*, present different facets of a similar gray world. The appeal of this ruined Earth may lie not only in sweeping away civilization as we know it but also in choosing what will abide. The postapocalyptic story, like Eliot's poem, is an exercise in discernment; it is a genre that dwells not only on destruction but also on what is worth saving.

Works Cited

Browning, Robert. "Childe Roland to the Dark Tower Came." 1855. *The Major Victorian Poets: Tennyson, Browning, Arnold.* Ed. William Buckler. Boston: Houghton Mifflin, 1973.

Eliot, T. S. "Tradition and the Individual Talent." *Selected Essays, 1917-1932.* New York: Harcourt, Brace, 1932.

_____. *The Waste Land*. 1922. *The Complete Poems and Plays: 1909-1950.* New York: Harcourt, Brace & World, 1962.

King, Stephen. *The Gunslinger.* New York: Signet, 1982.

Lauter, Paul. "Melville Climbs the Canon." *American Literature* 66.1 (March 1994): 1-24.

Litzinger, Boyd, and Donald Smalley. *Browning: The Critical Heritage.* New York: Barnes & Noble, 1970.

McCarthy, Cormac. *The Road.* New York: Alfred A. Knopf, 2006.

Shakespeare, William. *King Lear.* 1605-1606. *The Riverside Shakespeare.* Ed. G. Blakemore Evans. Boston: Houghton Mifflin, 1974.

CRITICAL READINGS

Surviving the Ride

Clive Barker

> The tygers of wrath are wiser than the horses of instruction.
> —William Blake: *The Marriage of Heaven and Hell*

First, a confession: I have no thesis. I come to these pages without an overview to propound; only with a substantial enthusiasm for the work of Stephen King and a *potpourri* of thoughts on fear, fiction, dreams and geographies which may bear some tenuous relation to each other and to King's fiction.

Theoretical thinking was never a great passion of mine, but ghost-trains are. And it's with a ghost-train I begin.

It's called—ambitiously enough—*L'Apocalypse*. To judge from the size of the exterior, the ride it houses is an epic; the vast, three-tiered facade dwarfs the punters who mill around outside, staring up with a mixture of trepidation and appetite at the hoardings, and wondering if they have the nerve to step out of the heat of the sun and into the stale darkness that awaits them through the swinging doors.

Surely, they reassure themselves, no fun-fair ride can be as bad as the paintings that cover every inch of the building suggest: for the pictures record atrocities that would have turned de Sade's stomach.

They're not particularly good paintings; they're rather too crudely rendered, and the gaudy primaries the artists have chosen seem ill-suited to the subject matter. But the eye flits back and forth over the horrors described here, unable to disengage itself. In one corner, a shackled man is having his head sliced off; it seems to leap out at us, propelled by a geyser of scarlet blood. A few yards from this, above a row of arches that are edged with canary-yellow lights, a man watches his bowels being drawn from his abdomen by a Cardinal in an advanced state of decomposition. Beside the entrance booth, a crucified woman is being burned alive in a chamber lined with white-hot swords. We might be tempted to laugh at such *grand guignol* excesses, but we cannot. They are, for all the roughness of their presentation, deeply disturbing.

I've never ridden *L'Apocalypse*. I know it only as a photograph, culled from a magazine some dozen years ago, and treasured since. The photograph still speaks loudly to me. Of the indisputable glamour of the horrible; of its power to enthrall and repulse simultaneously. And it also reminds me—with its sweaty-palmed punters queuing beneath a crystal blue sky for a chance at the dark—that nobody ever lost money offering a good ride to Hell.

Which brings us, inevitably, to the architect of the most popular ghost-train rides in the world: Mr. Stephen King.

It's perhaps redundant, in a book celebrating Stephen King's skills, for me to list his merits at too great a length. We, his readers and admirers, know them well. But it may be worth our considering exactly *what* he's selling us through the charm and accessibility of his prose, the persuasiveness of his characters, the ruthless drive of his narratives.

He's selling death. He's selling tales of blood-drinkers, flesh-eaters, and the decay of the soul; of the destruction of sanity, community and faith. In his fiction, even love's power to outwit the darkness is uncertain; the monsters will devour that too, given half a chance. Nor is innocence much of a defense. Children go to the grave as readily as the adult of the species, and those few Resurrections that circumstance grants are not likely to be the glory promised from the pulpit.

Not, one would have thought, a particularly commercial range of subjects. But in King's hands their saleability can scarcely be in question. He has turned the horror genre—so long an underdog on the publishing scene—into a force to be reckoned with.

Many reasons have been put forward for King's popularity. A common element in most of the theories is his *plausibility* as a writer. In the novels—though rather less in the short stories—he describes the confrontation between the real and the fantastic elements so believably that the reader's rational sensibilities are seldom, if ever, outraged. The images of power, of loss, of transformation, of wild children and terrible hotels, of beasts mythological and beasts rabid and beasts human—all are dropped so cunningly into the texture of the world he conjures—morsel upon morsel—that by the time our mouths are full, we're perfectly willing to swallow.

The net effect is akin to taking that ride on *L'Apocalypse*, only finding that the dummies on either side of the track, enacting over and over their appalling death scenes, closely resemble people we know. The horror is intensified immeasurably. We are no longer simply voyeurs, watching some artificial atrocity unfold in front of our eyes. We are intimately involved with the sufferers. We share their traumas and their terrors. We share too their hatred of their tormentors.

This is by no means the only approach to writing dark fantasy, of course. Many authors choose to plunge their readers into the world of the subconscious (which is, surely, the territory such fiction charts) with scarcely a glance over their shoulders at the "reality" the reader occupies. In the geography of the *fantastique*, for instance, Prince Prospero's castle—sealed so inadequately against the Red Death—stands far deeper in the world of pure dream than does the Overlook Hotel, whose rooms, though no less haunted by violent death, are far more realistically evoked than Poe's baroque conceits.

There are, inevitably, losses and gains on both sides. Poe sacrifices a certain accessibility by his method; one has to embrace the fictional conventions he has employed before the story can be fully savored. He gains, however, a mythic resonance which is out of all proportion to the meagre pages *The Masque of the Red Death* occupies. He has, apparently effortlessly, written himself into the landscape of our dreams.

King's method—which requires the establishing of a far more elaborate fictional "reality"—wins out through our commitment to that reality, and to the characters who inhabit it. It also earns the power to subvert our sense of the real, by showing us a world we think we know, then revealing another view of it entirely. What I believe he loses in the trade-off is a certain *ambiguity*. This I'll return to later.

First, a couple of thoughts on subversion. It has been argued, and forcibly, that for all the paraphernalia of revolution contained in King's fiction—the weak discovering unlooked-for strength and the strong faltering; the constant threat (or promise) of transformation; a sense barely hidden beneath the chatty surface of the prose, that mythic elements are being juggled here—that, despite all this apocalyptic stuff, the author's world-view is at heart a conservative one. Is he perhaps a sheep in wolf's clothing, distressing us with these scenes of chaos in order to persuade us to cling closer to the values that his monsters jeopardize?

I admit to having some sympathy with this argument, and I admire most those of his tales which seem to show the world irredeemably changed, with no hope of a return to the comfortable, joyless, death-in-life that seems to be the late twentieth century ideal. But if there is evidence that gives weight to such argument, there is also much in King's work which is genuinely subversive: imagery which evokes states of mind and conditions of flesh which, besides exciting our anxieties, excites also our desires and our perversities.

Why, you may ask, do I put such a high value upon subversion?

There are many reasons. The most pertinent here is my belief that fantastic fiction offers the writer exceptional possibilities in that direction, and I strongly believe a piece of work (be it play, book, poem) should be judged according to how enthusiastically it seizes the opportunity to do what it can do *uniquely*. The literature of the fantastic—and the movies, and the paintings—can reproduce, at its best, the texture of experience more closely than any "naturalistic" work, because it can embrace the complexity of the world we live in.

Which is to say: our minds. That's where we live, after all. And our minds are extraordinary melting pots, in which sensory information, and the memory of same, and intellectual ruminations, and nightmares, and dreams, simmer in an ever-richer stew. Where else but in works called (often pejoratively) *fantasies* can such a mixture of elements be placed side by side?

And if we once embrace the vision offered in such works, if we once allow the metaphors a home in our psyches, the subversion is under way. We may for the first time see ourselves as a *totality*—valuing our appetite for the forbidden rather than suppressing it, comprehending that our taste for the strange, or the morbid, or the paradoxical, is contrary to what we're brought up to believe, a sign of our good health. So I say—*subvert*. And never apologize.

That's one of King's crowning achievements. From the beginning, he's never apologized, never been ashamed to be a horror author. He values the *genre*, and if horror fiction is in turn more valued now than it was ten or twenty years ago it is surely in no small degree his doing. After all, the most obsessive of rationalists must find it difficult to ignore the man's existence: he's read on buses and trains; in Universities and Hospitals; by the good, the bad and the morally indifferent.

At this juncture it may be worth remembering that the dreams he is usually concerned to evoke are normally known not as dreams but as *nightmares*. This is in itself worthy of note. We have other classes of dreams which are as common as nightmares. Erotic dreams, for instance; dreams of humiliation. But it's only the dream of terror which has been graced with a special name, as though we recognize that this experience, of all those that come to us in sleep, carries some essential significance. Is it perhaps that in our waking lives we feel (rightly or wrongly) that we have control over all other responses but that of fear? Certainly we may use the word nightmare freely to describe waking experience ("the traffic was a nightmare," we casually remark), but seldom do our lives reach that pitch of terror—accompanied by the blood-chilling sense of inevitability—that informs the dream of dread.

In reading a good piece of horror fiction, we may dip into the dreaming state at will; we may even hope to interpret some of the signs and signals that nightmares deliver to us. If not that, at least there is some comfort in knowing that these images are *shared*.

(An aside. One of the pleasures of any fiction is comparing the intricacies of response with other readers, but this process takes on a wonderfully paradoxical quality when two horror enthusiasts are exchanging views on a favorite book or film. The gleeful detailing of the carnage, the shared delight, as the key moments of revulsion and anxiety are remembered: we smile, talking of how we sweated.)

There are many kinds of nightmare. Some have familiar, even domestic settings, in which commonplace particulars are charged up with uncanny and inexplicable power to intimidate. It is this kind of nightmare that King is most adept at evoking, and the kind with which he is probably most readily identified. It is in a way a natural progression from rooting outlandish horrors—*Carrie*; *'Salem's Lot*—in settings so familiar we might occupy them, to making objects *from* those settings—a dog, a car—themselves the objects of anxiety. I must say I prefer the earlier books by quite a measure, but that's in part because the Apocalypses conjured seem so much more comprehensive, and I have a practically limitless appetite for tales of the world turned inside out.

The other kind of nightmare is a different experience entirely and it is not—at least in the conventional sense—about threat. I mean the kind of dream voyage that takes you out of any recognizable context, and into some other state entirely. The kind that lifts you up (perhaps literally; for me such nightmares often begin with falling that turns into flight) and whips you away to a place both familiar and utterly new, utterly strange. You have never been to this place in your waking life, of that your dreaming self is certain; but there are presences here familiar to you, and sights around every corner that you will recognize even as they astonish you.

What actually happens on these voyages will run from the banal to the Wagnerian, depending on the dreamer's sense of irony. But the way this second sort of nightmare operates upon your psyche is totally different from the first. For one thing, the fears dealt with in the first sort are likely to be susceptible to analysis. They are fears of authority figures, or terminal disease, or making love to Mother. But the second kind is, I believe, rooted not in the specifics of the personality, but in something more primitive; something that belongs to our response as thought-haunted matter to the world we're born into. The images that come to overwhelm us in this region are not, therefore, projections of neurosis: they are things vast; contradictory; mythological.

King can conjure such stuff with the best of them; I only regret that his brilliance as a creator of domestic demons has claimed him from writing more of that other region. When he turns his hand to it, the effect is stunning. *The Mist*, for example, is a story that begins in familiar King territory, and moves through a variety of modes—including scenes which, in their mingling of the monstrous and the commonplace work as high, grim comedy—towards a world lost to humanity, a world that echoes in the imagination long after the book has been closed. In the final section of the story the survivors encounter a creature so vast it doesn't even notice the protagonists:—

. . . Its skin was deeply wrinkled and grooved, and clinging to it were scores, hundreds, of those pinkish 'bugs' with the stalk-eyes. I don't know how big it actually was, but it passed directly over us. . . . Mrs. Reppler said later she could not see the underside of its body, although she craned her neck up to look. She saw only two Cyclopean legs going up and up into the mist like living towers until they were lost to sight.

There is much more of breathtaking imaginative scope in *The Stand*, and in a more intimate, though no less persuasive, fashion in *The Shining* and *'Salem's Lot*. Moments when the terror becomes something more than a fight for life with an unwelcome intruder; when the horror reveals itself, even in the moment of causing us to recoil, as a source of fascination and awe and self-comprehension.

This is the root of the ambiguity I spoke of before, and to which I said I would return. *Wanting* an encounter with forces that will change our lives—that will deliver us once and for all into the regions of the gods ("I had a dream that I saw God walking across Harrison on the far side of the lake, a God so gigantic that above the waist He was lost in a clear blue sky."—*The Mist*)—yet fearful that we are negligible things and so far beneath the concern of such powers that any confrontation will simply kill us.

Charting that ambiguity is, I would suggest, a function that the fantasy *genre* can uniquely fulfill. It is perhaps the liability of King's virtues that such ambiguity is often forfeited in exchange for a straightforward identification with the forces of light. King's monsters (human, sub-human and Cyclopean) may on occasion be *comprehensible* to us, but they seldom exercise any serious claim on our sympathies. They are moral degenerates, whose colors are plain from the outset. We watch them kick dogs to death, and devour children, and we are reinforced in the questionable certainty that we are not like them; that *we* are on the side of the angels.

Now *that's* fiction. We are not. Darkness has a place in all of us; a substantial place that must, for our health's sake, be respected and investigated.

After all, one of the reasons we read tales of terror is surely that we have an *appetite* for viewing anguish, and death, and all the paraphernalia of the monstrous. That's not the condition of the angels.

It seems to me vital that in this age of the New Righteousness—when moral rectitude is again a rallying-cry, and the old hypocrisies are gaining acolytes by the hour—that we should strive to avoid feeding delusions of perfectibility and instead celebrate the complexities and contradictions that, as I've said, fantastic fiction is uniquely qualified to address. If we can, we may yet keep from drowning in a wave of simplifications that include such great, fake dichotomies as good versus evil, dark versus light, reality versus fiction. But we must be prepared to wear our paradoxes on our sleeve.

In King's work, it is so often the child who carries that wisdom; the child who synthesizes "real" and "imagined" experience without question, who knows instinctively that imagination can tell the truth the way the senses never can. That lesson can never be taught too often. It stands in direct contradiction to the basic principles which we are suckled upon and are taught make us strong in the world. Principles of verifiable evidence; and of the logic that will lead, given its head, to terrible, but faultlessly logical, insanities.

I return again to the list of goods that King is selling in his fiction, and find my summary deficient. Yes, there is death on the list; and much about the soul's decay. But there's also *vision*.

Not the kind laid claim to by politicians or manufacturers or men of the cloth. Not the vision of the *better* economy, the *better* combustion engine, the *better* Eden. Those visions are devised to bind us and blind us. If we look too long at them we no longer understand what our dreams are telling us; and without that knowledge we are weak.

No, King offers us another kind of vision; he shows us adults what the children in his fiction so often take for granted: that on the journey which he has so eloquently charted, where no terror shows its face but on a street that we have ourselves trodden, it is not, finally, the stale formulae and the trite metaphysics we're taught from birth that will get us to the end of the ride alive; it is our intimacy with our dark and dreaming selves.

From *Kingdom of Fear: The World of Stephen King,* edited by Tim Underwood and Chuck Miller (1986), pp. 55-63. Copyright © 1986 by Underwood-Miller Publishers. Reprinted by permission of the author.

King and the Critics_____

Michael R. Collings

To talk about King and critics is tremendously difficult, if only because of the enormous range of statements made about King by critics and about critics by King—to say nothing of King's own contributions to social, cultural, and literary criticism. Each perspective on King results in different possibilities; each works under different (and often mutually exclusive) presuppositions about art and literature; and each addresses radically differing audiences. In this chapter, I have divided an otherwise impossibly cumbersome topic into several more manageable subtopics, beginning with the most accessible and vocal forms of criticism—popular criticism as epitomized by reviews, review articles, and interviews in daily, weekly, and monthly publications as diverse as the *New York Times Book Review*, the *Kirkus Review*, and *The Orange Country Register*.

1. Popular Mainstream Criticism

In *The Valley Advocate* for 21 July 1986, Stanley Wiater borrowed the title of this study for an article examining the extent of King's influence and of the increasing critical interest in King.

Wiater outlines the three most important recent directions in King scholarship and criticism: Underwood-Miller's collections of essays, *Fear Itself: The Horror Fiction of Stephen King, Kingdom of Fear: The World of Stephen King*, and a third volume currently in preparation; Douglas E. Winter's 1982 *Stephen King* (which he refers to as *The Reader's Guide to Stephen King*) and its subsequent enlargement as *Stephen King: The Art of Darkness* (1984; 1986); and the Starmont series, which he notes is "on a somewhat more 'scholarly' level" than the others. Ostensibly an overview of criticism, Wiater's article serves equally well as an introduction to the difficulty of working with (and writing) King criticism. The article seems oddly schizophrenic, at once inviting and mildly disapproving of such endeavors. While acknowledging that King is a cultural phenomenon, Wiater refers sarcastically to the increasing intensity of critical study: "Yet for the millions of devoted readers who won't leave home without him [King], comes some erudite relief—even more books, not written by King, but about the man and his work." Such books may well become the "next cottage industry in the publishing world," he continues, as they "dissect every corner of the 'Stephen King Phenomenon.'"

Wiater even includes a brief quotation from King relevant to this critical attention. In a tone somewhat moderated from his earlier statements about critics (in the *Adelina* reviews, for example), King defers judgment:

> It's a little bit like Huck Finn and Tom Sawyer going to their own funeral. I'm aware of them. I've read them. For example; Collings's book, *The Many Facets of Stephen King*, which is the latest volume in this parade, has a marvelous and insightful essay on *The Eyes of the Dragon*, which is the children's book that I wrote that will be out in a year or two. That's a good piece. But beyond that, what can I say? They're there, and some of them are good, and some of them are bad, and I'm not going to pick them apart. It's not my place.

Criticism, King concludes, is "their business, not mine. I just write stories."

The article is symptomatic of a difficulty that has followed King's writing from the beginning. At first it was difficult to find neutral—to say nothing of favorable—criticism of King's novels; now, when critics have begun to take him seriously and to explore the complexities of the worlds he creates, they are themselves not taken quite seriously; the prevailing attitude seems to be that there must be something self-serving in someone who devotes this much time and effort to a writer who is himself "academically" suspect.

As a writer, of course, King has confronted this attitude innumerable times; in an interview with Loukia Louka for the *Maryland Coast Dispatch* (8 August 1986), when asked how he responds to attacks that he is "not very literary," King answered:

> I don't spend a lot of time worrying about it. If people ask me if I will ever do anything serious, my response is that I'm serious every time I sit down to write. You decide whether or not what I've done is serious. I try as hard as I can. It is not really for me to say or judge what I do. I do the best I can and the rest of it is up to the critics. Much of it will be decided 50 years after I'm dead. Either the stuff will still be knocking around or it won't. I think some of it will be. It might not be taught in upper level English classes. I'm not sure that is its place. But I think it will be there. Kids will still be checking *'Salem's Lot* out of the library. Horror stories have an incredible staying power. (86)

The comment is apt and appropriate; on the other side of the coin, however, King is not entirely satisfied with commonplace judgments about himself and his writing. Steven Beeber asked what King thought about the fact that for the past decade every novel he has published became a best seller. King replied:

> It upsets me in a way sometimes. By being a bestseller I get the feeling that there's just some kind of composite of the average American sitting between my ears, that I fall into the midground of literature—I guess I'd like to think I'm a little better than that. (16-A)

Perhaps he is; but he is undoubtedly in a difficult situation as far as critical reactions go. Since he has chalked up such remarkable commercial successes, it has become almost an article of faith among mainstream critics that he is not a writer worth talking about.

During late July and early August, 1986, a number of articles appeared that discussed two films: *Maximum Overdrive* written and directed by King; and *Stand by Me*, based on "The Body," a novella from

Different Seasons. The reactions to the films aptly define the current state of criticism.

Associating King's name with a film almost automatically endangers the project. Susin Shapiro focuses on this problem in her "One Picture Is Worth a Million Words." "No matter what I do," she cites King as saying, "the odds are good that people are gonna turn around and cream me" (10). In Shapiro's words, this tendency relates to

> the age-old dilemma of commercial success vs. fine art; the twain rarely meet. King's brand of kink and kineticism has brought him a popular success that's rivaled by very few, but there are killjoys out there who feel that "mass culture" is a contradiction in terms. No one is as keenly aware of this as King: in fact, I've never heard someone so finely attuned to his own drawbacks, so spot-on about the repercussions of the limelight. (10)

In a forthright conclusion to the discussion, King talks about his fears for *The Talisman*, including the sense that critics would savage it because he and Straub were too successful: "When you get too big and too many people like your stuff it must be mediocre. A mass mind is supposedly ordinary, not sensitive, literate and smart like the mind of a critic. Of course, it's possible to dismiss all criticism by saying they're just jealous" (10). He does, however, listen to critics; and he is aware of his faults as a writer—that his work is derivative, some of it is simplistic, and that he's not "an original thinker." On the plus side, he attempts to overcome more of these problems with each new novel.

Still, his understanding and openness did not help when *Maximum Overdrive* was released. It was not just a flawed film, according to many of the reviews available—it was a *personal* failure for Stephen King. Larry Ratliff begins his consideration of the film with the confusing assertion that "While it may be some consolation to Stephen King, this generation's one-man horror gristmill, 'Maximum Overdrive' only proves that the author himself can turn gore into bore just about as well as more experienced directors." The film is a short story padded to "an excruciating 97 minutes"; it is a "clunker"; King's promises to "scare the hell out of us" turn into King "grinding gears . . . even for his type of audience—the kind who think it's incredibly 'cool' to watch a movie with feet propped on seats in front of them." The review concludes by comparing *Maximum Overdrive* with the "ultimate 'truck run amok' film," Steven Spielberg's *Duel* (1971), even though there is little evidence that the two were intended to be compared.

What emerges from the review is not so much an assessment of a film as an implied critique of Stephen King, of his chosen genre, and of his status as a best-selling writer.

Robert Garrett begins his discussion of *Maximum Overdrive* by calling it a "factory reject," its narrative flawed by a "comic book-style [sic] idiocy that at times is charming." King's debut as a director is "boneheadedly direct and banal," resulting in a situation that is a "pale reminder of the beleaguered townies who hid in a diner in 'The Birds,' although the tiniest of Hitchcock's sparrows is spookier than King's big wheelers."

It is well and good to compare King's first film to Spielberg and Hitchcock and find it wanting; what Ratliff and Garrett seem to have ignored is King's own assessment of the film. He has frequently. called it a "moron movie," meaning that

it isn't a serious picture. You can go to the theater, sit down with a box of popcorn and a drink and believe everything you see for the next two hours. It isn't a serious movie in any way. Just leave your brains outside. (Louka 11)

In another response to the "moron film" reference, King simply said:

This movie is about having a good time at the movies, and that's all it's about. Believe me, it's not 'My Dinner With Andre.' And little Stevie is not rehearsing his Academy Award speech for *this* baby. (Burkett H1)

Even such disclaimers did not assuage one reviewer, who noted that King had called it a "moron movie," but that he had *over*estimated its effect.

Early reactions to *Stand by Me* also indicate King's difficulties. The film was superbly directed by Rob Reiner, who made several changes in King's original narrative, even commenting that "Stephen's novella was set in 1960, but since I was twelve in 1959, we moved it back a year, because the references seemed even more natural to me. The film became a blend of Stephen's story and mine. . . . The film only came into focus after I made my own personal connections to it" (Holden C8). The screenplay was written by Raynold Gideon and Bruce A. Evans, who, with Andrew Scheinman, also produced the film.

King's contribution to *Stand by Me* was thus diluted as the material passed through several hands; in fact, it seems probable that King's connections with the original narrative were purposely downplayed. Daniel Cziraky notes that "as bankable as King's name has become in the publishing world, the poor performance of past films based on his works was most likely a very big factor in Columbia's releasing the film as 'Stand by Me,' 'A Rob Reiner Film,' instead of Stephen King's 'The Body.'" While such thinking might be logical, Cziraky writes, it has the unfortunate side effect of distancing King from the finest film adaptation of his works yet produced.

In spite of that distancing, however, a number of reviewers seem intent on bringing King into the discussion. Generally speaking, according to several early reviewers, where the film succeeds it shows Reiner's hand; where it fails, it shows King's. Rex Reed disliked the film, noting that "rarely have 90 minutes of screen time been devoted to anything more trivial or pointless." He carefully includes the comment that the film was based on a story by King, "who publishes everything but his grocery list and calls it literature"—a comment that may have some validity in terms of King's reputation as a writer but seems to have little direct bearing on a film several steps removed from

King's prose. The implication is that the film is suspect simply because of its relation to Stephen King.

Kevin Lally finds the film much stronger, a "delightful sleeper," a "raucously appealing portrait of 12-year-olds." Yet he also insists that the underlying narrative is atypical of King, improved by strong directing by Reiner and equally strong writing by Gideon and Evans. Overall, the review is positive and helpful—until Lally feels it necessary to discuss King directly. *Stand by Me* is told from the point of view of Gordon Lachance, a successful writer:

> But if Gordie is meant to be King's alter ego, his pensive style gives no clue that it belongs to someone who's made his fortune from pulpy, grungy horror stories.
>
> Still, the one yarn young Gordie tells his friends—about a fat boy's disgusting revenge on his hometown—is in tune with the King that America has taken to heart.

King's novella might have seemed to portray Lachance as "King's alter ego," particularly since the two stories interpolated into "The Body" were in fact juvenilia by King; he is himself aware of the suggested connection, as is evidenced by a comment in a letter discussing *It* that "Derry is no more Bangor than Gordie Lachance is the young Steve King" (31 March 1986).

Stand by Me is even less transparent in this regard than was "The Body." The film's Gordie seems to reflect Rob Reiner as much Stephen King: "The feelings Gordie expresses in the film were very much like the feelings I've had for most of my life," Reiner said in an interview (Holden C8). Lally's attempt to find King within the film, and subsequently to use that discovery as a springboard for a negative statement about King's writing career, seems gratuitous and unfair to King, to Reiner, and to the film.

Richard Freedman uses the same technique in his review: the film is strong because of Reiner, weak when it depends on King's narrative.

"Considering what a disaster Stephen King's 'Maximum Overdrive' is," Freedman begins,

> directed by the best-selling horror novelist himself, it's a pleasure to report that "Stand by Me," based on his novella "The Body," is an almost unqualified success.
>
> But then it's directed by Rob Reiner . . . , as skilled behind the camera as King is a seemingly hopeless duffer.

Later, Freedman details several weaknesses in the film:

> Poorest of all, there's a kind of pity and self-aggrandizement on the part of the author that nearly spoils the tone of this dark idyl:
>
> "You're going to be a great writer some day, Gordie," Chris tells him, and one can just see King licking his chops as he set that line down (actually, in all fairness, the screen adaptation is by co-producers Raynold Gideon and Bruce A. Evans, but would Tolstoy have been capable of such self-preening fatuity?).

The parenthetical comment is itself confusing, since it seems at once to accuse King and to expiate him—and why the reference to Tolstoy in the first place? Nor, in the context of the film, is Chris's line out of place. Gordie has just admitted his deepest fears—that his father hates him, that he is no good—and Chris comforts him by admiring the one talent the film has clearly established that Gordie possesses: his ability to tell stories. At least three times prior to this scene, Chris has complimented Gordie on that skill; what better way to build up the younger boy's shattered self-image. To charge King with intruding "pity and self-aggrandizement" into the film works against the nature of *Stand by Me*.

The film is strong—with *Dead Zone* and *The Woman in the Room* among the most successful adaptations, with a fine screenplay and sensitive, careful directing. But to remove King from the equation entirely is as unfair as to blame him for every infelicity in the film. Yet many of the strongest responses to *Stand by Me* did precisely that.

Sheila Benson wrote in the Los Angeles *Times* that the film was the "summer's great gift, a compassionate perfectly formed look at the real heart of youth." She commends the writers, the actors, and especially the director; Reiner "has seen that the cast stays honest and his movie marvelously restrained." There is no mention at all of Stephen King.

Tom Cuneff does refer to King, but in the opening sentence, and then by way of establishing one condition for the film's success: "Though this movie is based on a novella . . . by scaremeister Stephen King, it's not just another one of his chillers." The remainder of the review is perceptive and positive, but ignores King.

Similarly, David Brooks's review concentrates on Reiner, on the narrative, on the actors, and on the relationships among the characters, but mentions King only once, in a paragraph that sounds a familiar chord: "Who could have predicted that a movie, let alone a very good movie, could be made from a story about four 12-year-olds hiking to find a dead boy? Set in 1959 and based on Stephen King's novella 'The Body,' 'Stand by Me' is an author's remembrance of his pivotal childhood adventure." The author in question is not even King; Brooks's next sentence speaks of Gordie Lachance, not Stephen King.

In the cases of *Maximum Overdrive* and *Stand by Me*, King's reputation is an almost impossible barrier to overcome. One film apparently failed because of King; the second succeeded in spite of him.

The situation with King criticism in general is equally diverse. In "King of Horror," Robert Hunt prefaces his discussion of film adaptations by arguing that

> King is the Steven Spielberg of horror. Like Spielberg, he's obsessed with popular culture, and particularly with those parts of it which he grew up watching: King would like to believe that his taste and sensibility have remained unchanged since the seventh grade. No pop culture revisionist, King deals with horror archetypes: if he writes about a vampire, you can be

sure he won't leave out the coffin, the stake, or the garlic; his werewolf, likewise, will be destroyed only by a silver bullet during a full moon. But King also recognizes that his subjects are archetypal, and knows just how much distance to keep from them. He knows his horror traditions, and knows better than to take them too seriously. (40)

Yet Hunt follows this paragraph with the disclaimer that he is referring only to the plots in the film adaptations; he has read few of King's novels, he admits, and those were "uninteresting stylistically." *Carrie* was a pot-boiler, a "routine entry in the then popular cycle of books about possessed kids" (40); *Cujo* is silly, and *Christine* even sillier, with the film's few impressive moments the result of John Carpenter moving away from King's "hot-rod version of *Carrie*" toward an emphasis on human characters. *Cat's Eye* succeeds better than did *Creepshow*, although largely because the later film is "perhaps the sort of thing that King . . . does best: simple, slightly familiar suspense situations that don't take themselves too seriously" (42). The point of Hunt's extensive analyses seems to be that the films are superior to the novels; yet even in discussing the films, Hunt carefully identifies *King*'s failings as a writer.

Many reviews of King's novels have paralleled these attitudes. *Kirkus Reviews* (15 August 1975) referred to *'Salem's Lot* as "super-exorcism that leaves the taste of somebody else's blood in your mouth and what a bad taste it is. . . . Vampirism, necrophilia, *et* dreadful *alia* rather overplayed. . . ."

Jack Sullivan's "Ten Ways to Write a Gothic," appearing in the *New York Times Book Review* in February, 1977, takes King severely to task for stylistic blunders: "To say Stephen King is not an elegant writer . . . is putting it mildly." He particularly dislikes King's use of parentheses, capitals and exclamation marks as points of emphasis in *The Shining*: "Sometimes non-punctuation or italics are used—quite arbitrarily— for gimmicky stream of consciousness effect." In addition, the novel's plot is obviously a re-working of Poe, Blackwood, and Lovecraft, as well as such films as *Diabolique, Psycho*, and the *Village of the Damned*; perhaps Sullivan might have discussed such internal referents as "allusions" in another writer, but for some reason, King is not allowed the liberty of building on the literary past, even though he acknowledges his debt to that past throughout the novel.

Michael Mewshaw similarly attacked King as stylist in "Novels and Stories," which also appeared in the *New York Times Book Review* (26 March 1978). The *Night Shift* stories may be imaginative, but they suffer from "twist endings that should have died with O. Henry, the hoariest clichés of the horror-tale subgenre . . . and lines that provoke smiles rather than terror."

Eight years later, King's most ambitious novel has come in for a similar drubbing. John Podhoretz's review of *It*, "Stopping 'It' Before It's Too Late," is written as a parody of the novel itself, with four parts and a narrative tone and style clearly based on King's own:

> *It can't be, it just can't be*, he thought wildly, *not again, not SO SOON!* He was quaking in his Nocona boots. For there, sitting right there, as though God or the devil
>
> (*it's the latter oh God it's the latter oh I know it's the devil*)
>
> had placed it there, was a gigantic book with a dark painting on the cover, and in large red type, the word "It." (68)

The article continues in this vein, criticizing the novel (as King had predicted) for its length: 1,138 pages (the hardcover *Stand* is only 823 pages long). As early as the *Adelina* reviews, King noted that as far as mainstream critics were concerned, the long novel had died long ago, and that since the 1950s, novels were more and more frequently discriminated against on the basis of length alone. "Many critics," he noted in 1980, "seem to take a novel of more than 400 pages as a personal affront." As evidence, he cites negative responses to *The Dead Zone* ("One critic was so put out by [its] length . . . that he wished I might contract a case of permanent dyslexia") and *The Stand* (King cites one comment to the effect that "Given enough rope, any writer will hang himself . . . and in this novel, King has taken enough rope to outfit an entire clipper ship") (King, "Love Those Long Novels" 9).

It was not surprising, then, that King would anticipate even more negative responses to *It* largely on the basis of its length. In one letter, he noted sadly that "the days when *any* novel as long as this gets much of a critical reading are gone" (31 March, 1986). In a lighter vein, he acknowledged the difficulty of reading such a massive work. After seeing the entire manuscript in a single stack, he writes, "a Great Postulate occurred to me: no manuscript weighing more than twelve pounds can *possibly* be any good. I also made my first New Year's Resolution in some ten years that night: *Never write anything bigger than your own head*" (Letter, 3 March 1986).

King was, therefore, prepared to some extent for reactions such as Podhoretz's to *It*, at least as far as the novel's length is concerned.

Podhoretz found more to quibble with in the novel than mere length, however. *It* demonstrates all of King's trademarks: a setting in Maine; quotations from rock songs; blood and gore; brand names; geographical accuracy to tie its horrors to the real world; "real get-down-in-the-gutter-and-sound-like-an-illiterate-moron-writing" set next to passages of more self-consciously elevated prose. The latter criticism sounds much like Mark Twain's condemnation of James Fenimore Cooper's literary offenses.

In despair, Podhoretz consults his own Van Helsing, a certain Dr. Smith, a mild-mannered University English professor by day and researcher into the occult by night. Smith warns Podhoretz that King must be stopped: "If you don't, this will go on forever. He'll publish longer and longer books. Two, three thousand pages. Five thousand. Your life will be devoted to reading his books. You will quit your job, you'll have no money, and you'll starve to death" (69).

The result is a quick trip to Maine, where Podhoretz confronts King to define the ultimate failure of *It*—it is boring. It depends upon the banality of blood, upon extensive passages of cruelty to create the interest that its implicit horror-elements cannot. King is no longer scary, Podhoretz asserts, so he had to fall back on unpleasantness (apparently ignoring King's claims that unpleasantness—what King refers to as the "gross out"—is inherent in King's theory of horror).

Not that King was always such, Podhoretz adds; once, in fact, he was a master of sorts—but Podhoretz carefully undercuts the positive with the negative. *The Stand* was a great novel, he says, adding the derogatory "in its own pulpy way":

> "The Shining" was genuinely imaginative and "'Salem's Lot" the only vampire novel worthy of comparison to "Dracula."
> But now where are you? You're hoping that prolixity will accomplish what your imagination can't. (69)

With *It*, King has given up on the supernatural and hopes to frighten by sheer bulk and page count. The novel is boring, King is boring, and Podhoretz warns that if this sort of thing continues, King will lose his fans.

There are, of course, positive reviews of *It*—many of them. But even there, a certain oddly lingering reticence attaches itself, often in unusual ways. The *Los Angeles Times Book Review* included a strongly favorable piece on the novel:

> I wait for each new King novel as an alcoholic waits for the next drink. I am addicted. If you are not, I suggest you introduce yourself to King's work through one of his earlier novels—"Carrie" or "The Shining." If, however, you are already a King addict, "It" will overwhelm you. (Goldberg 2)

The difficulty lies not so much in what is said (although the review is essentially plot summary rather than evaluation) as in who says it: Whoopi Goldberg, whose listed credentials are restricted to her work in film and theater. While she certainly has a right to an attitude toward King and King's novels, it unfortunately seems possible that her assignment to review the book was as much a mark of her reputation as a Hollywood personality as of her literary expertise.

This emphasis on personality leads to another form of popular criticism, which tends to ignore the works themselves and concentrate on *King* as personality—generally to his detriment. G. Wayne Miller begins his discussion of *Maximum Overdrive* not with references to the film but by describing King:

> Stephen King, the most popular horror writer of all time, is eating pizza—thick, oily, mega-calorie pizza with all the fixings. He's eating it the way a big hungry kid would—ferociously and noisily. Stephen King loves pizza, just as he loves scaring the pants off people.
>
> King, who has made enough money from what he calls a "marketable obsession" to buy Brooks Brothers' entire inventory, is dressed in jeans, work shirt, running shoes. Comfort is the thing for King, who sets many of his stories in rural Maine, the place he's lived for most of his 38 years.
>
> Would his visitor like a slice of that greasy monster masquerading as a pizza, he asks politely? No? Then have a seat. Feel at home.
>
> He sits—flops is probably a better word—onto an oversized chair in his hotel suite. King is well over six feet tall, and his long legs seem to stretch halfway across this elegantly furnished sitting room. He brushes his black hair off his face, grins mischievously, and peers from behind thick glasses, his "Coke bottles," as he's referred to them. (I-1)

Nothing in the passage seems directly relevant to *Maximum Overdrive* as film; everything, instead, points to Stephen King as eccentric celebrity.

For another writer, what seems most important is King's "long lantern-jawed face framed by a jet black bowl of hair that rises in two sweeping arcs around his forehead like the drooping wings of some bat" (Beeber 16A); for yet another, it is the hamburger he eats on the set of *Maximum Overdrive*, a greasy hamburger dripping with blood-like catsup.

The problem is, of course, that it is difficult to see exactly what his pizza and hamburger and hairstyle have to do with the quality of his writing or directing—and yet they are treated as if they were of paramount importance. John Coyne was speaking of this sort of pseudo-criticism, criticism by personality, when he commented that King was becoming his "own worst enemy"; Stephen King the writer was being replaced by Stephen King the visible personality. "You really shouldn't be known," Coyne says.

> J. D. Salinger has probably sold a lot more copies just because no one knows who J. D. Salinger is. If King or I wanted to play this game really well, we would be totally anonymous. We would be sending books in via UPS. King's problem—and it's a problem for all of us—is, what if he wants to write a love story? If he writes under his own name, he'll disappoint his readers, because they're expecting, if nothing else, that one lover will chop off the other's head or whatever. (Winter, "Coyne" 13-14)

In King's case, it has progressed even beyond that sort of disappointment. Now, a novel or film must live up to the media hype, and up to the popular image of King himself as the "titan of terror" and the "king of horror," and up to the impossible expectations generated by over thirty books and seventeen film adaptations in fewer than thirteen years.

Paradoxically, because of his popular and commercial successes it becomes more and more difficult for King to attain critical success.

2. Academic Criticism

Thus far, I have concentrated only on one sort of criticism—what might be called mainstream, non-academic, and popular criticism—and one sort of reaction to King.

There are, of course, others.

Academic critics have discovered King and are in many cases working diligently to place King within the framework of an acknowledged traditional literary heritage. In spite of references to such critical and scholarly endeavors as fostering a "cottage industry," collections of essays, such as Darrell Schweitzer's *Discovering Stephen King* (1985) and Underwood and Miller's *Fear Itself: The Horror Fiction of Stephen King* (1982; 1984) and *Kingdom of Fear: The World of Stephen King* (1986), include a number of valuable studies: Gary William Crawford's "Stephen King's American Gothic"; Robert M. Price's "Stephen King and the Lovecraft Mythos"; Debra Stump's "A Matter of Choice: King's *Cujo* and Malamud's *The Natural*"; Leonard Heldreth's "The Ultimate Horror: The Dead Child in Stephen King's Stories and Novels"; Bernadette Bosky's "The Mind's a Monkey: Character and Psychology in Stephen King's Recent Fiction"; and Ben P. Indick's "King and the Literary Tradition of Horror and the Supernatural."

One particularly useful piece, Michael McDowell's "The Unexpected and the Inevitable," begins by disparaging the "sapping methods of literary 'appreciation' taught in colleges and graduate schools," then proceeds to demonstrate graphically and convincingly King's mastery of pacing and rhythm. McDowell's chapter in *Kingdom of Fear* not only elucidates an important element in King's appeal to readers, but simultaneously provides an example of literary criticism that makes a difference for the readers.

Other articles on King have found their ways into periodicals— scholarly and academic journals not devoted to King studies or even to horror literature. James Egan's "'A Single Powerful Spectacle': Stephen King's Gothic Melodrama" appeared in the Spring 1986 issue of *Extrapolation*, a journal dedicated to understanding science fiction and fantasy. The article concentrates on King's relationship to a literary thread extending from Mary Shelley through Bram Stoker, Henry James, and Shirley Jackson, concluding that "King's treatment of the Gothic and the macabre are the opposite of impulsive meanderings— he consistently seeks to create a 'single powerful spectacle'" within a tradition that "has existed from the beginnings of literary history" (74). Two years earlier, Egan published "Apocalypticism in the Fiction of Stephen King," also in *Extrapolation*; in the same year *Clues: A Journal of Detection* published his "Antidetection: Gothic and Detective Conventions in the Fiction of Stephen King." In 1986, Gary William Crawford's new journal *Gothic* published Kenneth Gibbs's "Stephen King and the Tradition of American Gothic," a study of King in the context not only of Stoker, Poe, James, and Hawthorne but also of Herman Melville. Karen McGuire's "The Artist as Demon in Mary Shelley, Stevenson, Walpole, Stoker, and King," including an extensive discussion of Ben Mears in *'Salem's Lot*, appeared in the same issue.

This is not to argue that King has reached academic "respectability" as yet—or even that he wishes to do so. There are sufficient reactions to scholarly articles on King as fostering a "cottage industry," and to "instant criticism," that suggest academe still views the man and his critics with a jaundiced eye.

Gary K. Wolfe's review article in *Modern Fiction Studies*, for example, attempted an overview of recent scholarship in science fiction and fantasy. The pages devoted to King criticism argue that Winter's *Stephen King: The Art of Darkness* is the "only book on Stephen King anyone really needs" (148). The comment sets aside the fact that Winter's book is admittedly more of an appreciation than a critical or scholarly approach to King; in spite of its many excellences, it lacks a certain balance of perception and occasionally overstates its arguments. Gary Crawford, for instance, concludes his own critical overview of horror and the literature of the supernatural by noting that King has been the object of several studies, including Winter's. "Winter's book is sound," Crawford argues, "but one would think from reading it that King is another Shakespeare; his praise is unqualified" (103).

Still, what is most frustrating about Wolfe's essay is not his singling out an individual volume, but his general attitude toward King and King criticism as a whole. The essay approaches its stated subject, science fiction and fantasy, with a certain seriousness of tone that does Wolfe justice; certainly his discussions of the backgrounds to SF criticism and of such eminent figures in the field as Thomas Clareson, J. G. Ballard, and Philip José Farmer are carefully constructed and effectively argued.

Only with King does Wolfe allow the level of his discourse to alter. "As everyone knows," Wolfe writes,

> there are eight hundred zillion copies of King's books in print, which if lined up end-to-end would free up a considerable amount of shelf space in your local B. Dalton's. (147-148)

Later, in discussing the Starmont series, Wolfe uses such phrases as "flush on the heels of what must have been its greatest success," to comment that Starmont is "brandishing at us not one or two but *seven* more books about Stephen King!" On the basis of three, Wolfe feels able to comment on the entire series—and states so specifically.

The difficulty here is that almost everything related to King and horror fiction is treated with an entirely different tone than that which characterizes the rest of the essay. Colloquialisms, exaggerations, exclamations, italicized phrases suggest an underlying attitude not only toward the critics and their writings but toward King himself.

The uncomfortable fact is that King criticism is occasionally as suspect among academics as King's novels are. Certainly that is not the case everywhere; and equally certainly much of the academic establishment's antagonism toward King is softening. Yet the fact remains that many academic writers do not read King, have never read King, and have no inclination to ever read King—much less spend time on critical studies.

On the more positive side, King has participated in scholarly conferences, notably the fifth International Conference on the Fantastic in the Arts, held at Boca Raton, Florida, March 22-25, 1984. King served as Guest of Honor, delivering a lecture later published in *Fantasy Review*

(June 1984) as "Dr. Seuss and the Two Faces of Fantasy." Even more noteworthy for this discussion, he was the subject of a double session of academic papers chaired by Leonard G. Heldreth of Northern Michigan University at Marquette. The papers presented included "Stephen King's Vietnam Allegory: An Interpretation of 'Children of the Corn,'" by Anthony S. Magistrale of the University of Vermont, Burlington; "The Destruction and Re-Creation of the Human Community in Stephen King's *The Stand*," by Burton Hatlen, King's former professor at the University of Maine at Orono; "Stephen King's *The Stand*: Science Fiction into Fantasy," by Michael R. Collings of Pepperdine University; "Strawberry Spring: Stephen King's Gothic Universe," by Mary Ferguson of the University of Georgia, Athens; and "Monster Love; or Why Is Stephen King?" by Dennis O'Donovan of Florida Atlantic University. Several of the presentations were subsequently published; at least one first appeared in a scholarly quarterly and was then reprinted in a small-press fan publication. In general, the responses to King at this session indicate the range and scope of the more positive academic responses to his work.

Finally, in terms of serious literary responses to King, the Starmont series has attempted to indicate some possibilities for King criticism. Beginning with *Discovering Stephen King* and *Stephen King as Richard Bachman* (1985), each volume has explored a particular facet of King's works: pseudonymous novels, short stories, novels, films produced from King's fictions, and—in this volume—some extra-literary considerations in dealing with King and his reputation. The volumes are not specifically academic; they are, instead, intended for serious readers of King who might benefit from discussions, backgrounds, and generalized analysis. In addition, they try to bridge the often too-apparent gap between academic criticism and general readership by approaching King from two directions: first, by showing that the standards of traditional and contemporary literary criticism might be justifiably and beneficially applied to King's writings; and second, by showing readers that some familiarity with those standards may be helpful in appreciating and understanding more fully King's achievements.

3. Criticism within the Genre: Appreciations, Peer Criticism, and Fan Responses

On yet another level, some readers respond with personal, gut reactions, often displaying unalloyed adoration—one fan referred to the "orgasmic" experience of reading King's novels. Among fans, for example, criticism emphasizes what the individual reader felt while immersed in the works; there is in general less concern for establishing literary criteria for success or failure.

Paradoxically, Winter's *Stephen King: The Art of Darkness* to a degree falls within this category, since it is an appreciation and biography, coupled with literary criticism that emphasizes psychology and symbolism as well as King's own background. Winter's study has been justifiably influential in interesting readers and writers in King; much of the secondary work done since 1982 depends upon questions Winter posed, evaluations he made, assertions he brought forth. The book represents a fine blend of the fan and the academic, although given Winter's credits as a contributing editor for *Fantasy Review* he might lean more toward fan than academic.

Unfortunately, the dichotomy perceived by many as existing between fan response and academic criticism is rarely so neatly resolved. In an intriguing article published in *Castle Rock: The Stephen King Newsletter*, Christopher Spruce seemed intent on tackling the arbitrary definition of "literature" as "whatever college students study in literature classes, the works having been so deemed by a panel of self-appointed literary experts—usually college professors." Placing King in the context of contemporary American writers, including John Irving, Norman Mailer, and John Updike, Spruce wonders why King is simply disregarded as a writer of horror pulps who has committed the worst possible crime: he sells too many books.

Spruce's discussion is clear up to the point where he refers to those King works that he would nominate as true "literature": "The Reach" and *'Salem's Lot*. His judgment is not particularly the issue here; both are strong works, and "The Reach" does touch on important archetypal and mythic chords. The difficulty is that, after carefully breaking down the barriers separating King from "good literature," the article then evaluates these two works from a rather fannish perspective. The discussion of "The Reach" concentrates on plot summary and personal response. Spruce empathizes with Stella Flanders because she reminds him of many elderly women he has known in Maine and because she represents a certain sort of character that appeals to him. "Beyond that," he writes in the final paragraph devoted to the story, "my literary senses tell me that this is as good a story as I probably am ever going to have the pleasure of reading" (4).

What is missing is a clear discussion of *why* the story succeeds, not only as entertainment but as literature. And that is the point missing in many fan responses. Adulation is there, but without careful discussion and definition of relevant literary criteria; what is there besides the reader's "literary senses" that demonstrates King's mastery of language and form? Frequently, responses at this level concentrate on story line and on the sensation of fear King's stories and novels produce. These are certainly valid responses (and just as certainly not the only ones possible). The many appreciations, reviews, letters, and informal articles published in *Castle Rock: The Stephen King Newsletter*, for example, go far toward establishing the extent of King's popularity and the depth to which his works are capable of touching readers, regardless of the opinions of mainstream reviewers or academic critics.

As in so many other ways, King remains controversial when it comes to critics and criticism. This chapter represents only an overview of possibilities; it does not pretend to a definitive treatment of the issue. *The Annotated Guide to Stephen King* lists several hundred secondary works relating to King and his writing; each approaches the subject from a different critical and personal stance; each illuminates a slightly different perspective on the man and his works, and each defines for itself the importance—or lack of importance—King holds in contemporary American culture.

Works Cited

Beeber, Steven. "Stephen King: On the Dark Side With the Master of Horror." Atlanta GA, 19 July 1986.

Benson, Sheila. "Stand by Me." *Los Angeles Times* "Calendar" 31 August 1986: 27.

Brooks, David. "What Is Death, What Is Goofy?" *Insight* 1 September 1986: 57. Review of *Stand by Me*.

Burkett, Michael. "Shockmeister: King Takes a Run at Directing." *The Orange Country Register* (CA) 20 July 1986: H1-H2.

Collings, Michael R. *The Many Facets of Stephen King*. Mercer Island WA: Starmont House, 1985.

Crawford, Gary. "Criticism." *The Penguin Encyclopedia of Horror and the Supernatural*. Ed. Jack Sullivan. New York: Viking, 1986: 101-03.

Cuneff, Tom. "Stand by Me." *People* 1 September 1986: 12.

Cziraky, Daniel. "'Body' Praised." *Castle Rock* (October 1986): 8.

Egan, James. "Apocalypticism in the Fiction of Stephen King." *Extrapolation* (Fall 1984): 214-227.

_____. "'A Single Powerful Spectacle': Stephen King's Gothic Melodrama." *Extrapolation* (Spring 1986): 62-75.

Freedman, Richard. "Boys Will Be Boys in Refreshing 'Stand by Me.'" *The Star-Ledger* (Newark NJ) 8 August 1986: 49.

Garrett, Robert. "'Overdrive': Bodies by King." *Boston Globe* 26 July 1986.

Gibbs, Kenneth. "Stephen King and the Tradition of American Gothic." *Gothic* 1 (1986): 6-14.

Goldberg, Whoopi. "It." *The Book Review (Los Angeles Times)* 2 October 1986: 2.

Holden, Stephen. "At the Movies: Rob Reiner Films Unusual Teen Drama." *New York Times* 8 August 1986: C8.

Hunt, Robert. "King of Horror." *St. Louis* (August 1986): 40-41.

King, Stephen. *It* (typescript). March 1986.

_____. *It*. New York: Viking, 1986.

_____. Letter to Michael R. Collings. 3 March 1986.

_____. Letter to Michael R. Collings. 31 March 1986.

_____. "Love Those Long Novels." *Adelina* (November 1980): 9.

_____. *'Salem's Lot*. Garden City NY: Doubleday, 1975.

Lally, Kevin. "Here's a Movie to Stand By: Stephen King Adaptation Is a Sleeper." *The Courier-News* (Bridgewater NJ) 8 August 1986: C1.

Louka, Loukia. "Horror Stories Have Staying Power: The Dispatch Talks with Stephen King." *Maryland Coast Dispatch* 8 August 1986: 11, 73, 80, 86, 88.

McDowell, Michael. "The Unexpected and the Inevitable." *Kingdom of Fear: The World of Stephen King*. Eds. Tim Underwood and Chuck Miller. Columbia PA: Underwood-Miller, 1986: 83-95.

McGuire, Karen. "The Artist as Demon in Mary Shelley, Stevenson, Walpole, Stoker, and King." *Gothic* 1 (1986): 1-5.

Mewshaw, Michael. "Novels and Stories." *New York Times Book Review* 26 March 1978: 13, 23.

Miller, G. Wayne. "King of Horror: His Career's in 'Overdrive' as He Directs His First Film." *Providence Sunday Journal* 3 August 1986: I-1, I-3.

Podhoretz, John. "Stopping 'It' Before It's Too Late." *Insight* 25 August 1986: 68-69.

Ratliff, Larry. "Stephen King's 'Maximum Overdrive' Spins Its Wheels." San Antonio TX, 1986.

Reed, Rex. "'Stand by Me'—A Corny Kids' Caper." *New York Post* 8 August 1986: 22.

Schweitzer, Darrell, ed. *Discovering Stephen King*. Mercer Island WA: Starmont House, 1985.

Shapiro, Susin. "One Picture Is Worth a Million Words." *New York Daily News Magazine* 13 July 1986: 8-11. Review-article on *Maximum Overdrive*.

Spruce, Christopher. "Stephen King: The Critics' Non-Choice." *Castle Rock* (December 1985): 1, 4.

Sullivan, Jack. "Ten Ways to Write a Gothic." *New York Times Book Review* 20 February 1977: 8.

Underwood, Tim and Chuck Miller, eds. *Fear Itself: The Horror Fiction of Stephen King*. San Francisco CA: Underwood-Miller, 1982; New York: NAL Signet, 1984.

_____, eds. *Kingdom of Fear: The World of Stephen King*. San Francisco CA: Underwood-Miller, 1986.

Wiater, Stanley. "The Stephen King Phenomenon." *The Valley Advocate* 21 July 1986: 30.

Winter, Douglas E. "John Coyne: A Profile." *Fantasy Review* (October 1985): 12-14, 33.

_____. *Stephen King: The Art of Darkness*. New York: NAL, 1984; revised and expanded, 1986.

Wolfe, Gary K. "Strange Invaders: An Essay-Review." *Modern Fiction Studies* (Spring 1986): 133-151.

Do the Dead Sing?

Douglas E. Winter

> To the three Ds—death, destruction and destiny. Where would we be without them?
>
> —Stephen King

"The Reach was wider in those days," says Stella Flanders, the oldest resident of Goat Island, Maine. Ninety-five years old and dying of cancer, Stella Flanders has decided to take a walk. It is winter, the Reach has frozen over for the first time in forty years, and Stella Flanders has begun to see ghosts. And she has decided that, having never before left Goat Island, it is time for a walk across the Reach. The inland coast of Maine is a mile and a half distant, and so far as we know, neither the coast nor Goat Island has had occasion to move. But Stella Flanders is nevertheless right—the Reach *was* wider in those days.

The storyteller's name is Stephen King, and although he asks "Do the dead sing?" his story, "The Reach,"[1] is about a journey. Stella Flanders, having left her home behind, sets forth on an odyssey of discovery that, paradoxically, looks homeward with every step. The lonely crossing of the dark, frozen waters of the Reach means death for Stella Flanders; and the question "Do the dead sing?" asks what really lies upon the far side of the Reach.

That question, asked and answered in different guises, resounds throughout the fiction of Stephen King. Not very far from Goat Island, but in another version of reality called *The Stand*, Fran Goldsmith waits in expectation on the mainland coast at Ogunquit, Maine. She is pregnant, alone, and one of the few people left alive in a world decimated by the flu. Further south, in the fictional hall of mirrors known as *The Talisman*, twelve-year-old Jack Sawyer stands at Arcadia Beach on the tiny seacoast of New Hampshire. His mother is dying, and he senses that her fate—and perhaps the fate of the world—may soon be held in his young hands. Both Fran Goldsmith and Jack Sawyer have also decided to take a walk, and although the distances they must travel are considerable in miles, their journeys cross a Reach no different in meaning than that facing Stella Flanders—although each of them will return, for a time, to the near side of the Reach.

That Stella Flanders' journey is westward may be a fluke of geography, but that west is the prevailing movement of the travelers of *The Stand* and *The Talisman* is not. These stories enact the recurrent American nightmare—the terror-trip experienced by Edgar Allan Poe's Arthur Gordon Pym, Herman Melville's Ishmael, and a host of fellow journeyers: the search for a utopia of meaning while glancing backward in idyllic reverie to lost innocence.[2] It is a journey taken by Jack Torrance in *The Shining*, driving west to the promise of a new life at the Overlook Hotel; by Johnny Smith in *The Dead Zone*, who crosses time, if not space; by Louis Creed in *Pet Sematary*, carrying the body of his dead son along the uphill path to a secret burial ground; by character after character in Stephen King's fiction, all trapped between fear of the past's deadly embrace and fear of future progress in a world that placidly accepts the possibility of total war. It is a night journey, both literally and symbolically, and Stephen King is its foremost practitioner in contemporary fiction.

The story of Stella Flanders' crossing of the Reach provides an appropriate introduction to the night journeys of Stephen King. As an archetype of American nightmare, "The Reach" (originally published as "Do the Dead Sing?") suggests the principal reasons for the importance and popularity of modern horror fiction, and the writings of Stephen King in particular. It will serve as a roadmap of context, by which we will travel through ten years of Stephen King novels, from *Carrie* to his recent collaboration with Peter Straub, *The Talisman*. And the question "Do the dead sing?" will haunt us throughout these novels in literal and symbolic manifestations that may prove more frightening than the face of fear itself.

Asking whether the dead sing is much like offering Johnny Smith's rhetorical toast in *The Dead Zone*: "To the three Ds—death, destruction and destiny. Where would we be without them?" These questions have been asked since the first horror story was told by firelight, and they are as inevitable—and as unanswerable—as the question of why we tell and listen to horror stories. To suggest that the tale of terror is an inextricable element of the human condition—a guilty fascination with darkness and irrationality, with the potential for expanding human consciousness and perception, with the understanding of our mortality and our universe—would be true but insufficient. More pragmatic answers seem to be in order. Western society is obsessed with horror fiction and film—the past fifteen years have seen an eruption of interest in horror stories rivaled only by the halcyon days of the ghost story at the close of the nineteenth century.

To ask why we read horror fiction is to ask why Stella Flanders took that walk on that cold winter's day of the storyteller's imagination. Death stalks Stella Flanders, and her faltering steps onto the Reach are an adventure, an escape from a mundane life—and a mundane death. At a minimum, horror fiction is a means of escape, sublimating the very real and often overpowering horrors of everyday life in favor of surreal, exotic, and visionary realms. Escapism is not, of course, necessarily a rewarding experience; indeed, horror fiction's focus upon morbidity and mortality suggests a masochistic or exploitative experience, conjuring subjective fantasies in which our worst fears or darkest desires are brought into tangible existence. "It was the way things worked," says Officer Hunton in King's short story "The Mangler"—"the human animal had a built-in urge to view the remains."[3] But conscientious fiction of escape provides something more—an art of mimesis, a counterfeiting of reality whose inducement to imagination gives the reader access to truths beyond the scope of reason. As D. H. Lawrence would write of Poe's horror fiction: "It is lurid and melodramatic, but it is true."[4]

The escapist quality of horror stories and other popular fiction speaks in a conditional future voice. As King has observed: "Literature asks 'What next?' while popular fiction asks 'What if?'"[5] Despite its intrinsic unreality, the horror story remains credible—or at least sufficiently credible to exert an influence that may last long beyond the act of reading. One does not easily forget the thing that waits inside "The Crate,"[6] or the grinning, cymbal-clashing toy of "The Monkey."[7] This credibility is possible because horror's truths are judged not by the real fulfillment of its promises, but by the relevance of its fantasies to those of the reader or viewer. Although horror fiction appeals to the source of daydreams—and of nightmares—its context is waking reality.

The tensions between fantasy and reality, wanderlust and nostalgia, produce an intriguing paradox. Stella Flanders' escape across the Reach is a search for the ghosts of her past—the lives, and years, that have departed; it can lead only to her death. In the stories "The Ballad of the Flexible Bullet"[8] and "The Jaunt,"[9] King even more forcefully portrays how the active pursuit of the uncanny leads, with whirlpool inevitability, to destruction. As in many of the stories of the early-twentieth-century master of horror, H. P. Lovecraft, the uncanny provokes a self-destructive impulse, reflecting the alternately repulsive and seductive nature of horror fiction. "[W]hat is sought after—the otherworldly—makes us realize how much we need the worldly," writes critic Jack Sullivan, "but the more we know of the world, the more we need to be rid of it."[10]

The six o'clock news is sufficient to show our need to be rid of the world: assassination, rampant crime, political wrongdoing, social upheaval, and war are as much a part of our daily lives as the very air we breathe. And we can no longer trust that air—or the water that we drink, the food that we eat, our machines, or our neighbors. Just ask Richie Grenadine, who popped the top on a funky can of beer in "Gray Matter"[11]; or Harold Parkette, who employed "The Lawnmower Man"[12]; or the young woman who met "The Man Who Loved Flowers"[13]; or the characters of *Cujo*, whose reality is, in the final trumps, as inescapable as our own. And we live in the shadow of the atomic bomb, harbinger of our total destruction and the ultimate proof that we can no longer trust even ourselves.

Psychoanalyst and sleep researcher Charles Fisher once observed that "Dreaming permits each and every one of us to be quietly and safely insane every night of our lives."[14] His words apply as well to the waking dreams of horror fiction. In the tale of horror, we can breach our foremost taboos, allow ourselves to lose control, experience the same emotions—terror, revulsion, helplessness—that besiege us daily. If we fear heights, we can step out on "The Ledge"[15]; or if rats are our phobia, we can work "The Graveyard Shift."[16] The confinement of the action to the printed page or motion picture screen renders the irrationality safe, lending our fears the appearance of being controllable. The achievement of horror's conditional future is endlessly deferred; except within the closed environment of the fiction or film, the fantasy does not—and, perhaps more important, cannot—become reality. Our sensibilities are offered a simple escape from escapism: wanderlust fulfilled, we can leave horror's pages and shadowed theaters with the conviction that the horror was not true and cannot be true. Every horror novel, like every nightmare, has a happy ending, just so long as we can wake up, and we can say, with Herman Melville's *Pierre* (1852), that "It is all a dream—we dreamed that we dreamed we dream."

But horror fiction is not simply an unquiet place that we may visit in moments of need. Along with its obvious cathartic value, horror fiction has a cognitive value, helping us to understand ourselves and our existential situation. Its essential element is the clash between prosaic everyday life and a mysterious, irrational, and potentially supernatural universe. The mundane existence of Stella Flanders is never the same after she first sees the ghost of her long-dead husband. Her haunting is a traditional one, and Stephen King conjures an atmosphere of suspended disbelief by his very reliance upon the traditions of the supernatural tale. Just like settling into a comfortable chair, King's conscientious use of such traditions—both in terms of theme (as in the vampire lore of *'Salem's Lot* and the Gothic castle/hotels of *The Shining* and *The Talisman*) and of narrative technique (as in the Lovecraftian epistolary tale of "Jerusalem's Lot"[17] and the smoking room reminiscence of "The Man Who Would Not Shake Hands"[18])—lends credibility to the otherwise unbelievable. The supernatural need not creep across the floorboards of each and every horror story, however; reality itself often is sufficiently frightening—and certainly credible—as short stories like King's "Strawberry Spring"[19] and "Survivor Type"[20] prove through themes of psychological distress and aberration.

Then there are the stories that fall somewhere in between. Although Stella Flanders sees ghosts in "The Reach," these ghosts are no more adequately proved than the aliens who schoolmarm Emily Sidley believes have replaced her third-graders in "Suffer the Little Children."[21] To be sure, Stella Flanders follows the ghosts (just as Miss Sidley takes the little children, one by one, to the mimeograph room, where she kills them), but there is no extrinsic evidence of their reality. Do the dead sing? The question is not simply one of faith—how close does it come to reality?

The pursuit of realism suggests that horror fiction should follow a consequential pattern: that some semblance of reason, however vague, should underlie seemingly irrational or supernatural events. The leap of faith necessary to persuade the purblind skeptic that zombies can walk is made slightly easier by a springboard based in voodoo or—as in the classic zombie film, *Night of the Living Dead* (1965)—the strange radiation of a returning Venus probe, even if these explanations are themselves intrinsically illogical. And once that leap of faith is made, the reader may as well shout that the water's fine: if zombies can walk, then we have little additional trouble in accepting that they will feast upon the flesh of the living rather than serve as ideal elevator operators. The fact that the typical reader of horror fiction is willing to believe should render the author's task that much easier. There is a secret self—the eternal child, perhaps—lurking somewhere within each of us who yearns to be shown that the worst is true: that zombies can walk, that ghosts really beckon to Stella Flanders.

When the printed tale of terror was young—in those days of the "penny dreadfuls" and their more respectable kin, the Gothic novel—a rigid dichotomy was observed between fiction based in supernatural events and that based in rational explanation. The latter form, best exemplified by the novels of Ann Radcliffe—such as *The Mysteries of Udolpho* (1794)—and reprised briefly in the "shudder pulps" of the 1930s and the "Baby Jane" maniac films of the 1960s, proposed apparently supernatural events that were explained rationally at the story's end. As the modern horror story emerged in the late 1800s, however, neither a rational nor a supernatural explanation of events needed ultimately to be endorsed. Even formalist M. R. James would write: "It is not amiss sometimes to leave a loophole for a natural explanation, but I would say, let the loophole be so narrow as not to be quite practicable." Indeed, the archetypal ghost story, J. Sheridan LeFanu's "Green Tea" (1869), posed a mystifying dual explanation of its events, using the inevitable tension between the rational and the irrational to exacerbate its horror—a tension replicated nearly one hundred years later in the wholly inadequate interpretation of the psychiatrist at the conclusion of Alfred Hitchcock's *Psycho* (1960) and the straight-faced recommendation of exorcism by the physicians in the motion picture of *The Exorcist* (1973).

Stephen King's most pervasive short story, "The Boogeyman,"[22] suggests that explanation, whether supernatural or rational, may simply not be the business of horror fiction—that the very fact that the question "Do the dead sing?" is unanswerable draws us inexorably to his night journeys.

"I came to you because I want to tell my story," says Lester Billings, comfortably enthroned on the psychiatric couch of Dr. Harper. "All I did was kill my kids. One at a time. Killed them all."[23] So begins Lester Billings' journey through the retrospective corridors of psychoanalysis. He quickly explains that he did not actually kill his three children, but that he is "responsible" for their deaths because he has left certain closet doors open at night, and "the boogeyman" has come out. A rational mind must reject such a confessional, and Billings is an abrasive personality—cold, insensitive, filled with hatred for the human condition. Immediately, we doubt his credibility and his sanity. By the story's close, Billings has made it clear that it is he who fears "the boogeyman," and the reader can only conclude that he has murdered his children. Dr. Harper states that therapy will be necessary, but when Billings returns to the psychiatrist's office, he notices that the closet door is open—first, just by a crack, but it quickly swings wide: "'So nice,' the boogeyman said as it shambled out. It still held its Dr. Harper mask in one rotted, spade-claw hand."[24]

On a metaphorical level, the boogeyman's appearance may be an affirmation of Billings' psychosis—this is the loophole for a rational explanation. Symbolically, we see psychiatry, the supposedly rational science of mind—and, indeed, the science that explained as disease what earlier beliefs had held to be the workings of supernatural forces—succumb to the slavering irrationality of a "boogeyman." The retrogression to childhood, so intrinsic to Freudian solution, ironically affirms the correctness of childhood fears. And this very image is revisited again and again in King's fiction. When Father Callahan confronts "Mr. Barlow," the king vampire of 'Salem's Lot, he recognizes the face: it is that of "Mr. Flip," the boogeyman who haunted the closets of his youth. The thing that haunts Tad Trenton's closet in Cujo prefigures that rabid dog, the nightmare unleashed in daylight. And the Overlook Hotel of The Shining is revealed in the end as the quintessential haunted closet, from which the boogeyman shambles:

A long and nightmarish masquerade party went on here, and had gone on for years. Little by little a force had accrued, as secret and silent as interest in a bank account. Force, presence, shape, they were all only words and none of them mattered. It wore many masks, but it was all one. Now, somewhere, it was coming for him. It was hiding behind Daddy's face, it was imitating Daddy's voice, it was wearing Daddy's clothes.

But it was not his Daddy.[25]

On both the literal and symbolic levels, "The Boogeyman" shattered the distinction between the supernatural and the empirical, offering the chilling possibility that there is no difference. In its wake, King put forward a theme of "rational supernaturalism" in his novels—first seeded in *Carrie*, but brought to fruition in *The Stand*, *The Dead Zone*, and *Firestarter*—granting credence to unnatural phenomena through elaborate rationalizations not unlike those of science fiction, and simultaneously suggesting a dark truth that we all suspect: that rationality and order are facades, mere illusions of control imposed upon a reality of chaos.

Like the mask worn by the boogeyman, what Stella Flanders has left behind in the small community of Goat Island is deceptive. Surface appearances are not to be trusted, as two young men learn when they test the fledgling ice of the Reach on a snowmobile. The apparent serenity and pastoral simplicity of Goat Island are stripped away through Stella Flanders' memories of the town's complicity in the deaths of a mongoloid baby and a child molester. Artifice and masquerade are recurring themes in Stephen King's fiction, reminding us that evil works from within as well as from without—that, like the ravaged hulk of the 1958 Plymouth Fury that sits at the roadside at the beginning of *Christine*, we are clothed with the thin veneer of civilization, beneath which waits the beast, eager to emerge.

Horror fiction is thus an intrinsically subversive art, which seeks the true face of reality by striking through the pasteboard masks of appearance. That the lifting of the mask may reveal the face of the boogeyman, the new world of *The Stand*, or the nothingness of *Cujo* is our existential dilemma, the eternal tension between doubt and belief that will haunt us to our grave, when we surely must learn. But the lifting of the mask also strikes at the artifices of control that we erect against this dilemma—our science, religion, materialism, and civilization. That horror fiction evokes current events and religious and sociopolitical concerns should thus come as no surprise. The masterpieces of "yellow Gothic"—Robert Louis Stevenson's *Dr. Jekyll and Mr. Hyde* (1886),

Oscar Wilde's *The Picture of Dorian Gray* (1891), H. G. Wells's *The Island of Dr. Moreau* (1896), and Bram Stoker's *Dracula* (1897)—reflected the fears of an age of imperial decline. More recently, the "technohorror" films of the 1950s were obvious analogs of the doomsday mentality created by the atomic bomb and the cold war. As we shall see, the novels and stories of Stephen King exploit this subversive potential, consciously creating sociopolitical subtexts that add timely depth and meaning to their horrifying premises.

Stella Flanders does not read a horror story in "The Reach," but she does the next best thing—attend a funeral. Its ritual is not unlike a horror tale, organizing and packaging fears, giving meaning and value to death (and, in so doing, to life). And Stella Flanders helps us see something more; her attendance is compelled not so much by mere inquisitiveness, escape, catharsis, or the demands of society as by her memories of the past. Things were better then; after all, the Reach—indeed, the whole world—was wider in those days. When Stella Flanders embarks upon her journey, she understands what she is leaving behind in the "small world" on this side of the Reach: "a way of being and a way of living; a feeling."[26] Her glance backward is a fundamental aspect of all horror fiction; thus, Philip Van Doren Stern described the ghost stories of the early twentieth century as "singing the swan song of an earlier way of life."[27]

In an era of continuous social and technological revolution, however, contemporary horror fiction lacks a pretechnological culture to sentimentalize. Indeed, the horror lurking within certain of Stephen King's novels—particularly *The Stand*—is precisely the lack of an "earlier way of life" worthy of our sentiment.[28] Rather than indulge in a spurious attempt to recapture a social milieu, King's fiction often looks to our youth as the earlier way of life whose "swan song" must be sung. His stories are songs of innocence and experience, juxtaposing childhood and adulthood—effectively completing the wheel whose turn began in childhood by reexperiencing those days from a mature perspective. Indeed, several of his novels suggest that horror fiction performs the role of the modern fairy tale—*Cujo* begins with the words "Once upon a time," while *Carrie* and *Firestarter* respectively evoke the traditions of "Cinderella" and "Beauty and the Beast."

This is a powerful motif; it may cause the reader to look to his or her life as well as that of the characters. In King's works, we experience again those occasions in our lives when it has seemed important to understand what a person really is—to perceive the genuine identity beneath the social exterior of manner, habits, clothes, and job. Such moments are most common in childhood, when no one's identity is certain and when any exterior is likely to be impermanent or false. Uncertainty in our own sense of self renders the processes of knowing and communicating with others difficult and intense. We live in a world of emotion and moral significance, in which the business of life is the process of social relation and social judgment; we constantly attempt to fix our view of others, to do justice to emotions and judgments, yet language always seems inadequate to express what we *know*. We leave this world behind as we mature. As King wryly notes, "the only cure is the eventual ossification of the imaginary faculties, and this is called adulthood."[29] We lose our sense of the mysticism of life—of fear and fantasy, of unhindered and yet inexplicable vision, of unscalable heights and limitless possibilities. This lost world is sought by Ben Mears of *'Salem's Lot* in his nostalgic journey to the haunted house of his childhood, and found by Stella Flanders on the far side of the Reach. It is the world that we recapture in the fiction of horror.

Our haunted past offers one truth, one answer, that is often obscured by the countless rationalizations, psychological interpretations, and critical insights offered to explain the reading and writing of horror fiction. We knew that truth as children, on those nights when we feared the dark, the slightly open closet door, the certain abyss beneath our bed, yet we were drawn to the darkness and dread. It is the truth that anyone who steps upon a roller coaster—and anyone who reads a horror story—must recognize.

The truth is that it was fun—frightening ourselves, having nightmares, realizing that there is something that we do not and may not ever understand. The Reach was wider in those days, and the question "Do the dead sing?" did not need to be asked. Now that we are older, we may ask that question and offer explanations, but that one truth, that one answer, prevails throughout the night journeys of Stephen King: "We all had some fun tonight," says comedian Steve Martin, "considering that we're all gonna die."

Notes

1. *Yankee*, November 1981 (as "Do the Dead Sing?"); *Skeleton Crew* (New York: Putnam, 1985).

2. See Harry Levin, *The Power of Blackness* (New York: Alfred A. Knopf, 1958).

3. *Cavalier*, December 1972; *Night Shift* (Garden City, NY: Doubleday, 1978), p. 76.

4. D. H. Lawrence, *Studies in Classic American Literature* (New York: Penguin, 1977), p. 85.

5. Panel Discussion: "Horror in the Eighties: Still Alive and Well," moderated by Charles L. Grant, the Sixth World Fantasy Convention, Baltimore, MD, November 1, 1980.

6. *Gallery*, July 1979.

7. *Gallery*, November 1980; *Skeleton Crew*.

8. *The Magazine of Fantasy and Science Fiction*, June 1984; *Skeleton Crew*.

9. *Twilight Zone Magazine*, April 1981; *Skeleton Crew*.

10. Jack Sullivan, *Elegant Nightmares: The English Ghost Story from LeFanu to Blackwood* (Athens: Ohio University Press, 1978), p. 134.

11. *Cavalier*, October 1973; *Night Shift*.

12. *Cavalier*, May 1975; *Night Shift*.

13. *Gallery*, August 1977; *Night Shift*.

14. Quoted in "Sleep: Perchance to Dream . . . ," *Newsweek*, November 30, 1959, p. 104.

15. *Penthouse*, July 1976; *Night Shift*.

16. *Cavalier*, October 1970; *Night Shift*.

17. *Night Shift*, 1978.

18. In Charles L. Grant, ed., *Shadows 4* (Garden City, NY: Doubleday, 1981); revised version, *Skeleton Crew*.

19. *Ubris*, Fall 1968; revised version, *Cavalier*, November 1975; *Night Shift*.

20. In Charles L. Grant, ed., *Terrors* (New York: Playboy, 1982); *Skeleton Crew.*

21. *Cavalier*, February 1972.

22. *Cavalier*, March 1973; *Night Shift.*

23. *Night Shift*, p. 96.

24. Ibid., p. 107.

25. *The Shining* (Garden City, NY: Doubleday, 1977), p. 420.

26. "Do the Dead Sing?," p. 246.

27. Philip Van Doren Stern, "Introduction," *Great Ghost Stories* (New York: Washington Square, 1947), pp. xvi-xvii.

28. In King's words: "[W]e are the first generation forced to live almost entirely without romance and forced to find some kind of supernatural outlet for the romantic impulses that are in all of us. This is really sad in a way. Everybody goes out to horror movies, reads horror novels—and it's almost as though we're trying to preview the end." Quoted in Bob Spitz, "*Penthouse* Interview: Stephen King," *Penthouse*, April 1982, p. 122.

29. *'Salem's Lot* (Garden City, NY: Doubleday, 1975), p. 253. See James B. White, *The Legal Imagination* (Boston, MA: Little, Brown, 1973), pp. 245-46.

King, His World, and Its Characters_____

Heidi Strengell

The central aspects of Stephen King's fiction and his choice of genre can be analyzed in the context of both American society and the course of his personal life. Four factors have contributed to his worldview of the United States: Puritanism, the Gothic mode, "the Emersonian drive," and naturalism. King writes within the American cultural tradition in regard to all but the Emersonian drive, whereas some aspects and themes derive from his personal history. Since a writer with about 550 individual works has dealt with a great number of themes, my analysis is confined primarily to the aspects centering on the American literary heritage and on King's characters.

The roots of American Puritanism date back at least to 1630, when John Winthrop in his "Model of Christian Charity" used mild religious terror to create a particular political identity. Six years later John Cotton and his first-generation Puritan divines pursued a provisional polity to counter the nation's spiritual and civic decline and used the language of witchery (Ingebretsen, 10-13; for the origins of "persecuting society," see Moore). The unfortunate events culminated in the Salem witch hysteria of 1692-93, the echoes of which can be heard in King's first published novels, *Carrie* (1974) and *'Salem's Lot* (1975). These events show how closely connected religion and political identity actually were at the time. In those times of political "dis-ease," somebody had to be found guilty of witchcraft and punished accordingly to ease the minds of the Puritans. John Demos in *Entertaining Satan* argues that witchcraft was a necessary part of communal life, because it served the group by "sharpening its boundaries, reinforcing its values, and deepening the loyalty of its membership" (Demos, 14; Trevor-Roper 165, 189). Thus, although framed in religious terms as *maleficium*, witchcraft constituted a civil offense, and the witch's body became a site of public strife (Ingebretsen, 16; for the witch's person, see Thomas). Whereas witchcraft focused on social unrest within a divided community, it also "allowed Satan entrance to the self," thus underscoring the tension between internal conflict and social confusion (Hall, 146-47). In the same way, although silenced by law, such religious discourse still makes itself heard today, "surfacing in places presumed to be dismissible—particularly in the genres of the horror sublime, or those texts we call dark fantasy" (Ingebretsen, 12). The deeply religious framework of the American cultural heritage is explicitly about power and implicitly about fear, and, therefore, Puritanism and horror are often blended in popular fiction. In fact, Edward J. Ingebretsen goes as far as to claim that American popular culture begins with the Salem witch trials (12-13). Marion Starkey even notes that the "hangings were made a spectacle by intention" (208).

One might even venture to claim that religious discourse has in part been shifted from churches to horror fiction. Victor Sage in *Horror Fiction in the Protestant Tradition* offers a similar view and goes on to contend that the primary determinant in the formation of the Gothic is the religious one. In his historical reading, Sage points out that the formation of a Protestant orthodoxy essentially generated all the major symbols of the Gothic tradition (11). Ingebretsen distinguishes the two traditions by arguing that in Gothic lore monsters typically haunt the margins of society, whereas in political realities social deviants, such as witches, emerge from within communities (15). King's stories provide examples of how disowned theologies return, ghostlike, as moralistic social memory (14). King has been influenced by the Bible, and he professes a faith in the Christian God (Magistrale, *Decade*, 3; Underwood and Miller, *Feast*, 64). Brought up in the atmosphere of Methodism and "fascinated by the trappings and solemnity of Catholicism" (Underwood and Miller, *Feast*, 64), King has been preoccupied with religious themes throughout his writing career. Religious frenzy finds its expression in such characters as Margaret White (*Carrie*), Henrietta Dodd (*The Dead Zone*), Vera Smith (*The Dead Zone*), and Sylvia Pittston (*The Gunslinger*). Unworthy priests are represented by such characters as Father Callahan (*'Salem's Lot*), Reverend Lester

Lowe (*Cycle of the Werewolf*), and Sunlight Gardener (*The Talisman*). Good prophets are portrayed in the characters of Nick Andros (*The Stand*), Mother Abagail (*The Stand*), and David Carver (*Desperation*); evil in that of Randall Flagg (*The Stand, The Eyes of the Dragon,* and *The Dark Tower* series). Hence, King has been dedicated to religious themes both because of his national, Puritan heritage and for reasons of personal interest.

The concept of the Gothic is an emotional coloration, which may be called mood or more precisely mode, because, as Alastair Fowler in *Kinds of Literature* notes, "modal terms tend to be adjectival" (67, 106). In other words, although the Gothic began as a separate genre in the latter part of the eighteenth century, the genre no longer exists as such. Instead it is a mode that lends an atmosphere to literature, among other cultural artifacts. In fact, Leslie Fiedler in *Love and Death in the American Novel* argues that both the most serious and the funniest American writers have found the Gothic mode an apt one for telling the truth about the quality of American life (preface to the second edition, 2). Furthermore, he maintains that the Gothic atmosphere derives from the guilt that America's bloody past has produced. Not surprisingly the last desperate attempt to get rid of guilt is to pretend that all sinister events are nothing but jokes (6-7). Ingebretsen aptly links this guilt with the Calvinistic civic cosmology of expiation: the Salem witch trials, for example, were a means of self-definition (15). The witch-hunting rites were both expiatory and explanatory, socially just as clarifying and purgative as the Gothic literature less than a hundred years later.

The reasons for the proliferation of the Gothic may well be in part religious. Although most Americans believe in God, few seem to believe in his presence. In *Nightmare on Main Street*, Mark Edmundson argues that peace of mind can be gained by accepting the belief that the world is infested with evil, that all power is corrupt, that all humanity is debased, and that nothing can be done about it (67-68). The disenchantment with religion has caused a twofold reaction. Some seek confidence in the Gothic, others in naturalism—in either case, one ends up losing hope and dreams of benevolent, divine forces. Perhaps the essence of the Gothic mode is, however, the fall from innocence or the bargain with the devil, that is, the Faustian pact. These themes are visible in King's oeuvre from the beginning to the present. In particular they have found their direct expression in *Needful Things* (1991) and *Storm of the Century* (1999), where the pact is literally made. *'Salem's Lot* (1975), *The Shining* (1977), *Pet Sematary* (1983), *Misery* (1987), and even *The Dark Tower* series (1982-2004) are often referred to as Gothic novels because of their characters and settings. *The Dark Half* (1989) includes the Gothic motif of the double, and in *Gerald's Game* (1992) the same motif has been internalized in Jessie Burlingame's troubled mind. Finally, *Bag of Bones* (1998) can be labeled a Gothic romance, because it includes an unhappy love story. Of course, it takes more to make a Gothic novel than a single characteristic, and it seems more justifiable to argue that the Gothic mode is one important facet of King's oeuvre.

The third factor in King's American literary heritage is what I call "the Emersonian drive," namely, the self-reliance that, according to Harold Bloom, is "the Emersonian answer to Original Sin" (*Poetics of Influence*, 284) in the sense of personifying the confident spirit to clear whatever obstacles fate has chosen to put in one's way. The Emersonian drive seems to embody everything that eludes the Gothic: youthful drive and self-reliance. More significantly, for Emerson there is no fate to foil the efforts of a confident spirit, and each man is "greater than all the geography and all the government of the world" (*Nature*, 3). In fact, Emerson does not even believe in fate, and for him there is no original sin. In his view we succumb to fate out of fear, because in the Emersonian universe fate is an excuse and little more. The only sin is limitation; therefore, guilt, among other things, must go. Edmundson clarifies this point: "Whatever our faults in the past, we need to forget them or redeem them, if in sustaining them we're impeded from doing our work in the present" (72). By comparison, as an example of an anti-Emersonian, Bloom refers to Edgar Allan Poe, one of King's literary predecessors. He states that Poe's characters were never young (*Poetics*, 285). Edmundson, too, emphasizes that Poe's characters were struck by fate and Poe's "every story was a burnt offering on [fate's] altar" (72).

The Emersonian drive is continuously thwarted by fate in King. Born in 1947 to a lower middle-class family, King seems to exemplify the traditional American success story. However, the theme of success is rarely found in his fiction. In light of what we have learned from the contradiction between the Gothic and the Emersonian drive, this seems more than understandable. Although, for instance, the members of the so-called Losers' Club in *It* reach the top of the ladder in their individual lives, they are all haunted by their childhood memories. Not even King's most fantastic works have attempted to depict a truly Emersonian character. For instance, *The Talisman* (1984), which in Wiater, Golden, and Wagner's words is "about youth, hope, and innocence that harkens back to the simpler times depicted in Mark Twain's work" (66), finds its depressing epilogue in *The Tommyknockers* (1987). Here Jack Sawyer, the protagonist of *The Talisman*, heroically saves his mother's life only to see her killed by a drunk driver. Jack's journey to hell and back leads to nothing. Charlie McGee (*Firestarter*), Peter, the elder son of King Roland of Delain (*The Eyes of the Dragon*), and Trisha McFarland (*The Girl Who Loved Tom Gordon*) may provide the rare exceptions of this rule in King's oeuvre, but only by a very narrow margin. Obviously, Charlie will all her life be under constant surveillance, since she possesses an ability to start fires with her mind; Trisha, will not be able to reunite her divorced parents; and Peter will be in charge of a kingdom that sooner or later will again be attacked by Flagg. Thus, even in King's most fantastic works, his characters are shaped by deterministic forces and fate.

The fourth and final factor in King's literary heritage is literary naturalism. In *Backgrounds of American Literary Thought*, Rod W. Horton and Herbert W. Edwards call the genre "the product of despair," because it reflects the shattering of the optimism of the Enlightenment:

the faith in the democratic system, the hope for human growth, and the belief in the dignity of man (254). In its adherence to observed nature, literary naturalism is derived both from the natural sciences and from sociohistorical theories. As M. H. Abrams points out, the post-Darwinian thesis of literary naturalism holds that the human being belongs in the order of nature and does not have a soul or any connection with a spiritual world beyond nature. Therefore, a human being is merely a higher-order animal whose character and fortunes are determined by two kinds of natural forces, heredity and environment (Abrams, 153-54; Barton and Hudson, 117). Martin Gray, too, emphasizes that literary naturalism is a particular branch of realism with a focus on the miserable and poverty-stricken whose spiritual and intellectual aspirations prove meaningless, or on characters driven by their animal appetites, such as hunger and sexuality (135). As Horton and Edwards note, whereas the scholar of the Enlightenment probed the mysteries of nature as a means of self-justification, the naturalist found in scientific discovery only a confirmation of humankind's helplessness in the face of indifferent and inscrutable forces (255).

Since King has repeatedly acknowledged the existence of personal good and evil forces beyond human control, it is mainly the deterministic view of human beings that relates King to literary naturalism and which, according to Horton and Edwards, is regarded as the "most prevalent literary attitude [in the United States] during the first half of the twentieth century" (259). In *The World According to Kurt Vonnegut*, Bo Pettersson states that the origin of naturalism is manifold, including the modification of what is narrowly labeled as Calvinism into a philosophical determinism (29) and "the moral sterility of undisciplined material and political growth in America" (Horton and Edwards, 260). In King the following aspects of naturalism seem conspicuous: his view of human beings as a product of their environment, his view of humans at the mercy of indifferent forces, and his profound mistrust of scientific progress. Significantly, King shares the latter two attitudes with H. P. Lovecraft, one of his major literary influences.

The deterministic view of humankind also links the Gothic and literary naturalism in King's fiction. In Gothic fiction, fate rules human beings, and they are driven by their instincts; the deterministic view also holds these notions but assumes that humans, as rational beings, can make moral choices. Stephen J. Spignesi points out that in King's world "man possesses free will, but fate will often conspire to put things right" (*Lost Work of Stephen King*, 9). Apparently, King came to embrace the deterministic view of the world at a very early age, because it can be found in unpublished short stories such as "The Thing at the Bottom of the Well" and "The Stranger," both written as a young schoolboy. However, since King's naturalism is colored by the Gothic, the supernatural elements alternate between softening his naturalistic tones and making them even grimmer. At any rate, King's naturalism has kept its faith in the dignity of human beings and close-knit communities, within which emotional needs can be fulfilled and responsible acts committed. As Jeanne Campbell Reesman rightly claims, through supernatural realism King explores both the attractions and the failures of naturalism (109). Thus, he examines naturalistic themes by means of horror. In conclusion, King is a distinctly American writer in that he deploys motifs and themes deriving from the nation's common source of memory and experience and has continued to use the same motifs and themes throughout his career.

King has said about his work that "probably all the significant experience shows up in the fiction" (Magistrale, *Decade*, 2). The aspects of King's fiction that derive from his personal experiences are primarily (1) regionalism and the writer's home state of Maine and (2) character description, including outsider motifs, child depictions, female characters, and his fairy-tale Everyman. In this connection I will focus on the character-centered aspects of King's fiction, instead of, for instance, the more typical view of horror as an unexpected and catastrophic event, because the notion of character will be crucial to the development of my argument. Let us briefly consider the settings and people of King's formative years: After his father had gone out for a pack of cigarettes and never returned, his mother, Ruth, and adopted brother, Dave, led a restless life moving around the country. When Stephen was eleven years old, the family moved to Durham, Maine, where King stayed until he graduated from the University of Maine in 1970. In the following year he married Tabitha Spruce, whom he had met in college. The couple has stayed in the Maine area, and they have three children (Spignesi, *Lost Work*, xix-xx).

King can with good cause be called a regionalist with a distinct narrative voice, often colored by the Maine dialect. The close-lipped declaration of his love for Maine reads as follows: "For me, it has always been a case of being here, living in Maine all my life. The settings are here" (Magistrale, *Decade*, 10). Undoubtedly, the setting comes through, casting its own shadow over whatever King is writing, and for him the importance of region is linked with how people have been disconnected. *Dolores Claiborne* and *Storm of the Century* are set on an island, and through the fictional microcosms of Castle Rock, Derry, and Jerusalem's Lot, he examines a small-town pathology with its calm surface and rotten heart. James E. Hicks notes that the horror of, for instance, *'Salem's Lot* is the reader's "realization that the American pastoral is corruptible, that small town America is not a bulwark against depravity" (76). The xenophobia of small-town America has been dealt with in *Carrie, 'Salem's Lot, The Dead Zone, Cujo, It, The Dark Half, Needful Things, Insomnia, Bag of Bones*, and in several short stories. Equally, many of the names of King's characters have personal significance: while some appear as little more than jokes, others refer to the names of local people or allude to friends and acquaintances. King admits that he has used symbolic names since he was a writer in college: "I don't always do it, but John Smith was certainly the most obvious case, and I chose [that name] on purpose" (Magistrale, *Decade*, 3).

The roots of the outsider motif are also embedded in the writer's own childhood. All of King's works have been preoccupied with this motif, from *Carrie* (1974) to *The Dark Tower* (2004). Introduced to horror by a radio adaptation of Ray Bradbury's story "Mars Is Heaven" at the age of four, the writer has up to *It* (1986) explored "the mythic power that childhood holds over our imagination and, in particular, the point at which the adult is able to link up with his or her own childhood past and the powers therein" (Magistrale, *Decade*, 5). King has been depicting children throughout his writing career, regarding *It* as his "final exam covering the subject" (5). Despite such characters as Trisha McFarland in *The Girl Who Loved Tom Gordon* (1999) and the handicapped Duddits in *Dreamcatcher* (2001), it holds true that King's child characters have grown older at the rate of his own children. For instance, in *From a Buick 8* (2002), King introduces the eighteen-year-old Ned Wilcox, whose relationship to his deceased father is thematized in the novel.

For King imagination, in essence, separates a child from an adult. In *Danse Macabre* he points out: "The imagination is an eye, a marvelous eye that floats free. As children, that eye sees with 20/20 clarity. As we grow older, its vision begins to dim" (407). Adults without imagination are the worst of his monsters, and the child or adolescent protagonist can merely hope for an encounter with an adult who is able to reenter the world of childhood. Such adult characters are almost without exception represented as writers—they seem to have immediate access to their childhood memories and to be able to perceive other dimensions. Although perfect victims, children possess strength that adults have lost in the process of maturing. Thus, when Matt Burke faces a vampire, he is stricken by a heart seizure brought on by fright. But when Mark Petrie encounters one, he is able to fall asleep ten minutes later: "Such is the difference between men and boys" (*SL*, 243).

Ever since the publication of *Carrie* (1974), King has been blamed for depicting his women characters as stereotypes. Since eight of his novels feature female protagonists (*Carrie, Firestarter, Cujo, Misery, Gerald's Game, Dolores Claiborne, Rose Madder*, and *Song of Susannah*); seven depict them as wives or partners (*The Shining, The Drawing of the Three, The Tommyknockers, The Dark Half, The Waste*

Lands, *Insomnia*, and *The Dark Tower*); and four include them in minor roles (*The Stand*, *It*, *Needful Things*, and *From a Buick 8*), the accusation must be discussed in brief. Carol Senf notes the disagreement among critics commenting on King's portraits of women ("*Gerald's Game* and *Dolores Claiborne*," 92). At one end of the spectrum, Clare Hanson regards King as a misogynist who attempts to resolve his Oedipus complex by means of his fiction (150). In the middle we have Chelsea Quinn Yarbro, who in 1982 expressed how disheartening it is "when a writer with so much talent and strength and vision is not able to develop a believable woman character between the ages of seventeen and sixty" (65); Tony Magistrale, who in 1989 complained that King's oeuvre features few complex women, that is, "multidimensional blends of good and evil" (*Moral Voyages of Stephen King*, 51); and Mary Pharr, who in 1992 argued that although female characters are plentiful enough in King's works and although women clearly matter to him, they lack substance ("Partners in the *Danse*," 20). Finally, at the other end of the spectrum, Burton Hatlen considers King a feminist influenced by his feminist wife (Magistrale, *Voyages*, 104), and Mark Jancovich considers King's female characters at least as strong as his male characters (101-2).

In fact, Fiedler in *Love and Death in the American Novel* maintains that no American novelist has been able to treat the passionate encounter of a man and a woman, but instead they shy away from permitting in their works "the presence of any full-fledged, mature woman, giving us instead monsters of virtue or bitchery, symbols of the rejection or fear of sexuality" (4-5). Instead of love, American novels depict "comrades in arms" (5). King regards Fiedler's book as "a motivating force behind the writing of *Carrie*" (Magistrale, *Decade*, 5): "A lot of my efforts in writing about women were made because I wanted to understand women and try to escape the stereotyping that goes on in so much male fiction" (5). Although King has made an effort since the very beginning of his writing career to avoid female stereotypes, especially since *Gerald's Game* (1992), he has more consciously concentrated on women, the emphasis shifting from child characters to women characters.

As "the guru of the ordinary," King also celebrates ordinary men (Magistrale, *Decade*, 10). Like Johnny Smith in *The Dead Zone*, King's Everyman struggles against indifferent forces and triumphs over evil by discovering his inner strength. The victory is reached more by the protagonist's essence of being than by his heroic acts. As Magistrale notes, King has endowed most of his male protagonists with certain powers, such as imagination, which serve them in their struggles against evil forces (11). Several novels feature either outsiders (for instance, *Roadwork*, *The Running Man*, *The Dark Tower* series, and *It*) or writers (for instance, *'Salem's Lot*, *The Shining*, *Misery*, *The Dark Half*, and *Bag of Bones*) as protagonists. King argues that writing about writers has been an effort to understand what he is doing and what writing is doing to and for him (11). In fact, King's characters are developed in an unusual way, which in part results from the combination of archetypes and realism implicit in the characters. For instance, Johnny Smith epitomizes unselfish love for humankind, but he becomes flesh and blood through his realistic feelings and actions, such as the love for his girlfriend and the painful decision to shoot a maniac. Similarly, Norman Daniels, whose Christian name apparently refers to the protagonist of Robert Bloch's *Psycho*, personifies pure evil. Daniels is a police detective whose quick temper leads him to beat his wife and brutalize suspects and who becomes realistic through the detailed depiction of his hideous crimes.

King's writing has now been placed in the context of both American society and his personal life. Significantly, the central aspects of King's American heritage seem to center on the notion of fate. Fate played a decisive role in Puritan thought, bordering on the concept of God, who led the Puritans to the Promised Land of New England (Bercovitch, 136); in Gothic literature fate often implies evil destiny or even death, thus punishing the wrongdoings of such villains as Manfred of Otranto; and in literary naturalism parallels can be drawn with chance (as in King's Bachman books). In the section "Cosmological Determinism and Fate" in chapter 3, fate will be defined according to this tripartite division, but suffice it to note in this connection that the only aspect of the American literary heritage that cannot be applied to King, the Emersonian drive, focuses on life *after* fate has struck, thus providing an optimistic view of the future. When the exploration of fate intertwines with the central concerns deriving from King's personal experience, such as religion and human psychology, we have largely discovered the very essence of King's writing: the human being at the mercy of whimsical and indifferent forces where the best comfort can be found in empathy with one's fellow sufferers.

Works Cited

Abrams, M. H. *A Glossary of Literary Terms*. 1957. New York: Holt, Rinehart & Winston, 1984.

Barton, Edwin J., and Glenda A. Hudson. *A Contemporary Guide to Literary Terms with Strategies for Writing Essays about Literature*. Boston: Houghton Mifflin Company, 1997.

Bercovitch, Sacvan. *The Puritan Origins of the American Self*. New Haven, Conn.: Yale University Press, 1975.

Bloom, Harold. *Poetics of Influence*. New Haven, Conn.: Schwab, 1988.

Demos, John. *Entertaining Satan: Witchcraft and the Culture of Early New England*. Oxford: Oxford University Press, 1982.

Edmundson, Mark. *Nightmare on Main Street: Angels, Sadomasochism, and the Culture of Gothic*. 1997. Cambridge, Mass.: Harvard University Press, 1999.

Emerson, Ralph Waldo. *Nature*. 1836. In *The Essential Writings of Ralph Waldo Emerson*, edited by Brooks Atkinson and with an introduction by Mary Oliver. New York: Random House, 2000.

Fiedler, Leslie. *Love and Death in the American Novel*. 1960. New York: Dell, 1969.

Fowler, Alastair. *Kinds of Literature: An Introduction to the Theory of Genres and Modes*. 1982. Oxford: Clarendon Press, 2000.

Gray, Martin. *A Dictionary of Literary Terms*. Harlow, Essex: Longman, York Press, 1984.

Hall, David. *Worlds of Wonder, Days of Judgment: Popular Religious Belief in Early New England*. New York: Knopf, 1989.

Hanson, Clare. "Stephen King: Powers of Horror." In *American Horror Fiction: From Brockden Brown to Stephen King*, edited by Brian Docherty, 135-54. New York: St. Martin's Press, 1990.

Hatlen, Burton. "Beyond the Kittery Bridge." In *Fear Itself: The Horror Fiction of Stephen King*, edited by Tim Underwood and Chuck Miller, 45-60. 1982. New York: New American Library, 1985.

Hicks, James E. "Stephen King's Creation of Horror in *'Salem's Lot*: A Prolegomenon towards a New Hermeneutic of the Gothic Novel." In *The Gothic World of Stephen King: Landscape of Nightmares*, edited by Gary Hoppenstand and Ray B. Browne, 75-83. Bowling Green, Ohio: Bowling Green State University Popular Press, 1987.

Horton, Rod W., and Herbert W. Edwards. *Backgrounds of American Literary Thought*. 1952. Englewood Cliffs, N.J.: Prentice-Hall, 1974.

Ingebretsen, Edward J. "Cotton Mather and Stephen King: Writing/Righting the Body Politic." In *Imagining the Worst: Stephen King and the Representation of Women*, edited by Kathleen Margaret Lant and Theresa Thompson, 11-30. Westport, Conn.: Greenwood Press, 1998.

Jancovich, Mark. *Horror*. London: Batsford, 1992.

King, Stephen. *Bag of Bones*. 1998. New York: Pocket Books, 1999.

_____. *Carrie*. 1974. New York: Pocket Books, 1999.

_____. *Cujo*. 1981. New York: Signet, 1982.

_____. *Cycle of the Werewolf*. 1983. New York: Signet, 1985.

_____. *Danse Macabre*. 1981. New York: Berkley Books, 1983.

_____. *The Dark Half*. 1989. New York: Signet, 1990.

_____. *The Dark Tower: Dark Tower VIII*. London: Hodder & Stoughton, 2004.

_____. *The Dead Zone*. 1979. New York: Signet, 1980.

_____. *Desperation*. 1996. New York: Signet, 1997.

_____. *Dolores Claiborne*. New York: Signet, 1993.

_____. *The Drawing of the Three: Dark Tower II*. 1987. New York: Plume, 1989.

_____. *Dreamcatcher*. London: Hodder & Stoughton, 2001.

_____. *The Eyes of the Dragon*. 1987. New York: Signet, 1988.

_____. *Firestarter*. 1980. New York: Signet, 1981.

_____. *From a Buick 8*. London: Hodder & Stoughton, 2002.

_____. *Gerald's Game*. 1992. New York: Signet, 1993.

_____. *The Girl Who Loved Tom Gordon*. 1999. New York: Pocket Books, 2000.

_____. *The Gunslinger: The Dark Tower I*. 1982. New York: Plume, 1988.

_____. *Insomnia*. 1994. New York: Signet, 1995.

_____. *It*. 1986. London: Hodder & Stoughton, 1987.

_____. *Misery*. 1987. New York: Signet, 1988.

_____. *Needful Things*. 1991. New York: Signet, 1992.

_____. *Pet Sematary*. 1983. New York: Signet, 1984.

_____. *Roadwork*. In *The Bachman Books: Four Early Novels by Stephen King: Rage, The Long Walk, Roadwork, The Running Man*, 435-708. New York: Signet, 1986.

_____. *Rose Madder*. 1995. New York: Signet, 1996.

_____. *The Running Man*. In *The Bachman Books: Four Early Novels by Stephen King: Rage, The Long Walk, Roadwork, The Running Man*, 709-923. New York: Signet, 1986.

_____. *'Salem's Lot*. 1975. New York: Signet, 1976.

_____. *The Shining*. 1977. New York: Signet, 1978.

_____. *Song of Susannah: The Dark Tower VI*. London: Hodder & Stoughton, 2004.

_____. *The Stand*. 1978. Complete and uncut edition. New York: New English Library, 1990.

_____. *Storm of the Century*. New York: Pocket Books, 1999.

_____. *The Talisman* (with Peter Straub). 1984. New York: Berkley Books, 1985.

_____. *The Tommyknockers*. 1987. New York: Signet, 1988.

_____. *The Waste Lands: The Dark Tower III*. 1991. New York: Plume, 1992.

Magistrale, Tony. *The Moral Voyages of Stephen King*. Mercer Island, Wash.: Starmont Studies, 1989.

_____. *Stephen King: The Second Decade,* Danse Macabre *to* The Dark Half. New York: Twayne, 1992.

Moore, R. I. *The Formation of a Persecuting Society: Power and Deviance in Western Europe, 950-1250*. New York: Basil Blackwell, 1987.

Pettersson, Bo. *The World According to Kurt Vonnegut: Moral Paradox and Narrative Form*. Åbo, Finland: Åbo Akademi University Press, 1994.

Pharr, Mary. "Partners in the *Danse*: Women in Stephen King's Fiction." In *The Dark Descent: Essays Defining Stephen King's Horroscape*, edited by Tony Magistrale, 19-32. Westport, Conn.: Greenwood Press, 1992.

Reesman, Jeanne Campbell. "Stephen King and the Tradition of American Naturalism in *The Shining*." In *Modern Critical Views: Stephen King*, edited by Harold Bloom, 105-19. Philadelphia: Chelsea House, 1998.

Sage, Victor. *Horror Fiction in the Protestant Tradition*. 1988. London: Palgrave Macmillan, 1999.

Senf, Carol A. "*Gerald's Game* and *Dolores Claiborne*: Stephen King and the Evolution of an Authentic Female Narrative Voice." In *Imagining the Worst: Stephen King and the Representation of Women*, edited by Kathleen Margaret Lant and Theresa Thompson, 91-107. Westport, Conn.: Greenwood Press, 1998.

Spignesi, Stephen J. *The Lost Work of Stephen King: A Guide to Unpublished Manuscripts, Story Fragments, Alternative Versions, and Oddities*. Secaucus, N.J.: Birch Lane Press, 1998.

Starkey, Marion. *The Devil in Massachusetts: A Modern Enquiry into the Salem Witch Trials*. New York: Knopf, 1949.

Thomas, Keith. *Religion and the Decline of Magic*. New York: Scribner's, 1976.

Trevor-Roper, Hugh. *The European Witch-Craze of the Sixteenth and Seventeenth Centuries and Other Essays*. New York: Harper, 1969.

Underwood, Tim, and Chuck Miller, eds. *Feast of Fear: Conversations with Stephen King*. 1989. New York: Carroll & Graf, 1992.

Wiater, Stanley, Christopher Golden, and Hank Wagner. *The Stephen King Universe: A Guide to the Worlds of the King of Horror*. Los Angeles: Renaissance, 2001.

Yarbro, Chelsea Quinn. "Cinderella's Revenge: Twists on Fairy Tale and Mythic Themes in the Work of Stephen King." In *Fear Itself: The Horror Fiction of Stephen King*, edited by Tim Underwood and Chuck Miller, 61-71. 1982. New York: New American Library, 1985.

Taking Stephen King Seriously:
Reflections on a Decade of Best-Sellers_____

Samuel Schuman

I

I am not sure what it was that first suggested to me the notion that Stephen King was an author to be taken seriously. Three things happened in the late 1970's that somehow, separately or together, brought me to that rather unconventional conclusion.

First, I (and everyone else) began to notice that not only were King's works perpetual best-sellers, he was also beginning to generate multiple, overlapping works at the top of the popularity charts. Indeed, in 1980, King became the first American author to have *three* works simultaneously on the best-seller lists–*Fire Starter*, *The Dead Zone*, and *The Shining*. When I first began to contemplate writing this paper, King appeared in the most recent *New York Times* lists (Sunday, Feb. 3, 1985) for hardcover books (#3, *The Talisman*, written with Peter Straub) and paperbacks (#9, *Pet Sematary*). Today (Spring, 1987), *Misery* tops the best-seller charts, while the movie *Stand by Me* was the sleeper hit of the fall cinema season, and the author graces the cover of *Time* magazine. ANYTHING so popular for so long merits attention, whether it is Stephen King, the Beatles, the Ford Mustang, or Wm. Shakespeare.

Second, it was at about this same time that I met the author and had a (minor) opportunity to work with him. I was a new administrator at the University of Maine at Orono. King had graduated from that school, and, after his initial successes and, therefore, long after there was any financial incentive to do so, he offered to return to his alma mater for a year of teaching literature and writing. Since we were both affiliated with the English Department, we served on some committees together, and brushed up against each other in the studiedly casual way departmental colleagues do in larger American universities. Since we shared, as well, one very good friend—Dr. Ulrich Wicks, then Chair of the English Department—I had an opportunity to meet King on a number of social occasions. Although we were never particularly close, proximity to fame (of almost any sort) breeds a kind of respect and interest.

Thirdly, and most importantly, I began to take Stephen King seriously in the late 1970's because that was when, in a totally unstructured and non-academic way, I began to read his books.

II

Given King's unprecedented record of success—in film and television, as well as in print—it seems evident that anyone seriously interested in the state of contemporary American taste must pay substantial attention to his work. However, although King has written a lengthy work of criticism, holds a baccalaureate degree in English, and has taught literature, he is not much given to respectful kowtowing to the lit-crit establishment, and academic critics are certainly not enamored of his works. The general response to King's oeuvre amongst academics has been to ignore it or to consider it beneath contempt. Very occasionally, a literate reviewer will offer a back-handed compliment. [E.g., "King is too powerful a writer to go on indefinitely slinging his ink in cinematic verbal effects to no purpose. He has shown an acute understanding of human fears; if he can move toward an equally profound apprehension of our hopes, he may yet write a book that transcends its genre in the manner of all true art." Mary H. Rosenbaum, *Christian Century* 101 (March 21-8, 1984) p. 316.]

I want to suggest that, in fact, Steve King is a master of plot and setting; a skillful and self-conscious manipulator of the English language; a rather stern moralist; and a first-class creator of literary characters. King is not, and probably will not become, the Shakespeare of our day [although, as we all know, Shakespeare was not the "Shakespeare" of his day, either, if by that denomination we mean a recognized master of literary art—Shakespeare and his fellows in the Elizabethan theater were seen by educated and literary folk as popular hacks]. His greatest flaw seems to be the same that Shakespeare—and Dickens and

Thomas Wolfe—suffered from: he has a tendency to churn out enormous volumes of prose with great speed and without much of an inclination to go back over what he has written and make sure he has got everything just right. As a consequence, he is often "uneven." Portions of his works give the impression of immaculate craftsmanship, but they will be interspersed with other portions which are awkward, sloppy, hasty, and obviously not of very much interest to their author.

King's second major problem is a fairly regular and deliberate absence of taste. King seems to be the only important current writer other than Norman Mailer who can be very obscene without coming anywhere near the pornographic. He himself says that, when he can not achieve a higher effect, he will aim at revulsion:

> . . . I will try to terrorize the reader. But if I find I cannot terrify him/her, I will try to horrify; and if I find I cannot horrify, I'll go for the gross-out. I'm not proud. (*Danse Macabre*, p. 25)

This is an accurate description, and sometimes King seems too good at achieving this end. [One could make a case that in certain scenes Shakespeare seems to be "going for the gross-out," too. The cry of "Out, vild jelly" by Cornwall as he plucks out Gloucester's one remaining eye falls into this class (*King Lear* III. vii. 83). So does the scene in *Cymbeline* in which Imogen mistakes the body of Cloten for that of Posthumus—because it is without a head (*Cymbeline*, IV. ii. 295 ff, the lines and stage directions make it mandatory for Imogen to fondle and, finally, collapse upon, the gruesome corpse). So too does the scene in *Titus Andronicus* in which the ravished Lavinia, who has had her hands cut off and her tongue cut out, reveals the names of her rapists with this ingenious device: "She takes the staff in her mouth, and guides it with her stumps, and writes" (IV. i. 77 sd). Still, such scenes are the exceptions in Shakespeare's plays, and seem unfortunately common in King's novels. In this regard, he is perhaps akin less to the Bard of Avon than to Webster or Tourneur.]

III

In spite of these weaknesses, I believe Stephen King is a gifted and even important writer. To me, his particular strengths are:

—a surprisingly effective prose style, especially in the area of descriptive composition and dialogue;

—an ability to create characters at once unique and universal, and who therefore interest and engage us;

—a strong and clear ethical stance, which often generates a reassuring thematic message;

—most importantly, an ability to imagine and represent plots which is absolutely brilliant.

Perhaps the best manner to illustrate these gifts is through a somewhat detailed look at one particular bestseller. Because I find it his most effective novel, overall, I have selected *Pet Sematary* (1983).

IV

I think there are few if any descriptive passages in the English language that are any finer than this [the first paragraph of Shirley Jackson's *The Haunting of Hill House*]; it is the sort of quiet epiphany every writer hopes for: words that somehow transcend words, words which add up to a total greater than the sum of the parts. Analysis of such a paragraph is a mean and shoddy trick, and should almost always be left to college and university professors, those lepidopterists of literature who, when they see a lovely butterfly, feel that they should immediately run into the field with a net, catch it, kill it with a drop of chloroform, and mount it. . . . Having said that, let us analyze this paragraph a bit. (*Danse Macabre*, p. 268)

It should be clear from this citation that Stephen King pays close attention to the niceties of English prose style. In particular, I believe that he works very hard, and usually quite successfully, at building exactly the sort of descriptive passage he praises in Shirley Jackson's work—

the description which not only tells the reader *exactly* what some locale looks like, but goes beyond to convey its mood and its meaning. Here, for example, is the description of the pet cemetery which becomes a most important spot in the book named after it. *Pet Sematary*'s hero, Louis Creed, a physician and a newcomer to Maine, is taken, with his family in tow, to this spot by a native Mainer, on a pleasant weekend day outing:

They topped the second hill, and then the path sloped through a head-high swatch of bushes and tangled underbrush. It narrowed and then, just ahead, Louis saw Ellie and Jud go under an arch made of old weatherstained boards. Written on these in faded black paint, only just legible, were the words PET SEMATARY. He and Rachel exchanged an amused glance and stepped under the arch, instinctively reaching out and grasping each other's hands as they did so, as if they had come here to be married.

For the second time that morning Louis was surprised into wonder.

There was no carpet of needles here. Here was an almost perfect circle of mown grass, perhaps as large as forty feet in diameter. It was bounded by thickly interlaced underbrush on three sides and an old blowdown on the fourth, a jackstraw jumble of fallen trees that looked both sinister and dangerous. A man trying to pick his way through that or to climb over it would do well to put on a steel jock, Louis thought. The clearing was crowded with markers, obviously made by children from whatever materials they could beg or borrow—the slats of crates, scrapwood, pieces of beaten tin. And yet, seen against the perimeter of low bushes and straggly trees that fought for living space and sunlight here, the very fact of their clumsy manufacture, and the fact that humans were responsible for what was here, seemed to emphasize what symmetry they had. The forested backdrop lent the place a crazy sort of profundity, a charm that was not Christian but pagan. (*Pet Sematary*, p. 42)

Without bludgeoning these lines to death, it seems to me that this is a masterful description. The clearing in the woods is described precisely: we know its dimensions, its boundaries, its entrance, the character of the forest floor. King also conveys the *age* of this space—the boards are "old" and "weatherstained," the printing upon them is "faded." The underbrush is "head-high" and the trees "straggly." The blowdown is an "old blowdown." The passage is, obviously, emotionally loaded—the underbrush is "tangled" then "thickly interlaced." The jumble of trees is sinister and dangerous—it is dangerous in a way which makes the hero think about injury to his genitals. Vegetation fights for living space. But, along with this dense, dark, botanical aura, is a heavy emphasis upon the artifice of the cemetery—the grass is mown, the circle is "almost perfect." Items are "manufactured," "symmetrical." Obviously, King is trying to create a sense of a space which is at once childlike, a realistic man-made spot in the midst of the wild woods, and reverberating with a distinctly un-childish but also irrational and un-adult ominous sacramental presence. This is perhaps most effectively conveyed by the way in which the *Creeds* (their cat is named "Church!") *instinctively* hold hands, as if prepared for a rite, when they enter the cleared circle.

[As the novel develops, it turns out that the "PET SEMATARY" itself is not the "bad place"—the really haunted spot in the woods. Rather, that venue is on the other side of the sinister and dangerous blowdown. The cemetery serves as a gateway to the novel's site of genuine horror.]

This sense of a cleared spot in the midst of very rough forest which is not actively evil, but is certainly in no sense friendly or good, and which is invested with a distinctly non-Christian supernatural aura has literary precedents in similar locations in, for example, Hawthorne and "Gawain and the Green Knight."

Briefly, I also want to suggest that King's style is particularly sharp in the creation of dialogue. He has an excellent ear for the nuances of contemporary casual American speech, and he reproduces those rhythms and diction tellingly:

"Louis!" Rachel called. "She's cut herself!"

Eileen had fallen from the tire swing and hit a rock with her knee. The cut was shallow. . . .

"All right, Ellie," he said. "That's enough. Those people over there will think someone's being murdered."

"But it hurrrrrts!"

Louis struggled with his temper and went silently back to the wagon. The . . . first aid kit was still in the glove compartment. He got it and came back. When Ellie saw it, she began to scream louder than ever.

"No! Not the stingy stuff! I don't want the stingy stuff, Daddy! No—"

"Eileen, it's just Mercurochrome, and it doesn't sting—"

"No-no-no-no-no—"

"You want to stop that or your ass will sting," Louis said.

"She's tired, Lou," Rachel said quietly.

"Yeah, I know the feeling. Hold her leg out." (*Pet Sematary*, pp. 18-19)

The progression from "Ellie" to "Eileen" to "you want to stop that . . ." catches exactly Louis' mounting irritation, and sounds precisely like most any other harassed father in a similar situation.

Stephen King, is, in sum, a compositional craftsman. In dialogue and description, particularly, he is precise, controlled, evocative. In *Danse Macabre*, he notes:

. . . many writers of fiction seem totally unable to explain simple operations or actions clearly enough for the reader to be able to see them in his or her mind's eye. Some of this is a failure on the writer's part to visualize well and completely; his or her own mind's eye seems bleared half-shut. More of it is a simple failure of that most basic writer's tool, the working vocabulary. If you're writing a haunted-house story and you don't know the difference between a gable and a gambrel, a cupola and a turret, paneling and wain-scotting, you, sir or madame, are in trouble. (p. 361)

V

For "fright fiction" to work most effectively, it must focus upon a rather particular sort of character. The horror writer's protagonists must be sufficiently virtuous to win our sympathy, but sufficiently imperfect to seem recognizably human. They must be on the one hand interesting and unique, and on the other, "normal" and typical—otherwise, the evils which beset them will not be fully frightening to a readership which is, by and large, normal and typical. King's characters adhere exactly to these specifications. They are overwhelmingly middle-class, protestant, white, Americans. They are interested in earning a comfortable living. They are dutiful fathers, mothers, and children. They will err occasionally, but their sins are not gigantic (although they can plunge them into enormous nightmares) and seem almost comfortably domestic. Louis Creed, for example, has a rather sharp temper; he is permanently estranged from his father-in-law; etc. On the other hand, he is willing to take what seem heroic risks to preserve the integrity of his family. He is interesting and mildly unusual: Creed is a physician, but he has given up private practice to become a University doctor in Maine.

The work's second major character is Judson Crandall. Crandall comes close to appearing a stereotypical "Bert and I" New Englander: he is kindly, wry, tough, a man of few words. He is sincere, helpful, knowledgeable. He is saved, though, from saintliness by several frailties about which much of the plot of *Pet Sematary* revolves: He is, for example, so proud of knowing the secret of the pet cemetery that he can't resist showing off by revealing it to Louis Creed. At a crucial point at the end of the novel, Crandall falls asleep when he should have been keeping watchful guard. A glint of egotism, and a touch of dotage save Jud Crandall from becoming a *Yankee*-magazine Mainer, and leave him an individual for whom we can feel great fondness, pity, and a touch of kinship.

VI

Stephen King's novels (again, like Shakespeare's plays) do not ask us to stretch our moral imaginations. On the contrary, most of his books solidly and reassuringly reinforce conventional, middle-of-the-road ethical positions. Thus, on the one hand, King's works allow us to indulge ourselves in some wild fictive escapades (and to derive voyeuristic thrills at some fairly gruesome incidents!). But these events are usually packaged within a thematic structure which reinforces mainline Western moral traditions.

The Stand, It, Fire Starter, Cujo, The Shining, Misery, The Talisman and *Christine* all fall solidly within the traditional structure of a battle between good and evil. Sometimes the evil is human (e.g., *Misery, Fire Starter*); more commonly it is supernatural (*The Shining*; *It*), mechanical (*Christine*) or animal (*Cujo*).

Pet Sematary is, at its core, a version of the Frankenstein myth, the moral of which is that it is always immoral and very dangerous to tinker with the natural order of birth and death. The key to the story is a Micmac indian burying ground. Dead bodies buried in this bewitched spot return to the world of the living—but not exactly as they left. Depending upon how long they have been dead, they seem to take on an increasingly baleful and malevolent personality quite distinct from their original natures. Louis Creed is introduced to the Micmac Burial Ground by Jud Crandall after Creed's family's pet cat is hit by a car. Creed and Crandall make a midnight trip into the woods, bury the cat, and (like the old song) the next day, the cat comes back. It is sullen, it snaps, it smells bad, but it's back. Then Creed's young son is hit and killed by a speeding truck, and Creed exhumes him and carries his body to the magical burial place. The boy, like the cat, returns, but he was dead too long, and his child-body seems possessed by a maniacal and diabolic spirit. *Pet Sematary* is a long novel, and this summation does not do it justice. It should be clear, though, that the thematic center of the novel derives from the clear moral judgment that it is sinful for humans to tamper with mortality. Creed falls, through love, into a sin the mirror opposite of murder: he does not make the living into the dead; he tries to make the dead to live again, and in so doing brings down upon himself and his family a progressive nightmare from which there is no escape. Within a plot of considerable imaginative ambition, King embeds a thematic core which would be gratifying to the most ardent fundamentalist.

(It is worthy of note that the book begins with a citation from John's Gospel, in which Jesus announces his intention to raise Lazarus from the dead.)

VII

Stephen King's final novelistic strength is perhaps his most obvious, and most important: he is a master of plot, to Aristotle the most essential literary element. Although it would be great sport to illustrate this point with extensive summaries of King's plots, that entertaining step is really unnecessary. The one fact upon which all his readers agree is that Steve King's novels are page-turners. Their plots are engrossing and engrossingly unfolded. Beyond this general appreciation, two points are worth making briefly:

First, it is noteworthy that King's plots tend to be original with each novel: he does not rewrite the same best-seller over and over again. While most (but not all) of his works involve some element of the supernatural, that element varies wildly: an innocent and cute little girl who can set things on fire by the power of her mind; a car with a murderous personality of its own; wintering-over in a haunted summer resort in the Colorado mountains; a mad dog; vampires; a word-processor which can delete and create real things as well as words. So far, at least, King's imagination has been fertile, and he has admirably resisted the temptation to go back to the same lucrative story time after time.

Second, I want to conclude by suggesting that King is a master (really as a consequence of all the elements discussed above) of the most essential feature of the horror writer's craft: he embeds the weirdness and the horror of his plots within a framework of convincingly mundane realism. The bizarre is interwoven persuasively with the familiar. King's craftsmanlike compositional style, his solid grasp of character, and his mastery of plotting combine to draw us into a world which always seems comfortingly like our own. He makes the incredible credible: if there were a secret burial ground outside Orono, Maine, in which the dead could be brought back to half-life, *this* is exactly what it would be like.

This is an imaginary toad in a real garden. This is the essence of the fiction writer's craft, and it is more than enough reason to take Stephen King very seriously.

The Struggle for Personal Morality in America_____

Jonathan P. Davis

In the majority of his fiction, Stephen King seems to understand that while the world is broken up into societies and cultures for the sake of organization, individual people themselves are the driving forces behind change. An analytical interpretation of the human condition in King's fiction must begin with and focus on the individuals that join together to form larger collective bodies. After all, at the center of each and every issue facing people today is a question of moral choice: is it right to dump chemical wastes into streams and lakes? Is it right to abort an unborn child, and, if so, is it or is it not murder? Is it right to let one's sixteen-year-old daughter go on a weekend ski-trip with her boyfriend? Should one slip a candy bar in his pocket if no one is looking? The list of choices that call morality into play are endless. All of these questions have been subjectively called into debate in each and every American's mind, and they all center around the simple differentiation between right and wrong. While evil is a mainstay in the human heart, the magic of the human condition rests in its capacity to do good in spite of the adversities that prompt evil action. At the center of all things that result from human interference is the need to question what is right and what is wrong. It is the answers to these questions that have the largest impact on the human condition.

The appeal of King's fiction to his readers rests in the fact that it constantly raises the question of morality; it recognizes the pervasiveness of evil, but it also aims to prove that the forces of good, when formed behind a collaboration of human hearts to enforce good, will almost always reign over evil. It is only when the protagonists of King's stories alienate themselves from fellow human beings in their battles against evil while failing to recognize their own human flaws that they fall—a notion that reinforces the idea of strength in numbers, that the emphasis in a peaceful human condition is grounded in the collective will to do good. In other words, progress begins with the individual, but there must be a union of good will in order for the human race to further itself. This romantic notion of the potential good residing in the human heart is something that critic Deborah Notkin believes gives King his popular draw:

> Stephen King has achieved unprecedented popularity as a writer of horror fiction, largely because he understands the attraction of fantastic horror to the denizen of the late 20th century, and because, paradoxical though it may sound, he has reassurance to bring us. For whether he is writing about vampires, about the death of 99 percent of the population, or about innocent little girls with the power to break the earth in half, King never stops emphasizing his essential liking for people. He does not, of course, paint a rosy picture of a loving and flawless human race; he simply focuses, again and again, on people doing the right things in difficult situations, on people who behave slightly better than we expect. The overwhelming impression to be gained from reading King's books is that the kinks and the sadists are the exception, not the rule. In these novels, the average person is reasonably honest, caring and upright, and can be relied upon in most circumstances—not a fashionable concept, these days, but one which has obvious attractions for contemporary audiences. (232)

King's power in his fiction is an adamant belief in a personal moral code; those who behave morally and make correct moral choices when faced with adversities are those who are likely to win the fight against evil. Those characters in King's fiction who do not behave morally and rather surrender the well-being of others for evil or selfish motives are those who are ultimately destroyed. *Needful Things* is a prime reference of his idealized moral code. In the novel, entrepreneur Leland Gaunt opens shop in the town of Castle Rock. The name of his shop, Needful Things, is a primary indication of what is stored inside; his inventory consists of those material objects that each resident of Castle Rock most desires. As Gaunt predicts, Castle Rock's residents are willing to pay almost any price for their fancies. Gaunt's price includes two parts—a sum of money, and, most importantly, a trick to be played on a person of his selection. Each and every patron who steps through the door of Needful Things is faced with a moral choice: should they refuse access to the objects they desperately want and deny the risk of injuring their peers, or should they jump at the offer, abandoning any notion of brotherhood for the sake of personal gain? Unfortunately, most choose the latter, augmenting the mistrust among neighbors that had already been breeding prior to Gaunt's grand opening. Castle Rock's agreement to allow Gaunt, who capitalizes on their selfishness to corrupt it, turns neighbor against neighbor until widespread violence reduces the town to ashes. Two Castle Rockians, Polly Chalmers and Sheriff Alan Pangborn, who are engaged in a love affair, are also seduced by Gaunt's 'needful things,' but, after agonizing deliberation, reject his prizes and acknowledge his seductive scheme; their love for each other shines through the dark veil of their selfishness, and they join together against Gaunt. Likewise, Deputy Norris Ridgewick, although having played a major part in Gaunt's grand plan after performing a trick that triggers murder, also atones for his mistake by rushing to the rescue of Alan and Polly when Gaunt confronts them. In the end, Polly, Alan, and Norris are able to survive simply because they value human bonding over selfish motives. As Notkin's passage suggests, the concept of consequences arising from moral choice such as those portrayed in *Needful Things* is far from fresh or imaginative, but it is one that never loses its flavor or appeal with contemporary audiences. Inside the heart of us is a desire to see the selfishly wicked punished; this conviction is adequately exemplified in the real-life case of convicted serial killer Ted Bundy, who raped and tortured dozens of young girls from Florida to Washington. At his execution, when the switch was thrown, an audience standing outside cheered; he who acted selfishly and immorally against his fellow sisters was served his just deserts.

Yet another aspect of King's fiction pertinent to morality and the human condition is that his monsters and villains stem directly from human evil. His readers like to see his antagonists destroyed because they represent the human monsters that live among the real world— Rev. Jim Jones, Richard Speck, Charles Manson, John Wayne Gacy, Richard Ramirez, Jeffrey Dahmer: these are the extreme atrocities and perversions of the human spirit, the extreme examples of the breach in morality that threatens humankind. Burton Hatlen points out that:

> while King recognizes that serial killers truly do exist, he suggests that our fascination with them moves them into the same mythic territory where vampires live; and the myths we create about such people tell us as much about ourselves as they do about the psychopathology of sex murderers. Vampires, killer cars, and rubber-coated sex murderers—all crawl out of the "myth-pool in which we all bathe communally". . . . We, not King, have created these creatures; and he gives them back to us, to tell us something about ourselves. (84)

It may be that society's tendency to glamorize or raise to cult status psychopaths arises from a need to use those evil-doers as barometrical instruments measuring the sanity and morality of those who condemn their actions. An equally effective measuring device, King's fiction often allows readers to point fingers at the villains contained within and to cherish the truth or contemplate the untruth of each individual's morality.

As mentioned, King's fiction serves to argue that society needs a collective good will. However, that collective good will obviously starts at the individual level. While human beings make haste in accusing others of immoral actions, they often ignore consideration of how to obtain their own moral maturity—a paradox that reveals itself often in King's canon. Each one of King's novels portrays a protagonist or group of protagonists who must make moral decisions that will have impact on their fates. Without moral maturity, both people and King's characters suffer from their inability to heed the consequences of moral differentiation, therefore increasing the difficulty to act on behalf of goodness. Bernadette Lynn Bosky, making reference to one of King's most descriptive portrayals of moral choice, *Pet Sematary*, summarizes this concern of King's when she points out that:

> King realistically presents his characters with the choice of which interior voice to follow and which to silence. The tragedy of *Pet Sematary* is that Louis Creed begins to follow his intuitions only when he should begin to doubt them. His premonition regarding Gage and his visitation from Pascow are dismissed because they do not fit into his materialistic worldview. (231)

Without an individual's ability to make correct moral decisions, adverse conditions often become unavoidable. As Bosky brings to light, the fate of Louis Creed in *Pet Sematary* results from his anger with life for taking away his only son, Gage, who was struck by a semi-trailer truck when trying to cross a busy highway. Creed's reaction to his son's death is to exhume the corpse and bury it an ancient Indian burial ground behind the pet cemetery near his home, a ground that was once sacred to a tribe of Micmac Indians. Creed had already used the sacred ground to bury his cat, Churchill, when it was struck by a truck. The cat had come back from the dead, but was not the same cat: its spirit had been removed by the death process. What Louis saw in the resurrected Churchill was not the fluffy cat his daughter, Ellie, was fond of but rather an evil reincarnation. Rather than reviewing the results of the cat's return from the burial site and applying that knowledge to the horrible potential it could have with a human being, Louis ignores his wiser intuition not to play with death but rather confronts fate. What returns from the burial ground is a soiled, evil, blood-thirsty version of his son. Critic Samuel Schuman supports Bosky's observation when he suggests that:

it should be clear . . . that the thematic center of the novel derives from the clear moral judgment that it is sinful for humans to tamper with mortality. Creed falls, through love, into a sin the mirror opposite of murder: he does not make the living into the dead; he tries to make the dead to live again, and in so doing brings down upon himself and his family a progressive nightmare from which there is no escape. Within a plot of considerable imaginative ambition, King embeds a thematic core which would be gratifying to the most ardent fundamentalist. (113)

It is Creed's inability to make the distinction between the right and wrong courses of action that creates the fall of his subjective world. His fall is correlative with that of Victor Frankenstein—his failure to make the correct moral choice when pursuing a selfish goal brings destruction and sorrow to both him and his family.

Yet another example of a King character who suffers from a lapse in correct moral choice is Harold Lauder, one of the survivors of the flu epidemic in *The Stand*. Harold is a young social outcast much like the characters that find places in almost every King story. Harold is overweight, unattractive, and unable to communicate with other human beings intimately. When he falls in love with Frannie Goldsmith, his older sister's friend who also survived the epidemic, he cannot outwardly tell her of his feelings but rather keeps them trapped in a personal diary. When Frannie falls in love with Stu Redman, Harold's reaction is not to accept defeat but to allow his bitterness against both of them to mount. Frannie, Stu, and the rest of the Free Zone Committee (the representatives of the army of good will established in the postepidemic world) all try to make Harold a welcome member, but he rejects them. He cannot accept the fact that he is living in a new world, one needing reconstruction because of the massive population reduction from the superflu, and that the new world will give him an opportunity to become something that he never was in his previous life: a working cog in the mechanism of a meaningful society. As Bosky points out, "Harold will not let himself realize that his rejection of hope and change also murders his new, better self before it is born" (229). Harold is put in a position to accept the bond his Free Zone friends offer him or to reject it for the fulfillment of the destruction of the society he resented previously. His choice to reject human bonding in favor of the selfish goals offered by Randall Flagg, the adversary of the Free Zone, leads to Harold's downfall. Bosky supports this when she observes that:

> [one of the] most stunning scenes of "the free will to do evil or deny it" in King's fiction [has] little or nothing to do with the supernatural. Harold Lauder's acceptance of all-consuming hatred in *The Stand* . . . show[s] that no matter how much or little control we have over situations, we always choose whether or not to control our emotional reactions to these situations. (227)

Both Louis Creed and Harold Lauder may be seen as manifestations of real-life moral issues relevant to modern America. Creed's desire to interfere with the natural death process is applicable to the modern-day concerns about death control—euthanasia—while Harold Lauder's refusal to relinquish his rage over past wrongs can be applied to the continuous warring between countries on the national level and individuals on the domestic level. Both Louis and Harold serve to explicate King's interpretation of what happens when people fail to make correct moral decisions.

When readers are evaluating evil in King's books, they must be able to identify both the outright manifestations of evil and the sources of their power. No one can deny that characters like Randall Flagg, Barlow (*'Salem's Lot*), Pennywise the Clown (*It*), Morgan Sloat (*The Talisman*), and George Stark (*The Dark Half*) are purely concentrated evil; readers can reasonably dismiss any notion of moral redemption for these villains. These evil incarnations serve no other purpose than to destroy humanity and cloud their victims' moral discretion with their dark influences. The dark forces in King's fiction almost always derive their power from the weakness and vulnerabilities of their prey; were it not for human imperfections, these entities would not exert the degree of influence that they are able to carry out. In his book *Stephen King, the Second Decade:* Danse Macabre *to* The Dark Half, written for the Twayne United States Authors Series, Tony Magistrale argues that

> like the Overlook Hotel, the Tommyknockers, Christine, It, and other examples of maleficence in King's world, evil requires some element of human weakness—ignorance, avarice, anger, rejection, indifference, jealousy—as a means for the initial corruption of innocence. (244)

Burton Hatlen follows up on this when he suggests that "I am here proposing that King sees both Good and Evil as primarily subjective and intersubjective phenomena" (88). In other words, Hatlen is assuming that evil in King's fiction is not a sovereign body separate from humanity but rather is often the product of the accumulated negative impulses inside people, the same people who create their own monsters through their inabilities to love each other and act morally.

The tragedies in King's fiction lie not so much in the victims of evil manifestations but in the stories' central characters' tendency to bow to their human shortcomings, allowing evil to flourish. A majority of King's books place the central protagonists in positions to follow their moral or immoral impulses. Those who consider the implications of acting immorally and act accordingly are those who overcome evil; those who succumb to the immediate gratification that evil offers are those who eventually fall. Take the case of Arnie Cunningham in *Christine.* Arnie is another Harold-Lauder-type character who is rejected by his peers because of his peculiarity and unattractive looks. When he finds Christine, a '57 Plymouth Fury, he finds a new identity. He is able to stand up to his tormentors. He starts dating the most beautiful girl in his high school. The car, a symbol of identity in a young person's life, brings Arnie a sense of confidence. Yet while Christine has rewarded him with a fresh identity, she has also turned him into a hostile, self-serving individual. She kills all of those who have done or intend to do Arnie wrong; she brings his evil impulses to a horrifying reality. At first, Arnie is ignorant of Christine's malicious actions. But as the story continues, and Arnie becomes vaguely aware that since Christine has been in his life, people have been suffering, he must decide whether to scrap her, which would save lives and return Arnie to the thoughtful, caring boy he used to be, or to keep her and the self-fulfilling promises she offers him. Arnie makes his decision in the following scene:

> In fact, there were times when he didn't want the car at all. There were times when he felt he would be better off just . . . well, junking it. Not that he ever would, or could. It was just that, sometimes (in the sweaty, shaking aftermath of that dream last night, for instance), he felt that if he got rid of it, he would be . . . happier. . . . "Don't worry," Arnie whispered. He ran his hand slowly over the dashboard, loving the feel of it. Yes, the car frightened him sometimes. And he supposed his father was right; it had changed his life to some degree. But he could no more junk it than he could commit suicide. (264)

Arnie is in a position to make a moral choice: trash the car and save both others and himself from her evil, or keep her and continue to feed on the gratifications she can give him. His choice to keep her results in the deaths of several others and ultimately himself.

In another example where moral choice is called to question in King's fiction, Pop Merrill, the pawn shop owner in *The Sun Dog*, a novella in *Four Past Midnight*, has possession of a young boy's Polaroid Sun 660 camera that has caused some unrest due to the recurring picture it takes. Regardless of the person or object the camera is aimed at, the camera continuously produces an image of an angry dog. When Pop and Kevin Delevan, the camera's owner, put the pictures together in succession, it becomes apparent that the dog is turning and moving closer to the front of the picture, looking as though it is preparing to strike. Each successive snapshot brings it nearer until there is no doubt that the dog means to escape and exercise its rage. After becoming aware of the camera's oddity, Pop, a true capitalist, is drawn to its queerness and covets it with the intent of making a profit despite comprehending the implications of potential disaster accompanying it. At one particular point, as the possibility of the dog's intentions becomes more real to Pop, Pop begins to realize that maybe he could do the world and himself a favor by destroying the camera.

Why not get rid of the camera right here? he thought suddenly. You can. Just get out, walk to the guardrail there, and toss her over. All gone. Goodbye.

But that would have been an impulsive act, and Pop Merrill belonged to the Reasonable tribe—belonged to it body and soul, is what I mean to say. He didn't want to do anything on the spur of the moment that he might regret later, and—

If you don't do this, you'll regret it later.

But no. And no. And no. A man couldn't run against his nature. It was unnatural. He needed time to think.

To be sure. (711)

Pop becomes alert to the evil of the camera and is in a position to destroy it, but his choice to keep it for the selfish goals of either uncovering its secrets or reaping the profits of its sale results in his demise. His death comes after snapping the shutter the number of times needed to unleash the monster behind it.

While King often shows that those who reject their better intuitions sometimes fall, he balances his theory of the moral human condition by giving portrayals of heroes who defeat adversity when they choose to act with good will and kindness based on morality. Irv Manders, the old man who offers temporary sanctuary to Andy and Charlie McGee, refugees from a government operation called The Shop, in the novel *Firestarter*, is a prime example. When Andy and his daughter, Charlie, come to Irv's farm while on the run from the agency that plans to apprehend them with the intent of using their supernatural powers for government research, Irv is placed in a situation where he can either recognize their troubles and give them aid or refuse to interfere in the business of others, as many people tend to do, and turn them over to the authorities seeking them. Irv chooses to protect Andy and Charlie and acts on their behalf when The Shop representatives arrive at his home. As Deborah Notkin explains, "Irv seems to personify King's faith, for he can take people on their own recognizance despite contrary evidence, can stand up for their rights as if his own were in jeopardy, and can shelter them without regard for his own danger" (140). It is Irv's refusal to surrender the well-being of Andy and Charlie that serves as an obstacle in The Shop's attempt at apprehension. It is also Irv's selflessness that serves as a reference for the good that may result when one human acts on behalf of another for the remainder of the book. Irv is the extreme opposite of the novel's chief antagonist, John Rainbird, a Shop employee who pretends to be concerned with Charlie but is only misleading her with the intent of winning her trust so that he can get close enough to her to kill her. Irv, on the other hand, is truly interested in her well-being and is willing to sacrifice his own welfare for her. By creating characters like Irv and Rainbird, King offers readers the opportunity to evaluate the two extremes of the moral human condition, and in so doing, allows readers to comprehend the power of good over evil that results from sincere concern for other living creatures. Notkin points out of King, "very few writers of contemporary fiction would even create such a simply good character as Irv Manders, let alone imply that he might be the rule rather than the exception" (141).

While Irv and Rainbird serve to illustrate the scope of moral action arising from a general concern for others, another main cause of King's characters' failure to act morally comes from a combination of their inability to recognize their own shortcomings and their subordination of their human intuition for rational reasoning. These human flaws are innate; it is much easier to rationalize problems by adhering to reason than to trace fault back to the original source, oneself. Only those characters in King's fiction who are able to assert their imperfections can possess the power to change themselves and ultimately act in defense of moral righteousness. Bosky argues that:

> in King's fiction, natural human intuition is almost always correct and its results are often positive if followed—which it rarely is by the adult characters. Many of King's characters consistently refuse to trust their inner hunches, but there is usually at least one character in each story who does follow intuition, often with heroic results and probable, satisfying resolution. (212)

Those characters who acknowledge their weaknesses and trust their inner hunches, the ones innate in promoting the welfare of mankind, are those who acquire the power to fight evil. On the other hand, those characters who forsake intuition for human reasoning are those who are often incapacitated. The reason many of King's characters choose to ignore their intuition is that they have decided to shine a moral searchlight at others when what they really need to do is turn it back toward themselves. They believe in a rational explanation for everything that occurs as dictated by reason and have no faith in human individual choice, more specifically, their own choices. When acting on behalf of reason, they believe they cannot be wrong. Their subjective intuitions and impulses are almost always forfeited and subordinated to rational logic. In King's short story "I Am the Doorway," a story in *Night Shift*, it takes supernatural interference to show the protagonist, Arthur, that he is flawed. During an exploration of Venus, one of Arthur's crewmates ventures outside of the spacecraft. He comes back inside contaminated with an alien presence; that alien presence spreads to Arthur, who recognizes it later with the appearance of several tiny eyes that have been surfacing on his hands. The eyes ultimately force him to look inside of himself from an outsider's point of view:

It was a feeling like no other in the world—as if I were a portal just slightly ajar through which they were peeking at a world which they hated and feared. But the worst part was that I could see, too, in a way. Imagine your mind transported into a body of a housefly, a housefly looking into your own face with a thousand eyes. Then perhaps you can begin to see why I kept my hands bandaged even when there was no one around to see them. (97-98)

He says, describing the sensation received from the alien eyes in his hands: "But that was not what made me scream. I had looked into my own face and seen a monster" (101). Arthur, a representative of the common human being incapable of recognizing his own faults—one of the "Reasonable tribe"—needs the interference of an outside presence, a presence that is not human, to see that he is imperfect. A character like Arthur serves to reinforce one of King's general concerns about human beings—that personal introspection is sometimes impossible to achieve by oneself; the fact that King must create an outside supernatural force to hold up a moral mirror to Arthur's face should say something about King's recognition of some people's inability to evaluate themselves. Characters like *Pet Sematary*'s Louis Creed, *The Stand*'s Harold Lauder, *The Sun Dog*'s Pop Merrill, and *Christine*'s Arnie Cunningham—characters who aren't fortunate enough to benefit from an outside interference that causes them to question their own morality—are blunt examples of what happens in King's world when humans remain ignorant of their own shortcomings.

King's concept of moral degeneration arising from humans' indifference to their own flaws is not an original one. It is a theme that can be found throughout literature merely because of its universal truth; it does not apply solely to today's people and society but rather addresses the human condition as it has been throughout time. In drawing a comparison between King's protagonists and those created by other significant writers such as Herman Melville and Edgar Allan Poe, Tony Magistrale illustrates the universality of the idea:

There is a strong suggestion that Ahab and Poe's narrators secretly hate what they see to be a reflection of themselves found in the objects of their vengeance; for it is clear that in abandoning the most fundamental precepts of morality in order to accommodate the selfish urge to dominate and torment their fellow creatures, Ahab and Poe's narrators end up destroying themselves. (*Landscape of Fear* 21)

As the passage serves to explicate, the failure of people to successfully investigate their own morality, resulting in a self-destructive projection of internal flaws onto an external embodiment of those flaws, has been recognized by authors for years. In King's canon, the recognition can often be found in his portrayal of an adult world that persecutes its young; King's adults often subliminally despise both the exposure to worldliness and the access to evil brought about by their physical and mental growth, and they project that hatred to those that they no longer are: the young and innocent (*It*, *The Body*, *The Library Policeman*, *The Talisman*). In *Stephen King: The Art of Darkness*, Douglas Winter also points out that moral degeneration from lack of introspection is not an original King concept:

King's plague of vampires, like that of Jack Finney's "body snatchers," is less an invasion than a sudden confirmation of what we have silently suspected all along: that we are taking over ourselves, individuals succumbing to the whole. The relentless process of fragmentation and isolation—a progressive degradation of individuals to a one-dimensional, spiritless mass—has seen the moral disintegration of an entire town [regarding *'Salem's Lot*]. (47)

What Winter is referring to in citing *'Salem's Lot* is a town of people who are so busy finding faults in their neighbors that they are not able to unite in battle against the vampires that are preying upon them. The novel is not so much about vampires as it is about the fall of a community resulting from a breach of faith among brothers and sisters. King often details in the novel the ludicrousness of the exchanges between 'Salem's Lot's citizens. Rather than utilizing their energies to identify and change their own imperfections, they highlight those of others. These tendencies culminate in a state of isolation, denying any form of human bonding in the struggle, culminating in a complete lack of community action. The citizens have not been destroyed by vampires as much as they have destroyed themselves because of their inability to change and correct their own lives through moral maturity.

What English fiction, horror fiction, and specifically Stephen King's fiction have to teach their readers is that the first step toward mental maturity is gaining an understanding of the impact each and every person's moral standing has on the rest of society. As real monsters such as Ted Bundy and Jeffrey Dahmer have shown, even one person's breach of morality can affect the lives of an entire city or nation. Once an individual has learned the consequences of choice, learned to share the self with others, learned to see one's personal shortcomings, learned to believe in the good residing in the human spirit, then he or she will have taken a step toward becoming whole that may be more significant than any other emotional development imaginable. The fictitious characters Stephen King creates serve to present to King's readers images of themselves, calling to question issues of their own morality.

Works Cited

Bosky, Bernadette Lynn. "The Mind's a Monkey: Character and Psychology in Stephen King's Recent Fiction." *Kingdom of Fear: The World of Stephen King.* Eds. Tim Underwood and Chuck Miller. New York: New American Library, 1986: 211-37.

Hatlen, Burton. "Good and Evil in Stephen King's *The Shining*." *"The Shining" Reader.* Ed. Tony Magistrale. Washington: Starmont House, 1990: 81-103.

King, Stephen. *Christine.* New York: Viking Press, 1983.

_____. *Firestarter.* New York: Viking Press, 1980.

_____. *Four Past Midnight*. New York: Viking Penguin, 1990.

_____. *Needful Things*. New York: Viking Penguin, 1991.

_____. *'Salem's Lot*. New York: Signet New American Library, 1975.

_____. *The Stand*: The Complete and Uncut Edition. New York: Doubleday, 1990.

Magistrale, Tony. *Landscape of Fear: Stephen King's American Gothic*. Bowling Green, Ohio: Bowling Green State University Popular Press, 1988.

_____. *Stephen King, the Second Decade:* Danse Macabre *to* The Dark Half. New York: Twayne, 1992.

Notkin, Deborah L. "Stephen King: Horror and Humanity for Our Time." *Fear Itself: The Horror Fiction of Stephen King*. Eds. Tim Underwood and Chuck Miller. San Francisco: Underwood-Miller Publishers, 1982: 131-44.

Schuman, Samuel. "Taking Stephen King Seriously: Reflections on a Decade of Best-Sellers." *The Gothic World of Stephen King: Landscape of Nightmares*. Eds. Gary Hoppenstand and Ray B. Browne. Bowling Green, Ohio: Bowling Green State University Popular Press, 1987: 107-14.

Winter, Douglas E. *Stephen King: The Art of Darkness*. New York: New American Library, 1984.

Toward Defining an American Gothic:
Stephen King and the Romance Tradition_____

Tony Magistrale

In a recent edition of my favorite comic strip, "Bloom County," Opus, the obtuse penguin, suffers from a severe case of amnesia. Unable to remember even the most elemental aspects of his personality, he wonders aloud, "Do I prefer spinach salads for lunch? . . . or pistachio-nut ice cream? Do I read Saul Bellow or Stephen King?" The final frame shows Opus at home in a comfortable chair, dipping into a gallon tub of pistachio-nut ice cream and reading an enormous book entitled *The Gore* by Stephen King.

Perhaps better than any other comic strip currently in circulation, "Bloom County" achieves its humor in reflecting and parodying the manners of American popular culture. In the particular episode cited above, pistachio-nut ice cream and the brand-name fame of Stephen King are emblematic of America's junk food culture, while Saul Bellow is paired with the more respectable spinach salad. As the confused Opus acknowledges, pistachio-nut ice cream and Mr. King are clearly distinguished from the more substantial contents available in spinach salads and the fiction of Saul Bellow. King's novels may be more fun to devour than those of Bellow, but they are also perceived as being less significant, less "serious."

Despite an emerging corpus of film and literary criticism in the past few years that has treated King's fiction quite seriously, his long-standing artistic reputation is still considered in doubt. There are several reasons for this, the most frequently ascribed of which probably fall within this list:

(1) King makes too much money with his books (at this writing his yearly income is greater than the gross national products of most third world nations) and any popular writer can't be so good as his press;

(2) he produces nearly a book a year, so he must not work very hard at his craft;

(3) his predominant subject themes are the supernatural, the bizarre, and the occult, and he is therefore only tangentially concerned with the realities of contemporary life; and

(4) he needs an editor, presumably because many of his books are overwritten and badly organized.

It should not suffice for an *aficionado* of King's work to dismiss the above points as merely the cynical judgement of English teachers who are underpaid and unimpressed by creatures of the night. King himself has, to varying degrees, addressed each of these complaints in interviews, introductions to his fiction, and in his own analysis of the horror genre, *Danse Macabre*. In all honesty, much of King's *oeuvre* would benefit from the tough advice of a good editor; there are, for example, a number of instances where King's work could be substantially improved as a result of some judicious revising. However, it is both unfair and inaccurate when any or all of these laments serve as the basis for degrading King's importance as a serious American artist. Indeed, one of the primary motivations for the existence of this book is the resolute commitment on the part of its author to enhance the literary reputation—which, as we have seen, is often at odds with a popular one—of Stephen King's fiction by giving it the type of analysis it justly deserves, and for too long has failed to enjoy.

1

Who buys Stephen King's books and why?

In discussing the influence of the sociopolitical atmosphere of the 1950s on the evolution of the horror film, King argues in *Danse Macabre* that his generation represented

> . . . fertile ground for the seeds of terror, we were war babies; we had been raised in a strange circus atmosphere of paranoia, patriotism, and national *hubris*. We were told that we were the greatest nation on earth and that any Iron Curtain outlaw who tried to draw down on us in that great saloon of in-

ternational politics would discover who the fastest gun in the west was (as in Pat Frank's illuminating novel of the period, *Alas, Babylon*), but we were also told exactly what to keep in our fallout shelters and how long we would have to stay in there after we won the war. We had more to eat than any nation in the history of the world, but there were traces of Strontium-90 in our milk from nuclear testing. (23)

None of the issues King discusses above has changed much in three decades; the stakes are still high, the missiles more plentiful. The anxiety associated with the realities of modern life leads readers to King. His apocalyptic vision of a world in ruins (*The Stand*) or the nightmare of science unleashed beyond mortal control (*Firestarter, The Mist*, and "I Am the Doorway") are invented themes bordering on the very edge of possibility. The parallels between the world of King's novels and our own grow increasingly striking as we spin blindfolded toward the twenty-first century. In an age where it sometimes seems that to eat and drink and breathe is to be helplessly inviting cancer; where the constant threat of war in the Middle East and Latin America threatens to escalate into one final conflagration; where instruments of mass destruction increase in capability and sophistication, while those in charge of them seem less responsible and prudent; and where random and purposeless acts of violence have tacitly become an accepted element of Western life, King's fictional plots are appearing less and less surreal. And whether his audience reads to indulge a kind of perverse enchantment in imagining the destruction of humankind, or reads to reaffirm the importance of circumventing Armageddon, King's novels and tales are reminders of how far we as a collective society and culture have strayed from a balanced moral perspective. As a result, his fiction possesses a political and social relevance that is as serious and significant a contribution as anything Saul Bellow has yet to tell us.

King's tendency toward overwriting notwithstanding, his prose style remains deceptively simple and accessible, and the ease with which one of his imaginary worlds envelops the reader represents another reason for his popularity. In reading a novel such as *The Shining* or *Christine*, it is quite possible to withdraw from all commitments to family and friends, re-emerging after two or three days bleary-eyed and perhaps slightly paranoid, but nonetheless aware of having been transported into a fascinating realm. King himself acknowledges this very tendency in an interview he shared with Douglas Winter published in the book *Faces of Fear*:

In most cases, [my] characters seem very open and accessible. They seem like people that you would like to know, or even people you *do* know. People respond to that, and there is very little of that in novels today. . . . In most of the books, I think, there's a kind of Steve King hammock that you fall into—and you feel really comfortable in that hammock, because you know these people and you feel good about them. You don't have unease about who they are; you have unease about the circumstances that they find themselves in. And that's where the suspense comes from. (251)

King's best work employs many of the same techniques found in film, which is the most obvious explanation why his novels translate so well into movies. He possesses the ability to maintain levels of suspense because the imaginary world he portrays is so accurately visual. Consider, for example, this scene from the short story "The Ledge," a tale in which a jealous husband, who has discovered his wife's infidelity, torments her lover by forcing him to walk around the penthouse ledge of a high-rise apartment building:

I waited for the wind to drop, but for a long time it refused to, almost as though it were Cressner's willing ally. It slapped against me with vicious, invisible fingers, prying and poking and tickling. At last, after a particularly strong gust had made me rock on my toes, I knew that I could wait forever and the wind would never drop all the way off.

So the next time it sank a little, I slipped my right foot around and, clutching both walls with my hands, made the turn. The crosswind pushed me two ways at once, and I tottered. For a second I was sickeningly sure that Cressner had won his wager. Then I slid a step farther along and pressed myself tightly against the wall, a held breath slipping out of my dry throat. (190)

In this excerpt we see King's descriptive abilities at their very best. Not only does the reader clearly visualize the desperate plight of the narrator, clinging to the building with his legs and hands while the wind's personified "fingers" pull at his body, but his terrifying situation likewise fills us with pity and fear. As his journey around the building unfolds, his staccato breaths become ours, until finally we urge his survival, completely overlook his infidelity with Cressner's wife, and applaud the ironic conclusion as the narrator turns the tables on his tormentor and makes him walk the ledge.

King's many skills and liabilities as a writer are readily apparent. But his name has been elevated to brand-name status primarily because of his ability to create supernatural effects. As I will argue elsewhere in this book, I believe these extraordinary occurrences can be traced directly to King's sociopolitical perspective on contemporary America, but this is probably not an affiliation most readers make. As is the case with his general prose style, King's monsters are always highly visual manifestations—whether they occupy the form of rampaging trucks on an interstate highway, a malevolent deity who inhabits the cornfields of Nebraska, or the animated topiary outside a Colorado hotel. Once the reader is introduced to these creatures, he sleeps the worst for it.

King's most loyal readers belong to generations of moviegoers who have attended repeated viewing of Lucas' *Star Wars* trilogy, adults and children who were nurtured on television reruns of *The Twilight Zone* and *The Outer Limits*, individuals who have spent entire afternoons transfixed by the human-animal-vegetable hybrids in the paintings of

Hieronymus Bosch, and those whose literary tastes remain committed to annual readings of Tolkien's *Lord of the Rings Trilogy*. Several critics, most notably Douglas Winter and Don Herron, have reminded us of King's debt to the book and film success of *Rosemary's Baby* and *The Exorcist*. In the early 1970s these productions revitalized public fascination with the horror genre by focusing on its urban possibilities. Steering deliberately away from the science-fiction backdrops that characterized the genre's major contribution to literature and film in the 1950s and 1960s, Ira Levin's *Rosemary's Baby* and William Blatty's *The Exorcist* bring the terror back down to earth; indeed, their work is a reminder that the darkest evils are always those found in our neighborhoods, in our children, and in ourselves rather than in some deserted place out among the stars. As King reminds us in *Danse Macabre*, "the strongest watchspring of *Rosemary's Baby* isn't the religious subtheme but the book's use of urban paranoia. . . . Our dread for Rosemary springs from the fact that she seems the only normal person in a whole city of dangerous maniacs" (288-9).

King not only capitalized on the immeasurable public interest awarded to *Rosemary's Baby* and *The Exorcist*, as both novels and film adaptations appeared just before King's first publication (*Carrie*, 1974), but he likewise continued to emphasize the horror potential available in the everyday world. King's monsters are found not on planets light years away or in other exotic or foreign locations. Instead, they inhabit the ground floors of American factories, high schools, and rectories. Some of his creatures prowl the dark recesses of woods and swamps, but his most frightening creations can be found in neighborhood communities occupying positions of power and authority or in Washington controlling the fate of the nation. Like *Rosemary's Baby* and *The Exorcist*, King's world is an easily recognizable one, and when terror is unleashed in that world it becomes all the more terrifying because we comprehend its immediate relevance to our daily lives.

2

It is his awareness of the pervasiveness of evil—indeed, that it exists in ourselves, our social and political institutions, in short, in everything human—that links King to the literary tradition of American gothicism. In his essay "King and the Literary Tradition of Horror and the Supernatural," Ben Indick argues that King "has absorbed and utilized those qualities which characterize the different types of stories in the horror genre. In his own distinctive style are mirrored the major traditions he has inherited" (175). While Indick broadly outlines those gothic elements which have influenced King (e.g. the ghost story, vampire tale, etc.), he pays scant attention to the American romance tradition of the nineteenth century. Although he briefly includes mention of Poe in his analysis, Indick does not provide any thorough investigation linking King to Poe and other American writers from the nineteenth century. In fact, King owes as much to this earlier generation of writers—particularly Hawthorne and Twain—as he does to any German vampire legend or to his literary contemporaries, Blatty and Levin. The connection between King and the nineteenth century requires a critical forum for several reasons. The most important is by way of establishing King's place in the mainstream tradition of American literature. At the same time this relationship can also provide an appropriate context for discussing the origins of King's moralist vision.

The most obvious similarity that King shares with these nineteenth-century writers is his reliance on gothic settings and atmospheric techniques. Poe's haunted houses, Hawthorne's symbolic forests, and Melville's assorted workplace dungeons each bring to mind respectively *The Shining*, *Pet Sematary*, and "Graveyard Shift."

In Poe's tales of fantasy and terror, confined atmospheric environments are representative of the narrator's or main character's circumscribed state of mind. Thus, Prince Prospero's proud egotism in "The Masque of the Red Death" is illustrated by his seven-chambered castle sealed off from the world by metal doors and thick stained glass windows; the narrator's mental anguish in "The Pit and the Pendulum" is reflected in his dark, gradually narrowing prison cell; and similarly, the Usher mansion is emblematic of Roderick Usher's mental status: both its interior apartments and external facade exist in a state of chaos and disintegration.

The jump from Poe to King is really more of a skip, as their protagonists often find themselves in similar claustrophobic circumstances. In Poe's fiction, as Frederick Frank points out in his essay "The Gothic Romance," "Place becomes personality, as every corner and dark recess exudes a remorseless aliveness and often a vile intelligence" (14). King likewise employs physical settings as a mirror to a character's psychological condition, and *The Shining*, *'Salem's Lot*, "Graveyard Shift," "Strawberry Spring," "The Boogeyman," and "The Raft" are his most instructive examples. His gothic landscapes are animated by a terrible potency that appears out of all proportion to the small and vulnerable humans who are held within its bondage. Like Poe's buildings, King's architecture is imbued with a life of its own, an unnatural biology that reflects the character and history of its former inhabitants.

Although *The Shining* contains several explicit allusions to "The Masque of the Red Death," the Overlook's real inspiration is the Usher house, replete with its legacy of sin and death as well as its ultimate destruction. And similar to Poe's descriptions of the decayed mansion's relationship to its owner, the interior of King's Overlook hotel—with its dark, twisting corridors and infamous history—reflects Jack Torrance's own psyche. At the end of *The Shining* Torrance could no more depart from the Overlook than Usher could abandon the crumbling mansion that becomes his tomb.

Hawthorne's woods are a place of spiritual mystery; in them, young Goodman Brown, Reuben Bourne, and minister Arthur Dimmesdale must confront their own darkest urges. In *Pet Sematary*, Hawthorne's historical sense of puritanical gloom associated with the forest is mirrored in King's ancient Micmac Indian burial ground. Dr. Louis Creed, like so many of Hawthorne's youthful idealists, discovers in the Maine woods that evil is no mere abstraction capable of being manipulated or ignored. Instead, he finds his own confrontation with evil to be over-whelming, and like Hawthorne's Ethan Brand and Goodman Brown, he surrenders to its vision of chaos and corruption.

Melville's fiction, whether set on the sea or in the urban office, de-scribes the quiet nightmare of a capitalist economic structure devoid of humanitarian principles. The workplace as torture chamber is one of Melville's most frequent themes, and it is a vision that informs fiction as diverse as "Bartleby the Scrivner," *Benito Cereno*, and *Moby Dick*. The crew on board Ahab's *Pequod*, for example, is cajoled into blood oaths that force them to relinquish their humanity, becoming mere ex-tensions of their mad employer's quest for personal revenge against Moby Dick. King's descriptions of work experience in contemporary America bear close similarities to Melville's: in "Graveyard Shift," "Trucks," and "The Mangler," his characters are forced to perform la-bor under similar dehumanizing conditions. For both Melville and King, gothic settings and apparatus are often evoked as vehicles for un-derscoring a sterile and rotting economic system.

Melville's urban and seascapes and Poe's claustrophobic interiors make their regional influences difficult to pinpoint. Their use of gothic settings, while always specific and important to theme, could conceiv-ably take place anywhere in the world; in Melville's sea novels and Poe's *Narrative of Arthur Gordon Pym*, for example, the macrocosmic backdrop of the ocean, because of its sheer enormity, floats the reader in a sort of salt water vacuum. Hawthorne, on the other hand, was at his best as a regionalist author. His sense of Massachusetts—as a reposi-tory for historical events as well as a physical entity—is intrinsic to his most important fiction. Hawthorne's New England forests and puritan ancestry function as living beings in his work; they are always subject to his closest scrutiny, and often exert a profound influence over the lives of his protagonists.

At the Conference for the Fantastic in Arts, held in 1984 at Boca Raton, Florida, I asked Stephen King, who delivered the conference's main address, what effect living in Maine had produced on his writing.

He replied that "there's a Maine very few outsiders ever get to know. It's a place of rich Indian lore, rocky soil that makes it difficult to grow things, and incredible levels of poverty. Once you get out from behind the coastal resorts, the real Maine begins." King's Maine is a place of terrifying loneliness where nature seems antagonistic to human habitation and where men and women often feel the same degree of estrangement from one another as they do toward the supernatural creatures who threaten their lives. Burton Hatlen, perhaps the most persuasive critic on the regional influence on King, argues in "Beyond the Kittery Bridge: Stephen King's Maine," that in the writer's "myth of Maine," characters are confronted "with an overwhelming, terrifying challenge, and they won't survive it unless they can find within themselves some kind of courage that they didn't know they had" (59).

King is a regionalist in much the same way that Hawthorne was; each sensed that the real meanings behind the history and physical textures of a particular place could be fathomed only after great study—and what better laboratory than one's own ancestral past and regional legacy? Thus, *The Scarlet Letter* or "Young Goodman Brown" can no more be separated from their distinct puritan Massachusetts backgrounds than King's *'Salem's Lot* or *Pet Sematary* can be extricated from contemporary Maine.

King captures the native speech patterns, the local raw materials of a cold climate, and the specificity of place that set his readers firmly in a rural Maine world. His north country is a region of a particular people, language, and customs, all set apart by an awareness of their differences from cities even as near as Boston. King returns over and over to descriptions of his native state, and he does so for some of the same purposes Hawthorne used in writing about Massachusetts: each author understands that the universal themes of great literature—human sin, fear, and endurance—can only be rendered truthfully within settings and by personalities an artist has come to know on a firsthand basis. Much as Hawthorne relied on puritan New England as a setting to describe the foibles and sins that are the inheritance of humankind, King views Maine as a deliberate backdrop for his own allegories, enabling him to utilize specific elements from that culture in his portrayal of the moral conflicts common to us all.

3

In his book *The American Novel and Its Tradition*, Richard Chase defines the most important aspects of the romance tradition:

> Astonishing events may occur, and these are likely to have a symbolic or ideological, rather than a realistic, plausibility. Being less committed to the immediate rendition of reality than a novel, the romance will more freely veer toward mythic, allegorical, and symbolistic forms. (13)

Chase makes these points with reference to the work of Hawthorne and Melville, but it is immediately apparent, even from what has been said only so far in this opening chapter, that the description also applies just as well to King. Indeed, as we shall see, the use of the horror story as sociopolitical allegory is one of King's major contributions to the genre. Like King, the nineteenth century possessed a similar interest in portraying the discovery of self through metaphors of motion, the journey quest, and the conflict between ideologically opposing forces. "William Wilson," *The Narrative of Arthur Gordon Pym*, "Young Goodman Brown," "Ethan Brand," "My Kinsman Major Molineux," *The Marble Faun*, *Moby-Dick*, and *The Adventures of Huckleberry Finn* represent a blend of the literal with the symbolic, realism with allegory, and thus maintain certain similarities to King's canon.

The strength of King's stories is probably not to be found, however, in Melville's philosophical contemplations, nor in Poe and Hawthorne's speculations regarding the relationship between art and life. But the tentative and often precarious moral search for selfhood that characterizes the nineteenth-century romance tradition is likewise present in King. King's world-view is based on the complexity of modern life, and his protagonists begin the voyage toward moral wholeness only after experiencing the most disturbing encounters with evil. King relies on the journey motif in *The Stand*, *The Talisman*, *Pet Sematary*, and *Thinner* for the same reasons the nineteenth century did: the literal voyage—be it westward across contemporary America, downstream on the Mississippi River, or into the mysterious woods of a New England forest—becomes a metaphor for the journey into the self. This journey is fraught with danger along the way because King's young protagonists, like those of Twain and Hawthorne, learn that true moral development is gleaned only from a struggle with the actual, from confronting the dark legions of Morgan Sloat and Randall Flagg, rather than by avoiding them.

King writes fiction from the perspective of a fallen human world, and his characters commence their voyage to a moral comprehension of this world only at the very point where they become profoundly aware of the pervasive existence of evil. In Poe, Melville, Hawthorne and Twain, no individual is immune from the lure of evil—indeed, many of their characters succumb to its attractiveness and commit the most despicable acts of depravity. For example, neither Poe nor Melville satisfactorily explains why the narrators of "The Tell Tale Heart" and "The Black Cat" hate the old man and the cat, or why Captain Ahab feels the need to indulge his anger toward a white whale. However, there is strong suggestion that Ahab and Poe's narrators secretly hate what they see to be a reflection of themselves found in the objects of their vengeance; for it is clear that in abandoning the most fundamental precepts of morality in order to accommodate the selfish urge to dominate and torment their fellow creatures, Ahab and Poe's narrators end up destroying themselves. Most of the other central protagonists from the canons of Poe, Hawthorne, and Melville are measured by similar ethical barometers: evil triumphs when the individual fails to exert control over his darkest impulses.

An analogous set of moral principles is at work in King's fiction as well. In *The Stand*, for example, those few remaining humans immune to the superflu are pulled between the two allegorical forces of good and evil, represented by Mother Abagail and Randall Flagg. Most of the characters who align themselves with Mother Abagail to establish a community in Colorado maintain their allegiance throughout, but *all* of these individuals—even the leaders of the group, Stu Redman and Nick Andros—are visited by Flagg, the latter appearing frequently in dreams of temptation, fear, and confusion. Only in actively confronting Flagg's influence do King's characters affirm the principle of goodness; Nadine Cross and Harold Lauder, on the other hand, succumb to Flagg's machinations because they lack the self-discipline necessary to exert a moral will.

4

The discovery of evil is the central theme that writers in the American romance tradition share with King. The writers in this tradition have created characters who are a complex blend of good and evil, often committing their greatest sins in refusing to recognize the evil in themselves. This encounter with evil is frequently overwhelming; it does not always lead to a higher state of being. In fact its discovery often takes a violent shape—destructive of the central character or of others around him. Jack Torrance, Louis Creed, and Harold Lauder, like Benito Cereno, young Goodman Brown, and Poe's psychotic narrators in "William Wilson," "The Black Cat" and "The Cask of Amontillado," are not spiritually transformed by their discovery of the darker side of reality, but succumb to its horror and retreat into cynical pessimism.

On the other hand, the nineteenth century also supplies us with the possibility for spiritual regeneration within its strict moral precepts. Twain's Huckleberry Finn, Melville's Ishmael, and Hawthorne's Hester Prynne, Dimmesdale, Donatello, and Miriam, learn that there can be a certain strength derived from a descent into the abyss. King's protagonists suffer intensely to uncover a similar truth. His young heroes and heroines—Charlie McGee, Danny Torrance, Jack Sawyer, Mark Petrie, and those adults who are either affiliated with them or embody many of their attributes—inspire us with their efforts against despair and toward moral advancement. In this sense there exists a level of salvation available to King's characters that binds them to the "survivors" in the canons of Melville, Hawthorne, and Twain: the knowledge that moral maturity is a possible consequence from contact with sin. Their protagonists learn that they have within themselves the capacity for making ethical choices, and that these decisions will either enhance or retard their adjustment to the reality of evil. Once this awareness is established, the opportunity for a new and more confident personality emerges. It is the portrayal of this evolution that finally links King's fiction to the moral vision available in the nineteenth-century romance tradition—the ability to uplift his audience with the promise that painful insights into the horrors of our world can propel us beyond egotism or cynicism and toward the theory and practice of redemptive sympathy. Perhaps King's protagonists are unable to articulate it quite so adroitly, but they are nonetheless in a position to understand and share in the same spirit of transformation that informs Miriam's personality at the conclusion of Hawthorne's *The Marble Faun*: "'. . . sin—which man chose instead of good—has been so beneficently handled by omniscience and omnipotence, that, whereas our dark enemy sought to destroy us by it, it has really become an instrument most effective in the education of intellect and souls'" (840).

Works Cited

Chase, Richard. *The American Novel and Its Tradition*. New York: Doubleday, 1957.

Frank, Frederick S. "The Gothic Romance" in *Horror Literature: A Historical Sur-*

vey and Critical Guide to the Best of Horror, ed. Marshall B. Tymn. New York: The Bowker Company, 1981.

Hatlen, Burton. "Beyond the Kittery Bridge: Stephen King's Maine" in *Fear Itself*, eds. Tim Underwood and Chuck Miller. New York: New American Library, 1985.

Hawthorne, Nathaniel. *The Marble Faun* in *The Complete Novels and Selected Tales of Nathaniel Hawthorne*. New York: Random House, 1937.

Herron, Don. "The Biggest Horror Fan of Them All" in *Discovering Stephen King*, ed. Darrell Schweitzer. Mercer Island, WA: Starmont House, 1985.

Indick, Ben. "King and the Literary Tradition of Horror and the Supernatural" in *Fear Itself*, eds. Tim Underwood and Chuck Miller. New York: New American Library, 1985.

King, Stephen. *Danse Macabre*. New York: Viking, 1983.

_____. "The Ledge" in *Night Shift*. New York: New American Library, 1979.

Winter, Douglas, ed. *Faces of Fear*. New York: Berkley Books, 1985.

Technohorror:
The Dystopian Vision of Stephen King_____

James Egan

Stephen King has received considerable attention for his treatment of what Brian Ash calls the theme of a "darkening world" (Ash 86). Less familiar is the fact that, from the beginning of his career, King has concerned himself with the complex implications of science and technology, so much so that the horror he evokes often seems inseparable from the dangers of imperious science and runaway machinery of many sorts. The anti-technological slant of King's writing links it with one of the primary preoccupations of twentieth-century science fiction. Like many avowed science fiction writers, moreover, King shares the modern dystopian notion that calamity rather than enlightenment, peace, and security will result from the erroneous utopian premises of the technoscientific world view. Beneath the mayhem which permeates King's fiction lie interrelated, troubling questions about the power, extent, and validity of science and rationalism in contemporary society.

King, then, may be read as more than simply a writer of gothic horror fables. Douglas Winter points out that in 1954-55 King began to compose stories "emulating the science fiction that he read" (Winter 9). King's own analysis of the horror genre, *Danse Macabre* (1980), mentions Isaac Asimov, Arthur C. Clarke, and his favorite science fiction writer, John Wyndham. *Danse Macabre* likewise makes several important observations about science fiction, tales of terror, and kindred genres. Horror, King claims, explores fears "which exist across a broad spectrum of people. Such fears, which are often political, economic, and psychological rather than supernatural, give the best work of horror a pleasing allegorical feel" (*Danse Macabre* 18). Horror clearly can exceed the supernatural, and horror does not have to be nonscientific (*Danse Macabre* 30), for King stresses that science fiction and horror overlap, as do utopian and dystopian literature (*Danse*

Macabre 30).[1] Additionally, *Danse Macabre* offers a definition of technohorror which provides a useful perspective on his work. The sub-text of the technohorror film, King maintains, suggests "that we have been betrayed by our own machines and processes of mass production" (*Danse Macabre* 156). As examples of technohorror he cites the mutant and radiation movies of the 1950s; the more recent "vision of technology as an octopus—perhaps sentient—burying us alive in red-tape and information retrieval systems which are terrible when they work . . . and even more so when they don't"; and contemporary versions of an archetype: "the brilliant mind dangerously hypnotized by the siren song of technology" (*Danse Macabre* 159-60). Apparently, for King, horror can focus on major technological fears; the concern he voices in *Danse Macabre* over technological missteps rises to a clamor in his fiction (*Danse Macabre* 374).

Douglas Winter notes that the "technological horror theme is an obvious exploitation of the subversive tendencies of horror fiction" (Winter 82). These "subversive tendencies" have dystopian implications, though King does not explicitly discuss the contemporary assumption that technohorror sounds a dystopian cry of discontent. Paul Buhle's analysis of H. P. Lovecraft's fiction points out that horror has a dystopian ring because it calls into question "affirmative culture"; dramatizes the "increasingly empty faith in Progress" which has saddled society; implies a suspicion about the control mechanisms of the state; and articulates a fear that science and social knowledge are pushing aside humanity and nature (Buhle 120). King's work can, perhaps, best be characterized as a blend of anti-technological science fiction, gothic horror motifs and dystopian premises. This mixture of motifs and metaphors has distinguished precedents, for example, Shelley's *Frankenstein*, surely a prototypical horror story, but also an anti-technological, anti-utopian parable. A tenuous but definite link exists, moreover, between King's nightmare vision and the dystopian tradition of Zamiatin, Orwell, and Huxley.

Generally, King addresses what Harold Berger considers the "critical point in the interplay of man and science [when] man loses the savor of life or control of the course of events, or both." He articulates many of the primary fears generated by science and technology, especially mass anxieties about "man's survival, integrity, and compatibility with the natural universe" (Berger 6, 200). When read allegorically, much of King's work searches out a basic conflict: Can technological change be subordinated to human purposes? (Fogg 60). Specifically, King writes of malevolent machines, those which take on capacities their makers did not intend; of irresponsible and incompetent technology; of the monolithic, technocratic governmental apparatus; of the debilitating effects technology has on its users; of technology's ability both to cripple human awareness of the mystical and transcendent and to create illusory mythologies of its own; and of technology's ominous power to destroy the human race.

Malevolent machines stand out in King, who begins by focusing on devilish machines themselves and the threat they pose to civilization, then proceeds to an illustration of the complex, perilous relationship of the mechanical to the humanistic, placing particular emphasis on the destructive psychological interplay of machines and their makers. "The Mangler" (1972) features a mechanical antagonist, a Model-6 Speed Ironer and Folder, something which appears at first to be an ordinary piece of laundry equipment. A bizarre series of events, however, quickly differentiates the Mangler from ordinary industrial tools. Employees notice that the Mangler runs before anyone pulls the "on" switch. Soon it captures a victim and pulverizes her beyond recognition, and then a repairman loses an arm when the machine starts, apparently at its own command. These episodes lead detective Hunton, who has been investigating Model-6, to conclude that it is demonically possessed. Purely by accident it seems, the correct combination of magical ingredients fell into the Mangler and enchanted it. When Hunton tries an exorcism, however, he discovers that he has used the wrong formula, a mistake which multiplies the machine's power, allowing it to free itself from the laundry floor and pursue the now panic-stricken exorcist. In the closing paragraphs, Hunton waits, traumatized, for the "hungry" machine to devour him.

Anti-technology motifs permeate the story. The Mangler mimics the worst, not the best, qualities of its creators. As the fate of its first victim suggests, the Mangler has become a sadistic rapist and a murderer. The phallic-shaped machine leaves behind the bra and panties of the woman it has "mangled" with nearly orgiastic enthusiasm. Slowly, seemingly with pleasure, it pulls the arm of the repairman into its maw, though it apparently has the power to snatch him in an instant. Torture may be its objective. The Mangler likewise mocks naive, mechanistic assumptions about "machine" behavior. This machine operates itself rather than following human orders, takes the initiative, and acts unpredictably. Imagery completes the parody: the narrator consistently describes the Mangler as an animal which breathes like a dragon (80) and roars to life (82). Animism expresses a prominent anti-technological theme—the revenge of nature; clearly the Mangler displays many of the characteristics of a predator from the natural world. Finally, King's parable articulates yet another anti-technological motif, one of the darkest fears of a technological age, that machines can fall under the control of an evil, transcendent will which must eventually have its way with humanity. The demonic images of the story lend credence to this fear—at the end Hunton waits, trembling, to be swallowed alive by an angry, smoke-belching devil, an image which recalls medieval woodcuts of sinners punished by being turned into the food of demons.

"Trucks" (1973), which involves a small group of people stranded at a truck stop on an interstate highway, widens the ripple of technological terror. "Trapped" better describes their situation than "stranded" because, outside the diner, driverless trucks of all sizes patrol like vicious, hungry watchdogs. A large freight-hauler, which repeatedly tries to crush the nameless narrator's car, chases him into the truckstop. Parallels with "The Mangler" are manifest. Machines have revolted, pursuing their former masters the way a huge prehistoric animal might have hunted game. Yet "Trucks" seems a more foreboding story than its predecessor for several reasons. The Mangler was but one machine; now a remnant of humanity discovers that the entire world has apparently been taken over by machines. Though animistic imagery recurs, "Trucks" appears darker in tone than "The Mangler" since even the demonic rationale for machine behavior has been dropped. Moreover, "Trucks" is abrupt: when the story begins, machines are already out of control. "Trucks" illustrates the humanist premise that machines will lead to the "control of human life" (Hillegas 89).[2] The narrator and his fellow captives are forced to refill the gas tanks of a seemingly endless line of trucks, worked until they collapse. Worse, they get a glimpse of what the future holds, if they survive at all—they must be the servants of machines. Though the Mangler was horrific, it acted quickly. Now, machines and people have entered into a long-term relationship which thoroughly degrades humans. The narrator articulates still another humanist fear, that of human obsolescence, when he speculates about the extent of the rebellion, about the probability that machines will eventually dominate all life forms on the planet. Machines, he surmises, can find ways to replenish and repair themselves. People will become obsolete because a superior "species" has supplanted them.

In "The Word Processor of the Gods" (1983) Jon Hagstrom, a computer whiz who dies in an automobile accident, gives his Uncle Richard a word processor for a birthday present. Though the machine may be jerry-built of miscellaneous spare parts, thereby recalling the Frankenstein motif of much anti-technological science fiction, we are not dealing with a fire-breathing colossus. The word processor can, however, "process" far more than words—by means of its Delete button, it can radically rearrange reality, making objects or individuals disappear without a hint that they had ever existed. King removes animism and the demonic from the story, replacing them with involved psychological and moral questions which grow out of the machine-human relationship. Richard Hagstrom does eventually delete his disappointing son and wife, so that a machine can be said to have mastered humans once again. However, the word processor cannot press its own Delete button. A complex, ominous relationship has developed, involving the machine's maker, the machine itself, and Hagstrom. In "The Mangler" and "Trucks" humans were portrayed as the victims of machines; here a person cooperates with a machine to victimize other people. Yet the word processor cannot be called autonomous and that fact triggers substantive questions about evil and responsibility. Is the machine the primary villain, or should its human partners be faulted? True, the word processor permits Hagstrom's dubious, self-gratifying wishes to materialize, but those wishes existed before the machine did. Moreover, he could have used his birthday present for higher purposes. Ultimately, "The Word Processor of the Gods" poses intricate problems of moral legitimacy and limitation.

Christine (1983) represents King's most detailed treatment of the machine-human relationship. Arnie Cunningham, a lonely high school senior, becomes obsessed with a 1958 Plymouth in terrible condition, which he purchases from an eccentric, foreboding old man, Roland LeBay. On the surface Arnie's association with Christine looks normal enough: he is a passable mechanic and Christine is his first car, one he has paid for by himself. Yet as the novel progresses Christine proves to be a most unusual vehicle. The car's odometer runs backwards, and when it does so Christine repairs or renews herself, seeming to grow new parts the way an exotic species of animal grows new limbs. Christine also appears to have an uncanny connection with Roland LeBay. Dennis Guilder, the story's narrator, Arnie, and Leigh Cabot, Arnie's girlfriend, all see the rotting corpse of LeBay in the car at one time or another. LeBay was an evil character in life and his evil has not only survived him, but has allied itself with Christine, who appears to do LeBay's bidding in his vendetta against society—Christine acts as a focusing device for transcendent evil. Thus, the animistic and demonic images of the short stories reappear in *Christine*.

Arnie's liaison with Christine appears more complex still, for King develops in greater detail the man-machine interaction he had touched on in "The Word Processor of the Gods." Christine it seems, has feminine qualities, and she appears distinctly jealous of Arnie's contacts with human females. For his part, Arnie treats Christine as if she were a lover. He spends a great amount of time with the car, allegedly restoring her; but often he loses track of the time he devotes to Christine, occasionally discovering that hours have passed which he cannot account for. After several toughs who have vandalized Christine die mysteriously, Arnie steadfastly defends his car from a prying detective, though he knows that she has the power of restoring herself and therefore erasing the clues to her crimes. He and Christine share the car's black-magical powers as though they were a lover's secret. When Leigh Cabot, Arnie's human girlfriend, demands that he get rid of Christine, he refuses to cooperate; it seems that a lovers' triangle has emerged. As Christine's list of victims grows and the police pressure Arnie, his union with Christine becomes more intimate, more overtly sexual. He feels comforted when he is "inside" Christine and draws strength simply from touching her. She develops into his closest companion and a strong ally when Leigh falls for Dennis Guilder.

King has written a parable rich in implications for the man-machine alliance. Christine and Arnie have undergone the familiar role reversal: he serves the car's needs instead of the opposite. Arnie devolves into a technology addict who cultivates a sexually symbolic liaison with a machine. King's metaphoric suggestion of sexual bondage seems less familiar and more intricate than the standard machine-seizes-power motif. In short, *Christine* depicts a perverse form of animism. The car serves as Arnie's means of striking out against the annoyances and misfortunes life has dealt him, destroying his enemies and acting as a surrogate for human companionship. Christine brings to life nineteenth- and twentieth-century humanistic fears about machines (Hillegas 90). The car obviously exceeds "the intentions of those who created it" (Fogg 64). Christine is "indifferent to [human] values," even to Arnie's, though he refuses to acknowledge the fact (Fogg 64). She clearly destroys the "sense of community" in Arnie's life and alienates Arnie from everyone around him (Fogg 64). Christine becomes all things to

Arnie; his relationship with her makes human relationships obsolete. Arnie has gone so far as to make an idol of Christine, and thus he has symbolically lost his soul because he worships a metal demon. Of course, Christine does not work alone. Unless there were latent evil qualities and lingering frustrations in Arnie, her attraction would not have been so strong. Christine, a haunted technological derelict, animates Arnie's darkest dreams and the most ominous aspects of his personality. That Christine has given form and power to Arnie's potential for evil seems as disturbing a fact as autonomous machinery itself.

The Stand (1978) and *The Mist* (1980) offer extensive treatments of another anti-technological, dystopian motif—the "destruction and transmutation of nature." Both illustrate the far-reaching effects of technological irresponsibility and support the notion that "the new [scientific] knowledge and the power it brings represent an act of rebellion that goes beyond the order of things" (Fogg 67-68). Complex systems rather than specific machines are the culprits in each case. King dramatizes overt and easily recognized technological damage brought about by the systems themselves and the people who operate them.

The matter of wholesale destruction of nature and human society in King's fiction has been discussed elsewhere in some detail, so that only a few points remain to be made.[3] In *The Stand* military technology releases an apocalyptic plague of deadly germs, but technology cannot control what it has created and the plague virtually destroys the human race, turning civilization into a ruins of deserted streets, burning buildings, and rotted corpses. *The Mist* again singles out reckless technological tampering in the form of the mysterious Project Arrowhead, which has drastically altered the conditions of life on earth by apparently tearing a hole into another dimension and releasing an army of carnivorous creatures.

Mutations of human and animal life are widespread in both novels. Moreover, King implies that a vague but definite, and potentially more disruptive, mutation has occurred as well. In *The Stand* nearly all of the surviving population experiences a marked increase in psychological sensitivity, dreaming, for example, the same recurring dream of a faceless man, Randall Flagg, their demonic antagonist. The narrator of *The Mist*, David Drayton, observes that "new doors of perception were opening up inside" (93) for him and for several of the others trapped inside the Federal Foods supermarket. King uses this heightened perception as a metaphor of the mutation of the human subconscious whose powers have been altered and magnified by technological "fallout." The mutated psyches of characters in each novel have complex, powerful, and unpredictable qualities, lending credence to the idea that "when man is radically reshaped it is at a price" (Walsh 166). The process of mutation has, figuratively, transformed human nature itself and now a great ambivalence prevails, in which primordial forces hold sway, the by-product of meddling with human nature, but what those forces may lead to remains an open question. Could runaway mutation occur? Has the human psyche been so radically reshaped that the species must grope around in a mystical shadowland like a primitive tribe? Technology has been responsible for plunging human nature at quantum speed into the unknown, and the newly mutated psychological environment appears appropriately "mist"-shrouded. Potentially at least, despite the seeming post-apocalyptic utopia hinted at in *The Stand*, new types of monsters have been created, monsters who will be shaped by the as yet undetermined impulses and needs of their mutated psyches. The vast, ambiguous powers such monsters possess may be viewed, animistically, as yet another version of nature's revenge because previously untapped or repressed instinctive drives have forced humanity to reckon with them, with its own "wild talent." Put another way, the "return to the primitive" in both novels is "characterized by the lapse of science into magic and religion" (Fredericks 152); the amorphous "primitive" could well be as dangerous as the rationalistic excesses it replaced.

Technocracy, a more remote, ambivalent and elusive species of technology than those discussed earlier, receives attention in *The Stand* and *Firestarter* (1980). Roger Williams defines technocracy as a "mutation of bureaucracy" which "refers to the actual and potential political power of technical administrators, economists, engineers and related groups," and Bernard Gendron argues that technocracies employ not only overt coercion of many types to achieve their ends, but also more devious, "nonpunitive techniques of control," which include reward giving or genetic engineering (Williams 24; Gendron 99). A subplot of *The Stand* and the main plot of *Firestarter* detail the struggles of an individual or a small group against a technocracy. While the superflu decimates civilization in *The Stand*, the government tries desperately to control the plague, and at this point Stu Redman, one of the novel's protagonists, falls into the grasp of technocracy. Immune to the plague, Redman is given over to technicians who study his metabolism in order to isolate the source of his immunity. However, the so-called medical authorities who look after him soon prove to be an arm of the collapsing police state whose scientists are in collusion with the military. Though Redman undergoes tests constantly, test results are not provided and human amenities are not an issue. He has been turned into a guinea pig, but "that wasn't even the worst. The worst was the guns. The nurses who came in to take blood or spit or urine were now always accompanied by a soldier in a white-suit, and the soldier had a gun in a plastic baggie. . . . If they were just going through the motions now, then he had become expendable. He was under detention" (114-15). Redman eventually breaks out of the plague-control center, but he cannot fully comprehend the fact that he had been dealing with a subtle, insidious technocratic enemy which had seized him before he was sufficiently aware to defend himself (Nelson 178).

Firestarter takes its name from Charlie McGee, a young girl with mental abilities so advanced that she can start fires at will. Charlie's pyrokinesis results from technological carelessness: a small group of scientists, with government cooperation, abuses science by conducting experiments on unsuspecting humans with Lot Six, a drug of unknown properties. Both of Charlie's parents had had their psyches altered by Lot Six, and they passed their "gift" on to her. A monolithic, technocratic "government" lurks in the novel's background, and this aspect of technology preoccupies King in *Firestarter*, for scientific abuse dovetails with political repression and manipulation. A shadowy domestic espionage operation called The Shop kills Charlie's mother and captures her and her father in order to examine and exploit their powers. In police-state fashion, The Shop keeps a thick dossier on the McGees and watches them in much the same way that Big Brother watched Winston Smith in Orwell's *1984*. Agents of The Shop are seemingly everywhere, and those agents include assassins in addition to surveillance operatives of all types. The Shop also has a paramilitary headquarters and intricate technological and computer assistance. As the experience of Andy and Charlie McGee shows, The Shop specializes in two of the forms of tyranny favored by technocracies, mind-invasion and spying (Berger 101). To say the least, ambiguity characterizes The Shop's chain of command. Despite the disaster of the Lot Six experiments, The Shop was not held accountable. Despite the fact that the McGees are imprisoned, deprived of their civil rights, and constantly in danger of death, no one intervenes on their behalf. Metaphorically, The Shop has become the government—remote, machine-like, sending out human robots with computerized instructions, the possessor of virtually all political power. The Shop does not answer to a President, or a Congress, or to the people at large, but only to itself. In theory, of course, The Shop operates on orders from those higher up in the government, but higher-ups are only faceless shadows lost in the complexity of a structure that combines technology with anonymity, massive size, and strength. Day-to-day control of The Shop rests with an elite of spies, technocrats, and elusive political manipulators.

Though technocracy preserves a semblance of order, in *Firestarter* the question of final political responsibility for the uses of technology remains open. Individuals ultimately count for less than systems. Technology has helped to create a vicious cycle, becoming a primary part of an immensely intricate governmental structure, so intricate that only technology can supervise it. *Firestarter*, then, evokes several anti-technological fears, the primary one being that it is virtually impossible to differentiate a "real" government from The Shop. Moreover, The Shop has apparently decided that "social stability and freedom cannot be combined, and has opted for stability," a decision reminiscent of those made by the rulers of Huxley's *Brave New World* (Walsh 112). An overriding anxiety remains, that in the future and perhaps in the present as well, "direct control" of society will be in "the hands of an elite of scientist technicians who will rule by their own norms . . ." (Fogg 69). Though Charlie eventually escapes, *Firestarter* suggests that the evil monolith of technocracy has entrenched itself.

Carrie (1974) and *'Salem's Lot* (1975) both illustrate the most subtle, pervasive, and, potentially, the most dangerous aspect of technology: the technoscientific world view. Walter L. Fogg has described that world view as follows:

> . . . a set of values and a way of thinking which has its roots in the very beginnings of western civilization. . . . The technoscientific world view has eroded other modes of thinking and lifestyles and has demythologized man's world in order to make it technologically manageable. Technology is mistrusted because the values which both created technology and are fostered by it are exclusive of all other values. (70)

Jacques Ellul, Herbert Marcuse, and others, whose arguments Fogg summarizes, maintain that the "technical order" can be thought of as a *"way of life."* If, as Langdon Winner argues, humans have indeed become "thoroughly technomorphic" and have "invested [their lives] in a mass of methods, techniques, machines, rational-productive organizations, and networks," then civilization has been trapped by the "givers" of the technological order. The two novels in questions play off the "charismatic, nonrational elements of history" against the "static designs of intellect" (Winner 201, 42, 200, 180).

Carrie points up the failures of systems, and of the technoscientific world views of which they are a major element, when systems confront the unknown. Technology cannot control Carrie White as she destroys the town of Chamberlain with her telekinetic powers, nor can science, theorizing after the fact, explain her behavior. Technology and the scientific method, King implies, have an arrogance about the unknown, a presumptiveness which causes the several types of researchers who study the White phenomenon to assume that their methods can explain all riddles, that a complex system of inquiry can surely solve one "simple" problem. Those who direct the White Commission investigation are overconfident about their procedures. They cannot imagine that they have failed to find the truth, and their naivete proves dangerous. In Herbert Marcuse's words, the researchers have overemphasized the "*therapeutic* function of . . . analysis" and have worked to eradicate "obscurities, illusions, and oddities" (Marcuse 170). The Commission perpetuates the delusion that a parapsychological power such as Carrie's cannot exist, and in so doing denies the mystical and transcendent. In effect, the technoscientific world view has dismissed metaphysical moral realities in order to make life more "manageable." At the least, King implies, such a perspective leads to narcissism and myopia in those guided by its assumptions. The Commission's lengthy investigation results in the glorification of false mythologies about the unknown.

'*Salem's Lot* dramatizes how unaware people are of the long-term consequences of what Jacques Ellul has described as "Technique" (see Ellul 3-23). King pits the archetypal American small town, 'Salem's Lot, against the vampire Barlow, and unifies the novel by means of death metaphors. Predictably, the technoscientific world view has prepared the way for Barlow's reign of terror. Because reductive empirical science has denied the very concept of vampires, it cannot cope with Barlow. Ironically, in fact, science and technology are two of the vampire's strongest allies—while doctors and medical labs waste time performing useless autopsies and studying blood samples from the undead, the number of vampires grows epidemically. Since a vampire comes from the shadowland of myth and legend, he stands beyond technology's reach; technology, by definition, deals best with the "death" of machines and systems. King shows how dangerously vulnerable the desacralizing premises of science leave those who have, by choice or forfeit, internalized them: there is no defense against the darkness in the world.[4] *'Salem's Lot* measures rationalism, scientism, and technology against myth and the supernatural, "superstition and ignorance." The novel's protagonists, Ben Mears and Mark Petrie, can defeat Barlow only by adopting a mythical and "superstitious" attitude, by resurrecting a world view which presumably had been discredited, one which antedates computers, medical advances, and high-powered weapons. Basic human emotional resources (particularly faith), along with simple ingenuity, are all that will work.

If the technoscientific world view holds no answers, its unwitting disciples in the Lot must be powerless. True, Ben and Mark finally destroy him, yet Barlow achieves considerable success: virtually the entire population falls victim to him and his presence remains in the form of the undead who still haunt the vicinity. Barlow succeeded because the Lot was an ideal target for him, a town whose inhabitants recognized "themselves in their commodities," who "found their soul in their [automobiles] and . . . kitchen equipment." People in the Lot had long been hypnotized by the false mystique of science, gadgetry, and materialism, so that Barlow's victims were, metaphorically, dead before he found them, zombie-like and reconciled to the status quo. Barlow was an ironic liberator who "rewarded" his followers with an alluring escape from a one-dimensional, desacralized world where dreams and anxieties could be "resolved and fixed" by psychiatry and where the population could indulge its materialistic impulses to the fullest extent (Marcuse 9, 70-71). That Barlow, who offered only a demonic half-life, could make such headway in *'Salem's Lot* stands as an indictment of the failures of rationalism. scientism, materialism—the corrosive technoscientific world view, in short.

King's technohorror motif links his fiction with some of the major dystopian themes of twentieth-century literature. Clearly, King denies "the utopian possibilities that modern technology offers mankind" because he can discover no apparent "link between technological development and human progress" (Winner 18-19). Rather, he mocks the notion of technological "progress"—progress devolves into horror. Walter L. Fogg identifies the "destruction and transmutation of nature," "manipulated man," and "manipulated society" as recurring dystopian concerns of the twentieth century (Fogg 67-69). King's handling of these issues in *The Stand*, *The Mist*, *Firestarter*, and *'Salem's Lot* focuses on the variety of crises created by technological tampering and by the technoscientific world view itself. Instead of an impressive era of human happiness, technology ushers in a new dark age of runaway machines, a vengeful nature, and apocalyptic destruction. Demonic allusions and imagery underscore King's attack on technology: typically in his work characters fight losing battles with the "demonic machine, its demonic inventor, or technology itself" (Nelson 174). Such losing battles point to a major argument of contemporary dystopian fiction, that if man is "unfit to be the custodian of his technology . . . he will be victimized by a destructive one . . . or he must submit to the dictatorship of a protective technology" (Berger 34-35). Technology, King implies, reckons inadequately with the Dark Fantastic in human nature and in the vast reaches of uncharted reality outside of the human mind. Since the technoscientific world view relentlessly desacralizes, it produces a psychological rigidity which makes civilization and its systems vulnerable to the unknown. Technology remains naive about the moral reality of evil, and consequently technological operations of all types, from the mechanical to the political, repeatedly suffer the consequences of naiveté. King's emphasis upon the power and extent of evil indicates that he holds a dystopian world view, that his cosmology is "retrogressive," that he considers civilization and its accomplishments precarious at best and dangerously delusive at worst (Fredericks 151). *Carrie*, *Christine*, and *'Salem's Lot*, in particular, stress that "man is only intermittently and partially rational" (Walsh 168). King shares with other dystopians a fundamental doubt that "man is basically good" and that man and his culture are "perfectible" (Walsh 166; Stupple 26). King's skepticism provides a final thematic link with the dystopian tradition, for he repeatedly voices a dystopian recognition "that there are built-in limits to how much we can change the physical universe, the moral order, and our nature . . ." (Walsh 163). Trespassing beyond those limits invokes horror.

Notes

1. See also Fredericks, *Science Fiction and Fantasy* (Bloomington: Indiana UP, 1982), 5. Fredericks also points to the generic overlapping of gothic literature, fantasy, and modern science fiction.

2. "Uncle Otto's Truck" (1983), anthologized in *Skeleton Crew*, features a sinister machine as well, a large Cresswell truck, but does so with less originality and force than the other "machines" treated in this essay.

3. See, for example, Douglas Winter, "The Night Journeys of Stephen King," in *Fear Itself: The Horror Fiction of Stephen King*, ed. Tim Underwood and Chuck Miller (San Francisco: Underwood-Miller, 1982), 183-229.

4. For a social and genre perspective on darkness in *'Salem's Lot*, see Tony Magistrale, "Crumbling Castles of Sand: The Social Landscape of Stephen King's Gothic Vision," *Journal of Popular Literature* 1 (1985): 45-59.

Works Cited

Ash, Brian. *Faces of the Future: The Lessons of Science Fiction*. New York: Taplinger, 1975.

Berger, Harold. *Science Fiction and the New Dark Age*. Bowling Green: Popular Press, 1976.

Buhle, Paul. "Dystopia as Utopia: Howard Phillips Lovecraft and the Unknown Content of American Horror Literature." *The Minnesota Review* 6 (1975): 118-31.

Ellul, Jacques. *The Technological Society*. Tr. John Wilkinson. New York: Knopf, 1964.

Fogg, Walter L. "Technology and Dystopia." *Utopia/ Dystopia?: Threats of Hell or Hopes of Paradise*. Ed. Peyton E. Richter. Cambridge, Mass.: Schenkman, 1975. 59-73.

Gendron, Bernard. *Technology and the Human Condition*. New York: St. Martin's Press, 1977.

Hillegas, Mark. *The Future as Nightmare: H. G. Wells and the Anti-Utopians*. New York: Oxford Univ. Press, 1967.

King, Stephen. *Carrie*. 1974. New York: Signet, 1975.

————. *Christine*. 1983. New York: Viking, 1983.

————. *Danse Macabre*. 1980. New York: Berkley, 1982.

————. *Firestarter*. 1980. New York: Signet, 1981.

————. "The Mangler." 1972. *Night Shift*. New York: Signet, 1979. 74-92.

————. *The Mist*. 1980. *Skeleton Crew*. New York: Putnam, 1985. 21-134.

————. *'Salem's Lot*. 1975. New York: Signet, 1976.

————. *The Stand*. 1978. New York: Signet, 1980.

————. "Trucks." 1973. *Night Shift*. New York: Signet, 1979. 127-42.

————. "The Word Processor of the Gods." 1983. *Skeleton Crew*. New York: Putnam, 1985. 271-87.

Marcuse, Herbert. *One-Dimensional Man: Studies in the Ideology of Advanced Industrial Society*. Boston: Beacon Press, 1964.

Nelson, John Wiley. "The Apocalyptic Vision in American Popular Culture." *The Apocalyptic Vision in America*. Ed. Lois Parkinson Zamora. Bowling Green: Popular Press, 1982. 154-82.

Stupple, A. James. "Towards a Definition of Anti-Utopian Literature." *Science Fiction: The Academic Awakening*. Ed. Willis E. McNelly. Shreveport, La.: College English Association, 1974. 24-30.

Walsh, Chad. *From Utopia to Nightmare*. 1962. Rpt. ed. Westport, Conn.: Greenwood Press, 1972.

Williams, Roger. *Politics and Technology*. London: Macmillan, 1971.

Winner, Langdon. *Autonomous Technology. Technics-out-of-Control as a Theme in Political Thought*. Cambridge, Mass.: MIT, 1977.

Winter, Douglas. *Stephen King*. Mercer Island, Wash.: Starmont House, 1982.

The Ending Is Only the Beginning:
Genre and Its Influence on Climax_____

Patrick McAleer

> I'm like one of the old people's robots, he thought. One that will either accomplish the task for which it has been made or beat itself to death trying.
>
> —Roland Deschain, from *The Dark Tower*

Perhaps the one question that is left in the mind of Stephen King's Constant Reader at the conclusion of the *Dark Tower* series is whether or not Roland Deschain will achieve some sort of victory at the end of his quest in that the gunslinger has repeated and resumed his quest many times before, losing his friends, lovers and even his own children while journeying for at least one-thousand years. With each renewal of Roland's quest to seek the Dark Tower, the world moves on and Roland brings with him not only a past that is nearly forgotten, if not presumed to be dead, but a sense of hope that he just might find something different than the sands of the Mohaine Desert behind the final door at the top of the Tower, the one marked "Roland." The gunslinger's near-eternal existence—"*May I be brutally frank*? You go on"—and his never-ending adventure keeps readers constantly wondering if Roland will ever find solace and if the world(s) must live on until he discovers whatever it is he needs to find in order to permanently keep the Dark Tower stable and safe from threat (King, *The Dark Tower* 828). But even among this repetition, the circular nature of the *Dark Tower* series that asks the Constant Reader to revisit the gunslinger's story, examining the text for clues as to how Roland may truly find an ending leads to the question as to why he seeks the Tower. Or, more to the point, for what *ending* does the gunslinger journey? To attempt finding an answer to this question, genre becomes the focus of this discussion.

Analysis of the various genres King employs in the composition of the *Dark Tower* story points towards some of the answers sought as examinations of the themes and formulas found within the distinct genres outline reasonable expectations of Roland's quest, especially in terms of the tale's climax. Even though it has been suggested that "*The Dark Tower*'s generic and thematic impulses, in fact, typically disrupt the reader's pattern of expectations, offering him questions, not solutions," the search for at least an indication as to the overarching purpose and scope of Roland's quest is not unfounded or entirely quixotic (Egan, "Gothic Western" 100). Instead, the search for answers, albeit shrouded in mystery, speculation, skepticism and doubt, takes the curious reader down several paths towards termination points that may not necessarily be the original envisioned destinations desired by King. Yet, each generic route provides vital considerations for attempting to understand why the last gunslinger ventures into the waste lands and on to the Dark Tower of both his dreams and nightmares.

In attempting to answer the inquiry as to why Roland pushes on to find the Dark Tower, beyond the feeble suggestion that he must do so because Maerlyn's Grapefruit told him to do so as implied in *Wizard and Glass*, the various genres King employs in creating this tale provide a clue. But it should be noted use of various genres in *The Dark Tower* has been a mild point of contention and worry instead of being seen as a pathway to some sort of interpretive conclusion. For example, one such criticism of the genres at use in the *Dark Tower* describes results of this experimentation as a rather strange creation, even by King's standards: "its choice of form and genre, its interweaving of reality and fantasy, and the backgrounds of its composition all break from King's norm, making *DT* an unusual book, even for a master of the unusual" (Collings and Engebretson 99). In conjunction with this, one book review of the third book in the series comments that, "*The Waste Lands* seems at times an uncertain hybrid of horror and fantasy," suggesting that the experimental implementation of genre King weaves into this story does not always succeed (Nicholls BR14). Considering how many types of fiction follow a general template, or, as Northrop Frye states, "both literature and mathematics proceed from postulates, not facts," the formulas that King uses and alters clarifies the direction of Roland's journey (351). In short, if the various steps of a particular genre can be examined and applied to *The Dark Tower* and its ending, the expected conclusion within this selected genre becomes known, as well as the requirements that need to be fulfilled in order to reach such an end. With this approach, the first step is to isolate a genre, examine its structure and its expected ending, and not only see if Roland's tale fits within the framework, but also how the steps leading to the ending help to explain the rationale for endeavoring to accomplish the goal in question.

With King employing many genres in weaving together the gunslinger's tale with several variations and deviations, it is a moot point to simply say that the *Dark Tower* series is part Epic, part Western, part Gothic, part Post-Apocalyptic, and part Science Fiction and then show how the themes and markers of each genre can be identified in the work. For that matter, Linda Badley claims that, "King exploits the power of archetypes. He tells ancient stories, filtering them through modern Gothic and fantasy conventions" (102). Links between King and, say, Shakespeare and even the Greeks are not uncommon among scholarship on his writings, and, surely, such connections can be found within most any writer's fiction. But the sense of apprehensiveness that resonates in Badley's observation certainly suggests a lack of originality in King's writing, or at least a critique of his manipulation of the reading public by, presumably, presenting old tales under new guises. Yet, as James Egan suggests that, "in the broadest sense, a formula story provides its readers with 'a clear and reassuring regularity' and follows a straightforward and fairly predictable pattern of expectations," *The Dark Tower* series is noted as a collection of books that hardly follows any strict pattern, at least in the sense of genre, and further indicates a sense of inventiveness in King's writing ("Gothic Western" 100). Therefore, it is reasonable to conclude that with a heightened awareness of the genres King uses in the *Dark Tower* series, it can be better speculated as to what the outcome of Roland's quest might be due to the expectations each generic formula raises. In sum, within the many genres King writes into his tale, alongside the subsequent adherence to and manipulation of these templates, there is an answer waiting regarding to what the gunslinger's quest is aimed. However, it must be noted that some paths that are to be unveiled under the genres used in *The Dark Tower* are more revealing than others.

Preliminary Foundations

One of the earliest realizations any reader of *The Dark Tower* series comes to is that the story is an atypical work in that it does not easily or readily fit into just one genre. Readers start with a gunslinger, a cowboy apparently of the American West, but as the story moves on, it is discovered that the main character (the term "protagonist" is hesitantly used to describe Roland at any point in the story) lived his childhood in a medieval setting in which remnants of broken technology indicate an old and broken world. More to the point, James Egan notes of *The Dark Tower* that "King's work can, perhaps, best be characterized as a blend of anti-technological science fiction, gothic horror motifs and dystopian premises" ("Technohorror" 48). But without any solid framework, or lenses, to guide an initial reading of the text, mystery is all that surrounds the tale. Suspense may be built into the tale through such vagueness, but the overwhelming ambiguity of the first book in King's series, *The Gunslinger*, whether in terms of defining and isolating genre or developing the characters, leads to several inquiries about the story, one of which is sustained all throughout Roland's journey: why does he seek the tower? A general response to this question is Heidi Strengell's assertion that "King seems unwilling and unable to offer straightforward solutions to his protagonists' problems and spiritual ponderings" (120). Ambiguity and lack of clarity, of course, can be a part of the joy and journey of reading any book as it is not the author's job to give the reader all the answers. Then again, when facing questions of motive in fiction, readers can usually find answers within the text. But with King's *Dark Tower* series, Roland's motive is a mystery that equals the mystery of the Dark Tower itself.

An ideal place to begin with this discussion is Robert Browning's poem "Childe Roland to the Dark Tower Came" as it is the piece on which King's tale is essentially dependent. King references much of Browning's enigmatic poem in the story of Roland Deschain—his companion Cuthbert, the "hoary cripple with malicious eye" (Joe Collins/ Dandelo), and the anticipated winding of the slug-horn at the very end of the quest by the adventurer—but Browning's poem is just as problematic, if not more so, than King's story (line 2). Since the 1855 publication of this poem in Browning's collection *Men and Women*, literary scholars still have not derived a generally unifying interpretation of the piece. Still, some aspects of the poem are helpful as a starting point in the discussion on King's story. For an initial and general comparison between the two works and their respective adventurers, Heidi Strengell suggests that

> Browning's protagonist has spent his adolescence dreaming of and training for the sight of the Tower. As a persevering knight, he presses toward this goal, disregarding the mental and physical dangers that he faces. King's Roland, too, seeks a vision he neither understands nor precisely knows where or how to pursue. [120]

Here it should be noted that each Roland is introduced as an individual on journey; nothing more, nothing less. The reader in each case is immediately left with many questions to ponder through the duration of the adventure. Who charged each individual with the quest is unknown, motive remains unseen, and the overarching goal of the quest is never stated. However, readers of King's tale begin to understand why Roland thinks he must travel to the Dark Tower in the fourth book, *Wizard and Glass*, after Roland recovers from his first look into pink Wizard's Glass: "'the Tower is crumbling, and if it falls, everything we know will be swept away. There will be chaos beyond our imagining.

We must go . . . *and we will go*'" (King 581). Although it is actually quite foolish for Roland to wholeheartedly believe something he saw in the Wizard's Rainbow, it can be concluded that Roland gives *himself* the quest of saving the Dark Tower. In *The Gunslinger* Roland says of his quest that, "'To find the Tower is my purpose. I'm sworn,'" which does gain some context by way of the graphic novel *The Gunslinger Born* in which it is revealed that Arthur Eld's descendants are charged with protecting the Dark Tower (King 228). But, without the information provided in the graphic novel, the gunslinger's justifications for his quest beg the question as to why Roland swore, exactly to what he swore, and even if the act of locating the Tower is enough to satisfy the conditions of his journey, which once again raises the question as to *why* he seeks the tower. Roland, like King's Constant Reader, may not entirely understand *what* he pursues, but in examining the thematic boundaries of his tale, and in looking at Roland as a crossbreed hero, readers are taken closer to an answer as to *why* he seeks the Tower, and, why the story ends as it does, with repetition, which hardly seems to be a conclusion informed by any genre.

The "Epic" Formula—Questions of Duty

The beginning point for analyzing the various genres and literary formulas at work in the *Dark Tower* series is with the classical, or rather the epic tale. Although many of the elements to be discussed fall into other categories, such as myth or romance, the term "epic" will serve as a meeting place, in name only, for these closely related variations in genre. To start, Thomas Greene suggests that "the first quality of the epic imagination is expansiveness" (194). Immediately, this can be applied to Roland's quest as his journey for the Tower is for *all* of the worlds, not just his own. And as the stature of the epic quest suggests the importance of Roland's adventure, readers are nonetheless at a loss as to why Roland is the one chosen to undertake this important journey, and also why several others all fall while the gunslinger survives. Still, the gunslinger's continued existence and persistence in his quest can be explained, by the epic formula to which King adheres in places, as suggested by David A. Miller, who says that "a barebones scenario for the [epic] hero and his part in the quest would be: Someone extraordinary / Goes or is sent / To search for and retrieve / Something important" (162). As Roland travels into the dangerous lands outside of Gilead to search for the Dark Tower, the nexus of space and time, it can be argued that Roland is merely following suit with respect to what is expected of a hero on an epic journey. Yet, is Roland an extremely special or an unusually endowed individual? *If* he is indeed such a character, one might see why he seeks the Tower: he simply has the mettle and wherewithal to undertake such a journey, and someone has recognized this in Roland thereby charging him with the quest, quite possibly just for the sake of the challenge. The story within the pages of the *Dark Tower* series, however, does not present Roland as this character, with the exception of his skills with a gun, but even this minute aspect of Roland's character hardly makes him extraordinary.

Expectations of Roland's position and status may be a bit overwhelming and exaggerated, but it cannot be denied that the gunslinger is, at the very least, one of the best "draws" who has ever lived. Roland's ka-mates—Cuthbert, Alain and Jamie DeCurry—all cannot believe how skilled he is with a revolver, but does this mean that Roland is truly extraordinary? Not at all, since, "the hero is always, *and must be*, a prodigy at weapon play," which suggests that the skills which mark Roland as not only a gunslinger but also an uncommon hero are simply expected of a man in his position and can be considered as normal within the epic scope (Miller 206, emphasis added). On the other hand, Roland is imparted with intriguing knowledge concerning his person when he resumes his quest at the end of book seven— "*You darkle, you tinct*"—suggesting an eternal nature exceeding the normal human boundaries which forces reconsideration of Roland's epic aptitude (King, *The Dark Tower* 828). Roland's state of near-immortality does place Roland in the company of the divine, but the source of Roland's almost-eternal existence is neither extraordinary nor noble. Roland's repetitious journey and subsequent near-immortal status, stemming from one failure or another, is not a reward for an exceptional person who has lived an exceptional life, and his lengthy life-span can neither be seen as an indicator of greatness nor divinity, meaning that he is certainly not a noble warrior with god-like powers, meaning that he fails to live up to the epic expectation of a hero. Even holding to a more basic outline of the epic hero's quest which consists of, "departure/separation, initiation, and reintegration," there are still problems with the epic as a lens of reading *The Dark Tower* because Roland never truly becomes reintegrated into his world, especially as resumption is not the same thing as reintegration (Strengell 121). Only once does Roland fulfill the requirements of this epic template: as a young man he leaves for Mejis, becomes initiated as a gunslinger with the defeat of Eldred Jonas and George Latigo, and then gloriously returns to Gilead. But this microcosmic triumph does not align with the importance of epic size, and with Roland failing to fit within the basic formulas of the epic quest, a shift in focus towards smaller components, such as the role of the hero within the epic framework, reveals more of the gunslinger's aims.

While conceiving of Roland Deschain as a remarkable hero is problematic, it cannot be assumed that Roland's quest is already out of the realm of the epic and that the climax of *The Dark Tower* is therefore inexplicable through this genre. In acknowledging King's deviation from the divine or wondrous protagonist as an acceptable move away from the expected formula of the epic hero, David A. Miller provides the following as an alternative guide as to what is reasonably expected of an epic hero on an epic quest:

1. The hero is unique and isolate. His mark is his strong and deadly arm, but a particular quest may demand a hero of cooperative venturing. [. . .] 2. The hero is devoted to combat and confrontation: he must be prepared to seek out, or at least never avoid, those aspects of the quest. [. . .] He is both phys-

ically and morally prepared for such violence: a risk taker, superlatively courageous, honorable, single-minded in purpose—and probably, or necessarily, without much imagination. 3. The hero is detached from cultural and social place, is mobile and uncommonly swift [. . .] easily capable of taking up the challenge posed by time and distance in this world or another. 4. Precisely because the hero is easily detached from the social matrix, he is often as dangerous to the social fabric as he is useful in defending it. Indeed, in the end, he is more useful outside of society and displaying his excellence elsewhere—that is, on a quest. [163-4]

While there are already reservations of denoting Roland as extraordinary, he is certainly distinctive in that he is a grudgingly likable anti-hero who kills his own mother and still earns the trust of his companions. Among all that, his nemesis Walter speaks of Roland's mind as truly unique: "'Your mind. Your slow, prodding, tenacious mind. There has never been one quite like it, in all the history of the world. Perhaps in the history of creation'" (King, *The Gunslinger* 228). As far as isolate, readers of the *Dark Tower* series find Roland on both page one of *The Gunslinger* and the last page of *The Dark Tower* all alone; and as the action between these pages is concerned, Roland may find people to accompany him along the way, but he admits to his companions Eddie, Susannah and Jake that "'I am not a full member of this *ka-tet*'" which suggests that Roland's friends do not negate his isolation (King, *The Waste Lands* 259). Despite Roland's detachment from this group, they are necessary for his quest, which, according to Miller's model, is not uncommon. But as Roland adds to this when he says that, "'It may take a great many *ka-tets* to finish one picture,'" he suggests that the epic quality of isolation is not the key or the way to the Tower (King, *The Waste Lands* 259). To finish this line of thought on the role of the companion(s), Miller adds that, "The hero frequently has partners, companions, as a supporting cast *fitted* to his feats" (102, emphasis added). Roland might call it *ka* in order to explain the adept nature of his companions, but he is nonetheless a solitary individual who incidentally finds companions along the way and finds use for them as they are supposedly a part of his ka, people who serve particular functions for the larger story, or quest.

The second of Miller's heroic traits is the most interesting and telling of the four elements listed. With the epic hero "devoted to combat and confrontation," this is easily seen as a part of the gunslinger's code especially as the events in Calla Bryn Sturgis and Algul Siento play out. What is prominent about Miller's point is that the hero who faces danger without consideration of retreat does so as a matter of course, almost without thinking of any other option. In Roland's case, he does not travel to the Tower out of a sense of morality or even from a semblance of medieval chivalry. Roland's adventure moves out of the romantic offshoot of the epic as he is not one who follows the romantic form which "purges life of impurities and presents chivalry in heightened and idealized form" (Pearsall 21). Assuredly, the gunslinger does not necessarily seek salvation or to heroically serve his fellow man; instead of functioning as a character who performs good deeds for the sake of securing a sense of nobility for his own character, Roland blindly journeys for the Dark Tower, and as this building draws him on, he becomes further separated from the romantic hero as romantic, "action has no external motivation" (Pearsall 22). As the distinctly epic hero whose motivation is not intrinsic and is aligned with Miller's second epic trait of being "single-minded in purpose—and probably, or necessarily, without much imagination" which describes Roland quite accurately—"'You have no imagination. You are blind that way'"—this purpose-driven individual melts into Miller's third point which says that the epic hero is culturally detached and able to move quickly from place to place; such would be easy, if not expected, of an individual who has a goal and whose field of vision focuses solely on achieving such an end (King, *The Gunslinger* 219). Last, as Miller says that the hero's position outside of society makes him a potential threat, the discussion arrives at a proposition that seems to fit Roland quite well. As an outcast, as a loner who comes from a forgotten time, the gunslinger's anachronistic character is seen as a threat to the modernity of Mid-World as he brings outdated ideals to the world at large, but also has the guns and resolve to enforce his own incongruous views. As Miller suggests that the socially dangerous epic hero best serves his world on a quest, therefore consistently placed outside of the community walls, one must consider exactly what this means with respect to Roland's quest, especially if the purpose of Roland's constant questing is to keep him from inflicting harm on those he believes that he is sworn to protect.

As long as Roland continually resumes his quest, and succeeds in saving the Tower each time, then it appears that his purpose is to keep the Tower well and safeguarded, and maybe even for the well-being of all existence. This allows him to be truly beneficial for the world in which he lives because he constantly strives to save its existing communities. Yet, two critical issues arise which the benevolence of Roland's constant questing brings into question. First, as Roland repeats his journey for the Tower, the world has, "moved on since then. The world had emptied," which is to say that each repetition of Roland's quest does not truly begin back in the Mohaine Desert on the trail of the Man in Black *for the first time* (King, *The Gunslinger* 3). Each time Roland ends up back in the sands of the West and on the trail of the Man in Black, time has slipped away as evidenced by the assertions that Gilead is long gone to destruction and not recently brought to ruin. And Mid-World, as well as the universe, must endure continual existence, for good or ill, until Roland determines how to avoid repetition of his quest. As Roland repeats each quest, and as time slips forward each time, it is reasonable to believe that each journey is just a little bit different, with different players and different outcomes along the path which leads to the Dark Tower. When Roland resumes his quest, the world moves on and he does not begin at the true start, with the people of Tull still alive, Blaine still waiting in Lud, and Donald Callahan still traveling the highways in hiding. The next time through there will likely be no Allie, no Jake, no Andy the Robot—all have passed on, and have left Roland alone to find a new path to the Tower and with new companions who will most likely bear uncanny resemblances to Roland's former friends; Roland will remember Cuthbert, Alain and Jamie de Curry, but it is not far-fetched to think that he will *not* remember Eddie, Jake and Susannah.

What this all implies is that while Roland journeys, supposedly serving his country to the best of his abilities by removing himself from the society to which he is a threat, he in turn endangers more and more people each and every time he travels only to climb the Tower and goes through the door at the top marked "Roland." As long as the gunslinger is on his quest, death and destruction will result; the danger may not be faced by the society of which Roland is no longer included, but death does result for others, which makes readers question whose lives are worth more. Perhaps death of those who reside outside of Roland's community is what he is to avoid in a successful trek to the Tower, thereby providing validity to Miller's last criterion of the epic hero regarding the gunslinger in that most everyone must benefit from the perpetual adventure of the hero. But, Roland is a constant threat to the general well-being of everyone whether he is questing or not, which suggests that Roland is not an epic hero and that his purpose cannot then be understood by means of the epic genre.

In a stark contrast to what has been proposed thus far, Heidi Strengell offers the view that Roland is a selfless individual whose journey does benefit humanity rather than serving as an imposition, one that situates *The Dark Tower* well within an epic framework. Strengell says, "As I see it, Roland chooses responsibility for humankind over personal wishes," but the extent of Roland's responsibility, especially for that of human kind, can be easily dispelled by his never-ending pursuit for the Tower (122). His reason for saving the Beams and thus the Tower does not stem from a deep-seated emotional tie to humanity; Roland only saves the Tower because it is his duty as a gunslinger, and because he feels the need to understand the Tower and enter it, which is a symptom of the epic genre as, "epic answers man's need to clear away an area he can comprehend, *if not dominate*" (Greene 194, emphasis added). Also to recall is that the duty that Roland has fulfilled comes as a matter of course as, "the central realities of heroic literature are not to love or honour but loyalty to one's kin or leader, revenge, and the imperative necessity of asserting self (especially self as embodying a nation or people) through acts of power" (Pearsall 21). As Roland cries the names of the fallen once he reaches the Dark Tower, he acknowledges that he has fulfilled his duty as a gunslinger, as a citizen of Gilead, as dinh of his ka-tet, and that his allegiance to his quest and his people has endured as he has accomplished the impossible by reaching the Dark Tower for the sake of those who have fallen during his quest. With this in mind, it should be concluded that Roland's quest is not a moral voyage at all. Besides, Roland's overarching indifference to death would seem to dispel any notions that he is worried about those who he encounters along the Path of the Beam as, "the hero deals in death, and for the most part he accepts that death will be his inescapable portion" (Miller 120). Or, when Roland says, "We deal in lead," he does not deny guilt and remorse as related to death and murder, but he does acquiesce to the necessity of death in his quest, which contradicts the overall scope of the epic quest, a seeking to ensure life instead of ending it (King, *Wolves of the Calla* 111).

Roland's desire to reach the Tower must be done so at any cost, and his responsibility for humankind is to contend with them in a manner that will ultimately help *him* along on *his* quest. After all, what is Jake to Roland but a means to an end, especially in the first book, despite Roland's evolving emotions and tearful goodbyes witnessed in later volumes? Heidi Strengell believes that Roland's initial relationship with Jake should be seen differently: "By sacrificing Jake, Roland has made himself worthy of a dream vision of the Tower and earned the right to continue the quest" (131). However, Roland's sacrifice of Jake does not make him worthy of any such reward; if anything, it justifies Walter's attempt to mentally ruin Roland through the vision of the cosmos at the golgotha in *The Gunslinger.* Roland had a choice regarding

Jake Chambers's life, and the sacrifice of an individual for information is anything but noble. Also to consider is that Roland's journey(s) to the Tower need not take place on a single road. If anything, deviations from the path seen in the seven books of the *Dark Tower* would bode well for Roland in any future journey to the Tower. Therefore, Roland does not need to sacrifice Jake, or anyone else for that matter. So, does Roland venture forth to vanquish the evil tyrant for his king and his kingdom? Is the sacrifice of Jake worth the loss as a means for Roland to prove himself as a knightly figure merely performing the duty assigned to him out of a sense of honor for those he serves? If so, then it would seem that Roland's quest fulfills the ultimate goal of the epic quest: performing one's duty. But, seeing that Roland's journey has not entirely fit within this epic framework thus far, it should be little surprise to see that Roland's quest, after all, is not reasoned or intended to be out of duty despite what he tells his companions and the reader.

Roland embarks on his journey neither out of a duty to a land that has passed nor for any sort of tribute or attempt at securing a particular reputation. Before the graphic novel versions of *The Dark Tower* were written, the original texts proposed that Roland charged himself with his quest, and that his duty was only to himself, which is an inversion of the gunslinger code as learned within the culture of Gilead. Roland also does not quest for the Tower for the sake of honor: storming the Tower, and even halting the destruction of Gan's navel, is not done for the sake of any one person, any one city, and neither is this quest undergone due to allegiance to an individual or an ideal nor is it for the sake of Roland's own personal distinction. While fame may be the goal for some epic heroes, as some might "assume that the hero usually but very dramatically dies in the earnest hope of a kind of survival or even a persistence close to immortality, as a name to live on in fame and glory," Roland does not charge himself with saving the Dark Tower to restore a lost sense of nobility or to negate his infamous deeds as a youth, like sacrificing Susan Delgado and killing his own mother, Gabrielle (Miller 131). Were Roland truly an epic hero, one devoted to duty and the preservation of the well-being of the kingdom, he could be considered a champion of sorts. With this distinction, however, it must be understood that, "the first role of the hero as *champion* is to stand for the king; he is the hero festered into the structure of kingship, usually placed between the sovereign and external threat, or sometimes taking the place of the king" (Miller 182). But Roland does not necessarily function as a champion for any king or kingdom. Of course, Roland's homeland of Gilead is the land to which he feels a connection, and a land for which he performs many of his questionable duties, especially as readers recall his war-cry in *Wolves of the Calla*: "'*For Gilead and the Calla*'" (King 679). Yet, it is impossible for Roland to fight for a land that has been dead for centuries; Roland may fight for the *memory* of Gilead, but he cannot claim that he truly fights for a land which lies in ruin, a place that, "has been dust in the wind for a thousand years" (King, *Wolves of the Calla* 30). In sum, Roland and his heroic quest may fulfill some of the epic requirements mentioned, and may merge into other similar genres, but his failure to adequately fulfill other ex-pectations proves to be too problematic for utilizing the epic genre as a means of understanding the purpose of his quest.

Westward Expansion—In the Name of Civilization

When readers first meet the gunslinger on the trail of the Man in Black, he is witnessed as walking through the Mohaine Desert on the edge of civilization. Immediately, the reader begins to think that a Western is about to unfold finding a gun-toting cowboy leading a mule through a land that only shows smatterings of life: "He had passed the last town three weeks before, and since then there had only been the de-serted coach track and an occasional huddle of border dweller's sod dwellings" (King, *The Gunslinger* 8). The sporadic and desolate pres-ence of life and sparse civilization gives the story a Western feel as, "obviously, the Western takes place in the West, near the frontier," but more interesting to note is that Roland and his fellow gunslingers from

Gilead always feared being banished from civilization, sent to the west and out of their homeland as failures (Egan, "Gothic Western" 96). Here, unfortunately, is the first problem with the Western formula: instead of encountering the promise of an underdeveloped land in need of the order and direction that a gunslinger cherishes and champions, the West of Roland's world is anything but a bastion of budding civilization. Instead, the West is a place for outlaws and failed gunslingers. In other words, as James Egan notes, "one expects clarity in a formula Western, but this is not the case with *The Dark Tower*" ("Gothic Western" 99). And while the formula of the Western is in some disarray when it comes to *The Dark Tower*, especially as the West is a locale of shame and of figurative darkness in the *Dark Tower* series, the Western formula does not completely fail in its potential in illuminating the gunslinger's ultimate ends. Or, at the very least, early problems noted in the Western should not halt an examination of this genre.

Although the West of Roland's world deviates from the ideal frontier of the stereotypical Western, much of the geographical aspects of *The Dark Tower* are undeveloped and in need of order. With this, Roland's presence becomes necessary in this setting as, "the Western hero of the early dime novels typically functions as an agent of civilization" (Jones 26). The frontier of Roland's West may not fit the expected mold of the American frontier, especially as the land has been inhabited before Roland arrives as evidenced by the abandoned technology found at the desert way station and beneath the Cyclopean Mountains. Yet Roland can function as a Western hero in that he comes from civilization and whose presence may prove to be advantageous to those living in the borderlands. Still, caution must be exercised in accepting Roland's perception of what constitutes civilization. Much like how the civilization of the Old Ones dies out due to overwhelming scientific innovation accompanied by a sense of hubris, the civilization which Roland represents and adheres to is long gone. Roland's role as a man of the civilized world who has come to spread a civilized way of life may be nothing more than a mirror-image of Randall Flagg's quest for dominance as clearly seen at the end of *The Stand* when the defeated demon stares down upon a new mass of people: "*They are simple folk. Primitive; simple; unlettered. But I can use them. Yes, I can use them perfectly well*" (King 1138). Flagg then goes on to say to his new herd, "'I've come to teach you how to be civilized,'" and the use of civilization as a means of dominance and control is seen, all of which Roland is guilty of using to further his quest, especially in marking his guns as machines of a civilization that has passed on yet which still exhibit a talismanic quality that affords a position of power (King, *The Stand* 1141). Roland is definitely known to most everyone he meets in Mid-World, identified as a gunslinger by the sandalwood grips of his firearms which tends to trigger a response of obedience or even reverence. But, Roland cannot be a man of civilization, its representative, when said civilization no longer exists.

Regardless of his failure to function as a representative of civilization, Roland can still fulfill the role of the Western hero in that he often acts on behalf of a town or a group of citizens who cannot defend themselves. And like the epic hero, many Western heroes employ a sidekick to aid in these harrowing situations, which Roland attains during his travels. With respect to the hero's role in the Western as a protector of sorts is the observation that "the hero himself seldom stays to participate in the functions of that system he has helped to establish," and in a similar fashion, Roland, the champion of Calla Bryn Sturgis, and even Blue Heaven, moves on once his task is finished in each locale (Westbrook 39). Still, the Western hero serves as more than just a hired gun, as Heidi Strengell suggests that "in his roles as a diplomat, a mediator, a teacher, and a soldier, Roland does not depart from the Western hero archetype" (126). However, Roland's roles as diplomat and mediator are questionable. While Roland does act as a protector of the Rose in New York City and as a soldier for the people of Calla Bryn Sturgis, consider James Egan's assertion that "at no point does he act as a mediator between conflicting groups, nor does he perceive himself as one. The essence of a formulaic definition of a Western hero, therefore, does not apply to Roland" ("Gothic Western" 99-100). Perhaps the quest of the Tower in and of itself prevents Roland from filling the role of the small-town hero, as "Roland and his quest go beyond the microcosmic battle of the Western to the macrocosmic proportions of myth" (Strengell 135). Roland may don a cowboy hat, wear weathered boots and carry the old-style revolvers of his father, but he is only a shadow of the Western hero. Still, the size of Roland's quest, beyond the small town and his departure from the triumphant and diplomatic hero of the people, suggests that within the Western formula the conclusion, the purpose of Roland's quest, overshadows the menial events of the common folk. Although Roland's quest occasionally necessitates the safety of the small town like Calla Bryn Sturgis, the safety of the Calla-folken is merely a means to an end as Roland needs to save the citizens of this town to ensure that the Tower remains standing for him to storm it. Whereas the Western hero might be satisfied with a job well done in the dusty streets of a dilapidated town, Roland decides to move on and forgo celebration because there is more work to be accomplished, like the chase of the Man in Black.

Within the plot of the Western, pursuit constantly draws the protagonist on, which is present in the *Dark Tower* series as James Egan notes that, "first and foremost, the plot involves pursuit: Roland intends to learn the Man in Black's secrets by tracking him down" ("Gothic Western" 98). Roland's hunt for the Man in Black, and even the Tower, may be what pulls Roland away from any meaningful connection with the people he meets during his journey, so one may be able to neglect the fact that Roland escapes the microcosmic stature of the Western *hero* as he fulfills one of the formulaic aspects of the Western *plot* in his pursuit of the Man in Black. But, before Roland chases the Man in Black, he is supposed to have been a part of at least two other components of the Western novel: "In the dime novel adventure usually derives from a recurrent pattern of capture, flight, and pursuit" (Jones 137). Roland does fit within this pattern as he was captured in Mejis, only to be later freed by Susan Delgado and pursued Eldred Jonas. Also, Roland is later captured by the Little Sisters of Eluria and again escapes only to return to his pursuit of the Man in Black, who is caught by the gunslinger yet not necessarily captured. But, the plot of *The Gunslinger* and the rest of the *Dark Tower* books break the Western pattern mentioned in that pursuit becomes the most consistent and highlighted element of his quest, which does not assist with fully understanding Roland's quest in light of his constant pursuit of the Tower.

Although the West of Roland's world has been previously described as being in violation of the prescribed frontier of a typical Western, providing little assistance with the overall goal of discovering the purpose of the gunslinger's quest, a few pieces of Roland's tale can be placed into the Western template to better understand his journey by way of generic analysis. First, as the frontier has a tendency towards unrest and criminal activity, it is a place without order despite its resemblance to or attempt at forming some sort of community. And in Roland's West, the promise of civilization looks to be impossible to bring about as the primary culture is gone and dead. Yet, the disorder and chaos of Roland's West calls for attention, if not for the creation of a new society but for the sake of order. And order, whether in reference to a town or the Tower, just may be Roland's true purpose. With this notion of order, in conjunction with Heidi Strengell's suggestion that "the Slow Mutants and the residents of Lud [act] as the Indians or the outlaws," one might anticipate these characters as the general threat to stability in this underdeveloped landscape (127). Moreover, Roland himself proposes the idea that these outlaws and their rampages have benefited from the decay of the Dark Tower and that his quest for the Tower is not only about restoring the Tower itself but the land and its people as well. With the degeneration of the White, and the fall of Gilead and the kingdoms of the light, the Slow Mutants, the warring Pubes and Grays, or even the Wolves and those under the rule of the Crimson King all have risen to a dangerous level of power, which not only threatens various communities and the existence of peaceful people like those of River Crossing and Calla Bryn Sturgis but also the entire world. Roland's quest to save the Tower and halt the discord which is strewn all over his world may then be seen as a move to re-civilize the world. If this were true, it is tempting to embrace Daryl Jones's assertion that "the Western may be viewed as a narrative construct whose unifying principle is the Western hero's quest to reorder reality in terms of his own vision of the ideal world" (137). But if Roland is attempting to bring a new order to the world, a new promise of civilization, it is likely that Roland is hoping to bring about *his* own view of what the ideal world should be, which suggests that this exercise of dominion and even authority is his ultimate goal.

Roland's conception of the ideal world would, of course, be highly subjective and likely take the reader and the citizens of Mid-World back to an age similar to that of Gilead; it is what Roland knows and what he mourns, which seems as likely a goal for him as anything else. The promise of such a renewal may urge Roland on in his quest, but a quest to re-shape the world according to his own vision takes the reader from civilization and more towards tyrannical exercises of power. Roland's Gilead may have been a distinguished society, but even he cannot be sure that a return to this past is the best move to make and in the interest of *all* involved.

Civilization, in its varied forms and multiple settings, is, however, problematic for Roland's quest for the Tower. Roland's endeavor to restore his land, and even the line of Eld, appears to be a worthy quest, but it may be more appropriate to look to the horizon for a broader climax than the aspiration of re-establishing Gilead. To that end, Daryl Jones claims that, "altered, inverted, even parodied, the popular Western formula nonetheless survives. And it will continue to survive as long as it extends to humanity some glimmer of hope that a golden age still lies ahead" (168). What this suggests is that while civilization is the apparent ultimate end of a Western, *hope* is the key. Roland may *hope* for restoration of his broken world, and Roland's quest does prompt the reader to also hope that Roland will somehow avoid the continuous repetition of his journey coupled with the continued disintegration of Mid-World as the land, like Roland, is constantly moving on and moving forward because in the Keystone Tower world and Keystone Earth, "time [runs] just one way" (King, *The Dark Tower* 473). Additionally, the Horn of Eld does give Roland, and even the reader, a *"promise that things may be different* [. . .] *that there may yet be rest. Even salvation,"* but while the Constant Reader may be hopeful that Roland's quest will one day come to an end, it is hardly appropriate to consider one man's success as the indication that a golden age is on the horizon (King, *The Dark Tower* 828). A personal golden age for the hero may come to pass, but what is to be reasonably expected of Mid-World's prosperity if Roland does find a way to succeed in his quest, or at least the quest intimated within the Western framework? Of course, Mid-World and its inhabitants would no longer have to endure Roland's treacherous and deadly adventures, but is this really something that can be considered as a golden age?

With the idea of the golden age on the horizon as being the ultimate end of a Western, the previous analysis of the frontier and the role of civilization as elements key to the formulaic climaxes of the Western genre is recalled in that this explanation lacks insight into Roland's quest and motivations. As it were, if Roland's quest is to fit comfortably into the Western genre, the establishment of a new age would be Roland's goal, and if this was what drives Roland to seek the Tower, the Tower becomes a key to unlocking a new future, especially, as Daryl Jones says, "often the plot of the dime novel seems nothing more than fast-paced, loosely connected sequences of fistfights, gunplay and hairbreadth escapes strung out interminably and tied together by a happy ending" (135). But, through all seven books of the *Dark Tower* series, the promise of the "happy ending" is not provided, in that Roland may have deluded himself into thinking that the Tower promises, with its restoration, the coming of a new age.

Without a guarantee of actual prosperity which stems from the survival of the Tower, Roland of Gilead becomes painted as a man who is ultimately out for power, a power unavailable in the Western but nonetheless desired in order to mold the world according to his whims and even delusions that result in anything but a happy ending. Randall Flagg may have been the only character in the *Dark Tower* series to explicitly display aspirations of becoming the, "God of all," but Roland may not be too far behind (King, *The Dark Tower* 174). But, if the gunslinger is a character who hopes to find a means of shaping the world according to his own designs, he would need a way to accomplish this feat, and the road to this kind of dominance is not found in the realm of the Western.

The Gothic—The Dark Path to Power

Entering the realm of the Gothic, a focus on civilization is left behind with the Western. Within this new framework, that of "the archaic, the pagan, that which was prior to, or opposed to, or resisted the establishment of civilized values and a well-regulated society," is the genre for which King is primarily known (Punter and Byron 8). Indeed, the *Dark Tower* series resonates with Gothic qualities, especially with the object of Roland's obsession being a dark building that is often portrayed as being a Gothic construction on the various book covers of the series and even in the paintings of the books. Focusing directly on the Gothic nature of the series, though, James Egan says:

> Several of the story's organizing motifs have a Gothic ring to them as well. Roland journeys into the nightland, into the dark side of existence, rather than into the bright sunshine and the Promised Land of the conventional Western. His journey involves a typically Gothic predicament—he sets out into an immense unknown destiny, and that territory is probably expanding, not stationary. ["Gothic Western" 101]

Immediately Egan provides several key items of the Gothic novel to work with—the dark, the unknown, and the unstable. Thunderclap is the quintessential "nightland" with it being a land of eternal twilight as suggested by the artificial light beaming down on the Devar-Toi, and the "thinnies" in *Wizard and Glass* serve as evidence of an expanding land, one that even integrates parts of worlds other than Roland's own. In addition, one can reasonably expect Roland's tale to abide by the following guidelines of the Gothic: "In its rejection of moderation, regularity, compromise, simplicity, and stability, Gothicism embraces the erratic, the complex, the convoluted, the excessive, the abnormal" (Bayer-Berenbaun 144). Stated elements of the Gothic are certainly descriptive of Roland's, and Mid-World's, eccentricities, but as with the previous genres, caution needs to be exercised before embracing the Gothic as the key to the gunslinger's quest.

In noting that "the word 'Gothic' [. . .] originally conveyed the idea of barbarous [. . .] and antique, and was merely a term of reproach and contempt," it would be easy to consider Roland as a Gothic character (Summers 37). The extermination of Tull's citizens certainly helps to attribute a brutish nature to Roland, and as readers learn Roland is, according to Blaine the Mono, a "HATEFUL GUNSLINGER OUT OF A PAST THAT SHOULD HAVE STAYED DEAD," questions of the ancient are easily recognized in the gunslinger (King, *Wizard and Glass* 55). Also to consider:

> Where the classical was well ordered, the Gothic was chaotic; where the classical was simple and pure, Gothic was ornate and convoluted; where the classics offered a world of clear rules and limits, Gothic represented excess and exaggeration, the product of the wild and uncivilized, a world that constantly tended to overflow the cultural boundaries. [Punter and Byron 7]

At first glance, the "chaotic," "convoluted," and "wild" side of the Gothic are clearly present in *The Dark Tower*. One need only to walk the streets of Lud to see a lack of order in the broken city, and the Great Western Woods traveled in *The Waste Lands* give a literal and figurative wild in which all things, especially mechanical, have come to ruination. However, if Roland's quest is primarily Gothic, it seems that the

Western is appropriately undercut as civilization crumbles within the Gothic genre. But, as the gunslinger's stated goal is to save the Tower, and all the worlds, the inherent wreckage associated with the Gothic creates a dilemma because Roland's journey faces failure in a Gothic template, that which points towards destruction rather than salvation.

To provide an overview of what could be expected in King's tale which has ties to the Gothic and helps to explain Roland's quest, geography is an important focal point. As geographic instability is clearly seen in *The Dark Tower*, confirmation of the Gothic treatment of this theme is noted in the following: "What we find in the numerous conjunctions of Gothic and the post-modern is a certain sliding of location, a series of transfers and translocations from one place to another" (Punter and Byron 51). Instability in the landscape plays out as a constant imposition to Roland's quest, one that implies confirmation in that the Gothic genre is more of a determining presence in *The Dark Tower* series than other seemingly minor genre creations and integrations. In addition to the expansive and tumultuous landscape within the Gothic there is "a certain attention to the divisions and doublings of the self" (Punter and Byron 51). Simplicity and singularity function as polar opposites to the Gothic, which concerns itself with the ornate and various, which leads to the eerie pairings of characters in the *Dark Tower* series—Roland/The Crimson King; Cuthbert/Eddie; Jake/Alain; Susan/Susannah; Sheemie/Bryan Smith—which suggests that Roland's final confrontation with the Crimson King is one of necessity as Roland must seemingly battle his double and triumph in order to proceed with his quest. Yet, the, "unimaginable final battle" which Roland is destined to fight is only a means to an end and not Roland's ultimate goal (King, *The Gunslinger* 231).

In continuing the search for Roland's purpose, other considerations of the Gothic novel must be looked at, including the suggestion that "Gothic novelists are particularly fond of hypnotic trances, telepathic communications, visionary experiences, and extrasensory perceptions," which helps to contextualize the paranormal activities witnessed in the *Dark Tower* series as occurrences which may not necessarily be of the science fiction model (Bayer-Berenbaun 25). Even with the allusion to the science fiction aspects of the *Dark Tower* series, there is a Gothic twist added to the extraordinary mental states and scientific innovation as "discoveries in the scientific only served to aggravate a sense of alienation and further disturb notions of human identity" (Punter and Byron 20). Science then becomes not solely a matter of speculation and the rational but an offshoot of the Gothic as the use of logic and technology leads the people of Mid-World farther and farther away from their own humanity, or what Roland calls the Prim. The Old Ones meet a Gothic ending in that their technology took over their lives and eventually destroyed them, and it is clear that the people behind the Sombra Corporation and North Central Positronics are taking the people of Keystone Earth in the same direction. While this is just one other instance of the repetitious nature of Roland's world and his quest, "for repetition is indeed a feature of many Gothic works," there must be some significant point to these Gothic connections and initial observations (Punter and Byron 284). As the Gothic can be viewed as a genre which fails to adequately sustain itself as something more than just a presence in the *Dark Tower* series, a genre which simply describes many aspects of Roland's journey, there is more to consider with regard to the applicability of this genre to the gunslinger's voyage. With confirmation that unstable geographies, double-identities/characters, exceptional mental abilities, repetition and the dark side of science are all present within the Gothic frame and are all witnessed in Roland's tale, there is most definitely something of importance to the climax of the story that can be concluded with this information.

With a prevalent theme of Roland's story being devoted to the Gothic, it stands to reason that his journey connects with that of the aimless wanderer, one who revels in the chaos and destitution surrounding him despite his sentiments to the contrary. This certainly keeps Roland's adventure in the realm of the Gothic, as "the Gothic quest is for the random, the wild, and the unbound," suggesting that

Roland's journey for the Tower has little direction and it takes him from the security of being an apprentice gunslinger in Gilead to the uncharted territory of his world, a space in which he loses his friends and becomes the *last* gunslinger (Bayer-Berenbaun 29). One of the causes for the instability which Roland encounters is the crumbling state of the Tower and its effects on his world, and with the sickness of the Tower seeping out and causing disarray, Gilead falls to the rebel forces of John Farson. The defeat of the Gunslingers and the deterioration of Gilead at the hands of Farson and his men, presumably enabled by the deteriorating state of the Tower, eventually leads the Constant Reader to a lonely and callous gunslinger, which comes about due to yet another Gothic twist as, "the Gothic novel has been continuously associated with revolution and anarchy" (Bayer-Berenbaun 42). As Roland witnesses such revolt and carries the affects with him, mostly in the form of nostalgia and even vengeance, his quest becomes devoted to restoring some sort of order. Yet, if the gunslinger were truly motivated and enamored with chaos and destruction, as might be expected of a Gothic protagonist, then the quest he describes to all he encounters as a journey to save the world brings about questions of the usefulness of the Gothic formula for discovering why Roland quests for the Tower.

It should be considered that "the Gothic mind at once admires the tyrant and supports the collapse of institutions" (Bayer-Berenbaun 44). The gunslinger can be seen as a tyrant in his endeavor to possibly raise himself to the status of a god in his pursuit of the Dark Tower, but Roland's quest is primarily concerned with the restoration of the Dark Tower. If Roland can be seen as one who is consumed with desire for power, then the Gothic genre certainly illuminates Roland's character and his motive within such a position. However, the role of the tyrant, or specifically the Crimson King, who wishes to bring about the destruction of the Tower, becomes Roland's sworn enemy once the Crimson King's identity and intentions are made known. Still, Heidi Strengell suggests reconsideration of Roland's position as he "also possesses qualities of the tyrant-leader at the beginning of the quest.

He is ready to sacrifice anything to reach the tower and uses others as tools to achieve this goal" (134). Roland's perpetual questing has brought nothing but death and destruction, and the losses of those closest to him do not deter Roland from continuing on his journey. Stephen King says as much in *The Drawing of the Three*: "Roland loved her [Susannah] because she would fight and never give in; he feared for her because he knew he would sacrifice her—Eddie as well—without a question or a look back" (402). While this confirms Roland's lack of humanity, Roland reneges on this sentiment in *Wizard and Glass*— "'What you call "the bottom line," Eddie, is this; I get my friends killed. And I'm not sure I can even risk doing that again'" (King 664). What is telling about Roland here is that he is not entirely convinced of his new attitude toward the purpose of his companions as a means to the end of the Dark Tower.

Roland's indecision and vague indication of change, that being the transition from cold-hearted loner to loving *dinh*, does not entirely settle the intimations of the Gothic presence in his story, as "the characters in Gothic novels are usually hyper-self-conscious. They scour the depths of their own intentions, questioning not only their actions and perceptions but their motivations and fantasies as well" (Bayer-Berenbaun 38). Whatever Roland's ultimate choice—stoic killer or compassionate leader—he remains a mystery to the reader, especially as he is more than willing to leave the Devar-Toi to save Stephen King moments after his friend and companion Eddie Dean dies, even though he also shortly afterwards shows a rare display of emotion when Jake Chambers dies, reluctantly leaving his surrogate son behind in the earth to, once again, move on in his quest. Even if Roland escapes the label of a tyrannical figure who seeks the Tower for his own personal ends, Roland still seeks the Tower despite the overwhelming uncertainty of what he will find at the Tower, and at the cost of losing his friends and companions. Death becomes an inevitable part of Roland's quest, with the exception of his own death, which is an implicit means of empowerment for the gunslinger. With Roland as the survivor, the most skilled of his class and the chosen leader of his ka-tets, the gunslinger is placed into a position of great power and even authority. In a Gothic context, this comes about as "the Gothic fascination with death and decay involve an admiration for power at the expense of beauty" (Bayer-Berenbaun 27). With that said, the goal of the Gothic hero, at least concerning the *Dark Tower* series, is to attain power.

The Epic hero is primarily concerned with honor and duty, traits specific to the individual, usually acting for the sake and benefit of his community, and in the Western tradition, as civilization becomes the focus of the hero, the aim of the hero moves beyond the self to the development of the world around him. With the Gothic there is not only an inversion of previous traditions but that the primary end of the Gothic hero is not just a return to the individual, but a return that allows the hero to act for himself or herself, complete with a newfound form of power, suggesting that the purpose of Roland's quest is the attainment of power. The Tower is perceived to promise this power within Randall Flagg's mind, and Roland, too, looks to have this thought in mind throughout the *Dark Tower* series. Unfortunately, the ambiguity of Roland's professed intentions prevents confirmation of this conclusion. For example, when Roland and Susannah reach the Castle of the Crimson King in the seventh book, it is suggested to Roland that he need not continue his search for the Tower despite his intentions and promise to do so: the Crimson King's steward Rando Thoughtful/Austin Cornwell asks Roland, "'To *whom* have you given your promise? . . . For there is no prophecy of such a promise'" (King, *The Dark Tower* 610). Roland then indicates that his quest is self-imposed, and is done so without any more reason than a child's response of *just because*: "'There wouldn't be [a prophecy]. For it's [the promise] one I made myself, and one I mean to keep'" (King, *The Dark Tower* 610). Even as Roland makes this promise to himself to seek and find the Dark Tower, and as Rando Thoughtful/Austin Cornwell seems to be genuine in his warning to Roland to "show sense before it's too late for sense and *stay away from the Dark Tower*," it is too speculative to conclude that Roland makes this promise for his own potential gain, or at least for the acquisition of power (King, *The Dark Tower* 617). However, when Tony Magistrale says of the Gothic genre that it is, "more than just atmosphere and indulgence; it is also a serious means of presenting the fundamental dangers—both personal and social—that are the consequences of amoral behavior," it can be concluded that while the gunslinger neither professes any desire to attain power nor directly plots to gain an elevated position, the atmosphere of morality linked to allusions of power is more revealing than a sustained focus on power itself within the Gothic template (*Second Decade* 145). All things considered, the gunslinger is a character whose morals and ethics come into constant question, but a study of his ideologies is almost as fruitless as the attempt to understand his motives and goals via the Gothic.

It may seem likely that Roland quests for power if his tale is isolated in Gothic restraints, but even more important to remember is the macrocosmic nature of Roland's quest—it is about more than one man and one world, and Roland admits this to Eddie in *The Drawing of the Three*: "There's more than a world to win, Eddie. I would not risk you and her—I would not have allowed the boy to die—if that was all there was" (King 405). If it is believed that Roland sacrifices the lives of his companions for a greater purpose, possibly negating the questions of morality connected with this genre, then the Gothic genre fails as a whole as the appropriate lens of understanding Roland's ultimate objective.

Post-Apocalyptic—A Time of Renewal

So far, three distinct genres have suggested three potential goals of Roland's quest—Duty, Civilization, and Power—and it has been claimed that none of these goals are the final aim of the gunslinger. Now that the progression has moved from the Gothic, a genre of the broken and deformed, the Post-Apocalyptic theme of the *Dark Tower* series enters the discussion with not a fascination with the broken in and of itself, but an examination and careful consideration of the causes and effects of ruination in the gunslinger's world. Early on in Roland's tale, readers see that the land through which he journeys has undergone some traumatic changes in the landscape and is also a scene in which various forms of technology have been rendered all but powerless. Even though Mid-World has seen its share of devastation and destruction, suggesting that Roland's world has already experienced an apocalypse of a sort, a better suited course of analysis is to view Roland's world as one that is in the middle of an apocalypse. In seeing the gunslinger's world leaning toward the End of Days, but not quite completely fallen to total destruction, his quest looks to be well placed within the *Post*-Apocalyptic novel by way of the allusions to some previous cataclysms. And the desolate land of the gunslinger's world implies that his quest of saving the Dark Tower is aimed at preventing the most common climax of an apocalypse—complete ruin.

Before focusing completely on the end of the world, it must be said that apocalypse is not just about a final judgment. As Heidi Strengell says, "although the apocalypse is frequently associated with the end of the world and the postcatastrophic scene, it also celebrates the birth of a new world" (132). What Strengell proposes is important in that as Roland may wish to prevent the end of existence by saving the Dark Tower, the anticipated result of his success is the salvation of Mid-World, complete with a hope that the saved world would prosper, similar to the golden-age promised in the Western genre. Even as the post-apocalyptic also deals with religious roots, there is a tendency to neglect the religious allusions of the apocalypse as it applies to Roland's world. Yet considerations of religion lead to a clearer understanding of Roland's world and his journey, especially as John R. May elucidates the necessity of religious exploration and clarification within the apocalyptic model by stating, "the import of the apocalypse as it developed in the Hebrew and Christian canons had nothing to do with holding the carrot of eternity before the believers' noses" (17). In thinking that the apocalypse does not represent an ending, or a completely religious ending, the conclusion that the apocalypse is more of a cyclical nature than one promising a true end may be believed, as suggested by John R. May's basic template of the apocalypse as being comprised of "judgment, catastrophe, [and] renewal" (209). Of course, the cyclical nature here seems to be a major influence on Roland's journey, especially concerning the last pages of *The Dark Tower*. Still, renewal and repetition are apparently inevitable in the apocalyptic/post-apocalyptic realm, especially as, "in Judeo-Christian apocalypse, time is irreversible" (May 210). The same is certainly true for the gunslinger: each time he resumes his quest—"'What do you mean, resume? I never left off'"—the world moves on with him (King, *The Gunslinger* 212). Gilead is never restored, Roland is not given a chance to go back to Jericho Hill to change the fate of his fellow gunslingers, or even pick up the Horn of Eld himself, and when he is seen in the Mohaine Desert once again on the trail of the Man in Black, he may not quite be exactly back at the beginning.

Traveling with Roland along the Path of the Beam towards End-World, a land that has seen its share of devastation, readers walk with Roland in an apocalyptic land that positions him to constantly move forward and yet still seek some sort of connection with the past. With the inevitable movement into the future—never backwards—the apocalyptic essence of Roland's quest takes on more than the typical feel of survival coupled with the constant questioning of *what went wrong*, or even what preventative measures could have been taken. In other words, "apocalypse is a response to cultural crisis. It grows out of that sense of loss that results from the passing of an old-world view" (May 19). If this claim is applied to Roland and his motivation for seeking the Dark Tower, readers would be essentially revisiting the role civilization plays as the ultimate end of the Western novel, but the twist within the post-apocalyptic thematic is that nostalgia and regret play more prominent roles than the attempted establishment of a particular way of life. While Roland may not be able to re-create the court of Gilead in Mid-World, the role he plays in adjusting and responding to the apocalypse may afford him an opportunity to at least renew the ancient way of life Gilead reflected, much like in the Western. But before accepting renewal as not just the second step in Roland's quest—the reformation of his ka-tet as implicated by the subtitle "Renewal" in *The Drawing of the Three*—the final destination and purpose of Roland's quest, and the basics of the post-apocalyptic genre, need to be examined.

Stepping back to see what leads up to the *need* and *desire* to recall a past that has been destroyed, the Post-Apocalyptic genre as a step-by-step progression initiates expectations of an apocalyptic text, and a ten-point template, as provided by R. W. B. Lewis, is as follows:

1. Periodic natural disasters, earthquakes and the like; 2. the advent and the turbulent reign of the Antichrist or the false Christ or false prophet; 3. the second coming of Christ and 4. the resulting cosmic warfare (Armageddon) that brings in 5. the millennium—that is, from the Latin, the period of one thousand years, the epoch of the Messianic Kingdom upon earth; thereafter, 6. the gradual degeneration of human and physical nature, the last and worst apostasy (or falling away from God), featured by 7. the second and briefer "loosing of Satan"; 8. an ultimate catastrophe, the end of the world by fire; 9. the Last Judgment; and 10. the appearance of the new heaven and earth. [196-7]

Right away heavy religious implications are seen in this model, but with simple substitution—like John Farson in the place of the False Prophet, or even proposing that "the Man in Black's actions identify him as a manipulative demonic agent, the apocalyptic False Prophet"—this formula can be secularized, but even with a few creative twists and interpretations, skepticism comes as no surprise as failure has already occurred with the three previous genres in adequately determining Roland's actual purpose (Egan, "Gothic Western" 103). Nonetheless, the discussion begins with the first step in the apocalyptic progression, natural disaster, and the claim can be made that the Beamquakes

Roland witnesses are an appropriate marker of the beginning of an apocalypse. Six Beamquakes will, as far as the Constant Reader knows, lead to the fall of the Tower and initiate the end of existence. Also, the thinnies Roland and his companions discover, "'places where the fabric of existence is almost entirely worn away,'" function as sporadic natural disasters of a sort (*Wizard and Glass* 66). The source of these disruptions in the natural order of Roland's world are easily recognizable and observed in the texts comprising the *Dark Tower* series, even including the presumed man-made disasters seen in the waste lands outside of Lud and in the badlands around the Castle of the Crimson King.

The second through the fifth points of the apocalyptic progression are ones that look outside of Roland's where and when and bring readers into the realm of the biblical where a stretch of the imagination is needed to find events and characters in the *Dark Tower* series to fit the post-apocalyptic mold and to foreground the end of renewal that has been suggested. With the arrival and the reign of the Anti-Christ, or the False Prophet, John Farson could represent this character. Farson's rhetoric—"'Ask not what the good man can do for you . . .'"—and the war he wages on the gunslingers places him and his politics well in the position of a False Prophet as he opposes the establishment, Gilead, and the sacredness and dignity for which this city stands to protect and honor (King, *The Gunslinger* 108). The third point in the apocalyptic model, however, poses a problem for the purposes of this exploration as the "second coming" of Christ does not occur in the *Dark Tower* series. Roland doesn't even hold to any faith worshipping this deity, despite the number of believers readers come across in Roland's journey. But, by the furthest stretch of the imagination, one might consider Roland to be a Christ-figure, one who acts as a conduit for the Prim and the White to return to Mid-World, which would make his quest appear as a second coming of sorts. Heidi Strengell takes the idea of Roland being a Christ-figure a bit further when she suggests that Roland and Jake are not completely separate characters, and that Roland's sacrifice of the boy Jake is almost like Roland sacrificing a part of himself: "Roland is also Jake. In this sense he sacrifices himself for human kind. [...] Like Jesus this Messiah is tempted: he could turn around and take Jake with him" (131). *If* it is accepted that the return of Christ occurs in King's tale through Roland, then the fourth point of the apocalyptic template can be approached as just another formula being adhered to in *The Dark Tower*: Armageddon.

The "cosmic warfare" that Armageddon suggests is usually the focal point of most discussions of the apocalypse as it is the event that brings about the destruction and desolation usually associated with apocalypse; also to note is that post-apocalypse typically implies a scene witnessed *after* the cause of the chaos has come to pass. In the *Dark Tower* series, however, the closest thing to Armageddon is the last stand of the gunslingers as Jericho Hill. Even though there are allusions to nuclear holocausts throughout Roland's story, these modern representations of Armageddon are never actually witnessed in *The Dark Tower*. Although it would be safe to say that these assumptions are most likely correct, the scale of these incidents becomes problematic for a general understanding of Armageddon, which would be *complete* ruin. However, Roland's world only experiences minor battles and events which suggest a minuscule reflection of what total Armageddon would cause. And as Roland's world does not necessarily experience Armageddon, there are further problems with the post-apocalyptic template in that the "millennium" which constitutes the fifth point in the apocalyptic progression never comes to pass. If there ever was a Messianic Kingdom in Mid-World, a period of roughly one thousand years of harmony, it might be considered the time of Roland's youth. But Gilead falls, and along with it a golden age ceases, which hearkens towards the sixth point of the apocalyptic template with the gradual degeneration of humanity. Various examples of the degeneration of mankind are seen as Farson comes to power in the West, the citizens of Mejis burn Susan Delgado at the stake in a display of mob madness, and even in what might be considered as an age of fidelity Gabrielle

Deschain strays from her husband's bed and into the arms of Marten Broadcloak. But, going further back in time before the fall of Gilead, the social decline observed in the *Dark Tower* actually begins with the Old Ones, whose reliance upon technology replaces an important element in the gunslinger's tale, that of faith.

When it comes to issues of faith, and not necessarily that of religious devotion, Cuthbert Allgood reminds readers that many of the gunslingers, those who are apparently charged with protecting the Dark Tower, do not even believe in the existence of this structure: "'There *is* no Tower, Roland,' Cuthbert said patiently. 'I don't know what you saw in that glass ball, but there is no Tower. Well, as a symbol, I suppose—like Arthur's Cup, or the Cross of the man-Jesus—but not as a real thing, a real building'" (King, *Wizard and Glass* 580). Even though readers and Roland later learn that the Tower does actually exist, Cuthbert's skepticism can be excused as the Tower was kept as a secret by the elder gunslingers. What this leads towards is an indication of the waning humanity in the court of Gilead as the gunslingers, perhaps shrouded in pride, would not let their own children know of the existence of the Dark Tower. While the senior gunslingers may be pardoned for this omission of information because there existed the possibility that their children would be sent west and possibly become threats to Gilead and the Tower, the implicit isolation of the gunslingers as the dominant individuals of Mid-World makes them susceptible to the onslaught of Farson and his men, who act on behalf of the Crimson King, a character some associate with the devil. As to whether or not the Crimson King's association with Satan and his plans for bringing the Dark Tower down fits the seventh point of the apocalyptical model—a return of Satan—is up to the reader to decide. But even as the last five premises of the post-apocalyptic model have proven to be problematic, the final three points of the apocalyptic model prove to be much more difficult to work with. As it stands, Roland's quest as seen in terms of the post-apocalyptic is certainly curious and interesting, but hardly enlightening.

In considering the last points of the post-apocalyptic model, Roland's journey into End-World shows no clear connection or even an allusion to a disastrous cataclysm facing the entire world, a Last Judgment, or even the appearance of a "new heaven and earth." Some may consider the scene at the end of the seventh book in the series when Roland is pulled through the door at the top of a Tower as a form of judgment, or even an accounting. Yet, even through a loose interpretation concerning the "catastrophe" and then considering Roland's resumption of his quest as a final judgment, it is difficult to regard the world in which Roland finds himself as one that is a "new earth." And although the *Dark Tower* is certainly out of place within a rigid adherence to the Post-Apocalyptic model, when Roland and his ka-tet liberate the Breakers of Blue Heaven and save the Shardik-Maturin Beam, the post-apocalyptic theme of renewal does come to pass. Additionally, with the regeneration of the Beams beginning, and the promise that the other Beams will begin to renew themselves in due time, Roland's quest comes to an end at this point in the Post-Apocalyptic genre. A new time is on the horizon, much like the "golden age" one comes to expect at the end of a Western novel, and Roland has saved the Tower. But this does not signal the end of the Post-Apocalyptic in *The Dark Tower*. Within the Post-Apocalyptic frame, there can be no renewal without the ultimate desiccation of the land by the "ultimate catastrophe" or the Last Judgment. Roland's quest, at this juncture, would have to be about salvation, and not necessarily personal salvation, as a true renewal cannot occur, theoretically, without the fulfillment of the final points of the apocalyptical formula. Renewal is at best a means to an end, but it is not Roland's climax, which is not saving the Dark Tower but entering it and even understanding its mysteries.

After four genres have been examined, and after four tries of attempting to find answers to questions as to why Roland seeks the Tower, one more genre remains: science fiction. And keep in mind that the progression of these genres also serves as a metaphorical template for Roland's own personal development: as each genre moves back and forth between a focus on the individual only to return to a concentration on the larger scope existing outside of the individual, a return to the individual waits on the horizon, and one of literature's outcasts will finally reveal what has been sought.

Science Fiction—The Pursuit of Knowledge

In nearing the end of the discussion, complete with previously unanswered questions concerning genre and its influence on climax, the realm of science fiction, unfortunately, poses plenty of problems as well. Above all else, Carl Freedman claims that concerning the science fiction genre, "no definitional consensus exists" (13). Moreover, Brian Stableford says that "science fiction is something of an anomaly. There is no typical science fictional climax which exists in parallel with the typical climaxes of detective stories, genre romances, thrillers, Westerns, horror stories, or heroic fantasies" (8). While this does not bode well at its most basic level, especially as "science fiction has no typical action or place," there are, nonetheless, various aspects of science fiction to work with in order to move on with a purposeful analysis (Gunn 6). In fact, science fiction is the most telling genre in terms of climax in *The Dark Tower* series.

First, there is the technological side to science fiction that asks for attention as Roland's adventure sees its share of scientific innovation—the Wolves, Blaine the Mono, Andy the Messenger Robot, and even the simple forms of technology like electric lights and gas-powered machines. But, beyond the common technological aspects of science fiction, consider the general foundation or beginning for most science fiction authors: "Most speculative writing is basically a response to the opening question 'what would happen if . . . ?'" (Ash 11).

With this question, science fiction considers imaginative realms that are unfamiliar but not entirely surprising; science fiction takes what is known and what is conceivable, regardless of its improbability, and takes "the reader far beyond the boundaries of his or her own mundane environment, into strange, awe-inspiring realms thought to be in fact unknown, or at least largely unknown, but not in principle unknowable" (Freedman 15).

Here science fiction takes on a mildly Gothic feel as the unknown comes into the picture, but, more importantly, science fiction delves into the realm of not simply what is unknown but rather what can be known and is awaiting discovery. In the context of Roland's quest, he may not be a scientist looking to develop or improve society through technological innovation, but as science fiction implicitly deals with discovery and knowledge, the mysteries of the Dark Tower ask for nothing less than exploration and contemplation if not outright comprehension. Also, Roland has promised himself to *find* the Tower, to discover it, and also to unravel its mysteries, and while this may not be what is typically expected of science fiction, it is certainly an appropriate lens through which his quest might finally be understood.

Science fiction should be treated and understood as not necessarily a genre which deals with future possibility, but one that places the characters in a scene which asks for immediate attention and uncanny cunning in order to survive a startling and surprising situation. While this view may be a bit convenient for the sake of application to the *Dark Tower* series, science fiction does involve, above all things, adaptability. In dealing with rampant machinery, questionable innovations, and even strange beings, all things one would typically expect in a science fiction work and things readers witness in the *Dark Tower* series, each of these scenarios involves the ability to adjust and adapt to a given scenario. As Carol Colatrella implies the same notion when she says, "while science fiction remains interested in the empowering possibilities of technology [. . .] it also tries very hard to figure out the mistakes we made getting here," science fiction is depicted as a genre that requires of its characters a keen curiosity aimed at embracing change and working to solve potential problems (562). Or, as Tom Moylan notes, "science fiction demonstrates our incapacity to imagine the future and brings us down to earth to apprehend our present in all its limitations"

(42). Fortunately for Roland, "he had in his long life been nothing if not adaptable" (King, *The Gunslinger* 4).

Adaptability is nothing, however, without knowledge: in order for the characters in a science fiction novel to succeed, they must have knowledge that facilitates their adaptability. In order to defeat the forces run amok found in a typical science fiction novel, one would have to know *how* the machine works in order to find its weakness. Or, for Roland to save the Tower, he would need to learn how to save it. Even after he learns to do so as he becomes aware of the Breakers in *Wolves of the Calla* and concludes that the Tower itself is ailing because of the weakened Beams, the Tower still promises knowledge, which stretches beyond Roland's initial goal of saving the Tower. And this lure of the unknown is common enough to classify as a science fiction motif. Sidestepping the primary objective of a science fiction novel—knowledge—for a moment, it is important to look at some of the other components of science fiction to validate this end and to show how Roland's quest moves in this direction.

To start, "it is quite possible to class almost the entire serious side of the [science fiction] genre under divergent headings of 'utopia' and 'anti-utopia' writing, in which the future is seen as more (or less) agreeable than the present day" (Ash 3). In thinking of science fiction as a genre which deals with states of social perfection, or at least a preferable state of a specific community, and that the quest in this scene is aimed at achieving perfection by any means necessary and most likely through technological innovation, the story of the *Dark Tower* serves as a parallel to this template with the history of the Old Ones. The attempt to better the world before the gunslinger's time was achieved by technological means, and with the direction Keystone Earth takes in the series as prompted by the Sombra Corporation and North Central Positronics, the world of Eddie, Susannah, and Jake moves towards a science fiction utopia. Even though the literal definition of the word utopia—no place, no where—implies that such a state of existence is impossible, Roland's quixotic quest is nonetheless focused on setting up a new world order based on what he has learned (which certainly resonates with elements of the Western and the Gothic). But Roland lacks the knowledge to do so, and there is much placed in Roland's road which certainly limits his attainment of this information.

Science fiction brings to the table the formula of obstacle/response, or rather that of escape/resolution. Science fiction also suggests a scene of failure in some form and the resulting response of those who are faced with this breakdown. Not only does science fiction constantly ask "what if" when shaping the plot of a particular tale, science fiction seems to also ask, beyond the basic plot element of conflict, the question of how one would respond in a rather extraordinary situation. The end result, whether the hero wins through or not, is that knowledge is acquired. Of course, many threats in science fiction come about due to unwieldy knowledge, and as science, in general, attempts to harness knowledge by breaking things down into understandable units, the attempt at some manner of mastery serves as a constant form of motivation. And Roland becomes a character in the *Dark Tower* whose lack of imagination becomes one of his biggest impositions; Roland cannot be satisfied with saving the worlds by saving the Beams, and he cannot simply wonder at the marvel of the Tower in and of itself. And this brings up a key theme of science fiction to situate alongside knowledge: the theme of wonderment.

Characters in a science fiction novel often lack imagination—they are comfortable to a point in that most critical thinking is cast aside, both logical and creative. As Jonathan Davis implies of science fiction, the people in these tales tend to "fail to realize what their mechanical babies will someday require of them" (*Stephen King's America* 71). In addition to this claim, Tony Magistrale asserts that "throughout the greater body of his fiction, Stephen King addresses the dual genies of science and technology gone bad—the dim results of man's irresponsibility and subsequent loss of control over those things which he himself has created" (*Moral* 27). Therefore, it is the regeneration of the imagination, accompanied by a sense of responsibility, which allows the characters to win through; science put these characters into a dire situation, along with a clear misunderstanding or misuse of whatever threat is running rampant, and their humanity is what will help them to succeed. However, the movement from the rationality of science back to the emotional nature of the human needs some sort of catalyst, and readers see this play out in the *Dark Tower* series, first with the Old Ones who thrived in an age of innovation but later renounced their ways and tried to recapture the magic that they had abandoned because they witnessed the folly of their faith in technology. Readers also witness complacency due to rationality as they travel with Roland into New York as he chastises the citizens of New York for having no sense of awe or imagination to balance out their overly rational minds that have begun to take technology as a matter of course:

> Here he was in a world which struck him dumb with fresh wonders seemingly at every step, a world where carriages flew through the air and paper seemed as cheap as sand. And the newest wonder was simply that for these people, wonder had run out: here, in a place of miracles, he only saw dull faces and plodding bodies. [King, *The Drawing of the Three* 366]

As Roland critiques the citizens of New York, he would do well to look at himself in the same light, but even if the gunslinger were to gain an imagination and a sense of wonderment that might aid him on his quest, one still must consider that Roland's enlightenment may not be needed, especially if it is suggested that the Tower should fall at the hands of the Crimson King and his son Mordred. With this thought, science and science fiction each seem to come with a cost/benefit scenario, and with Roland storming the Tower and ascending it, a backwards step must be taken in order to question what the cost of Roland's pursuit of knowledge is.

Knowledge, for all of its benefits within a science fiction model, carries with it some dangers and prompts caution. There is the idea that there are some things that individuals cannot or should not know, and that the pursuit of such knowledge is complete foolishness and encumbered with pride. If the Dark Tower is the great mystery of Roland's world, and if his quest is driven by knowledge more than anything else, questions arise as to whether or not Roland should even journey beyond the Castle of the Crimson King, if it is necessary for him to "'pass beyond ka itself'" (King, *The Dark Tower* 609). Perhaps the gunslinger may not need to actually enter the Dark Tower in End-World for his quest to be successful, which suggests that the knowledge Roland seeks by continuing his quest is not necessary, or that this knowledge is even purposely denied to Roland as each time he reaches the top of the Tower he is still left with all the questions he had at the foot of the building and no answers to take with him back into the desert. For the purpose of analyzing the use of knowledge in Roland's quest, his potential justification of seeking the Tower must be analyzed and critiqued to see if his search for knowledge is valid. With this prompting, focus shifts to what Roger Shattuck calls *forbidden knowledge*, the kind of knowledge Roland may be seeking, and of which Shattuck gives six categories: "1. Inaccessible, unattainable knowledge; 2. Knowledge prohibited by divine, religious, Moral, or secular authority; 3. Dangerous, destructive or unwelcome knowledge; 4. Fragile, delicate knowledge; 5. Knowledge double-bound; 6. Ambiguous knowledge" (327).

To explain the first category of forbidden knowledge, Shattuck explains it as follows: "Some aspects of the cosmos—of 'reality'—cannot be reached by human faculties. [. . .] inaccessibility springs either from the inadequacy of human powers or from the remoteness of realms presumed to exist in ways inconceivable to us" (328). If the Dark Tower is the daunting enigma it is reported as being, a vessel which encompasses and maintains existence, then the goal of comprehending the nature of *everything* is understandable, as such questions of existence cross most people's minds. Also, consider what Walter says to Roland in the golgotha: "'The greatest mystery the universe offers is not life but size. Size encompasses life, and the Tower encompasses size'" (King, *The Gunslinger* 221). And if the Tower encompasses size, it is certain that the Tower is the nexus of all the worlds and contains *everything* in existence. But, the knowledge that the Tower promises cannot be grasped by Roland as Walter generously warns Roland that, "'Size defeats us'" (King, *The Gunslinger* 221). If the Tower does promise knowledge of the infinite and the unknown, the adventurer who seeks such understanding may be better off knowing that, perhaps, "it is simply the nature of things, including ourselves, that prevents us from knowing everything" (Shattuck 328). The second category of forbidden knowledge that Shattuck provides, prohibited knowledge, makes sense within a civilized setting, but with respect to Roland's quest, nothing really prohibits him from attempting to gain the knowledge he believes awaits him in the Tower. Yet, considering the third category of forbidden knowledge, dangerous knowledge, one may hold on to the hope that Roland would exercise discretion at the prospect of learning what is to be learned, if anything, upon a successful completion of his quest that might prove to be perilous.

Regardless of the substance and nature of the knowledge Roland may find at the Tower, Shattuck states that, "simple prudence should impel us to take careful account of such dangerous forms of dangerous knowledge" (331). The unknown danger that may result in Roland's acquisition of knowledge, despite the potential benefits, lends credence to the claim that, "in some circumstances, the truth survives better veiled than naked" (Shattuck 331). If Roland were to learn of the great mysteries of the universe, and even comprehend them, his suspect nature makes it clear that he may not use his newfound knowledge for the best reasons. The gunslinger may not strive to be the godhead like Randall Flagg, but Roland's character is certainly questionable enough to wonder, with caution, as to what he might do with the knowledge he seeks.

Moving on to Shattuck's fourth category of forbidden knowledge, fragile knowledge, this is an area of knowledge with which Roland actually has much experience. He has dealt with this brand of knowledge several times throughout his quest, most notably concerning his knowledge of Susannah's pregnancy with Mia's child, Mordred. As Roland discovers Susannah's pregnancy before the others in his ka-tet, he keeps to his own counsel for the sake of keeping cover if Mia proves to be an enemy (which she does) and to keep his ka-tet intact as the information is certainly precarious. Roland undoubtedly knows that some knowledge is better left alone, or at least unstated, due to its volatility and potential for chaos, and he would then do well do remember that, "fragile knowledge finds its natural home in the domains of discretion and privacy" (Shattuck 332). The key word to this claim is "privacy," especially as it relates to the gunslinger's goal; Roland does not even consider that the reason for the Dark Tower's location, wheels and wheels from civilization, may be for the purpose of seclusion, which would help ensure the safekeeping of the fragile knowledge it presumably contains. However, Roland does not consider this as he pushes on to End-World in his never-ending pursuit of the Tower. Perhaps this can be explained by Shattuck's fifth category of forbidden knowledge, knowledge double-bound, or knowledge that seeks to reconcile the subjective and the objective. In this type of forbidden knowledge, Shattuck explains that, "we cannot know something by both means at the same time. The attempt to reconcile the two or to alternate between them leads to great mental stress. [For example] Losing culture while being immersed in another" (332). Roland's quest, and the knowledge he desires, comes from a completely subjective point of view. As he charged himself with his quest and initially learned of the Tower from no source but his own poorly-drawn conclusion as prompted by the Wizard's Rainbow, Roland then tries to present his quest from an objective standpoint. He believes he knows what he must do, but without the confirmation from an outside and impartial observer, Roland's quest is undertaken with the zeal and purpose drawn from within and with no true purpose other than what Roland himself attributes to the quest. And Roland does so even though, "hard as we may try, we cannot be both inside and outside an experience or life—even our own" (Shattuck 334). Still, the nature of Roland's quest tries to understand his quest from both positions. Even if Roland were to abandon his endeavor to be both inside his own life, the quest for the Tower, and outside of it, looking at it in an objective manner to give the quest purpose and even meaning, he would still be faced with the last category of forbidden knowledge, ambiguous knowledge.

Shattuck explains the last classification of forbidden knowledge as "a condition in which what we know reverses itself right under our noses, confounds us by turning into its opposite" (335). Surely, there is no clearer indication of the futility of Roland's quest for knowledge it would have to be the ambiguous nature of the Dark Tower: it appears as a building, it is thought of as Gan's Navel, and while the Tower functions as both a symbol and a living being, every time Roland reaches the Tower it changes. Recall that as Roland ascends the stairs to the top of the Tower and looks into each room, they compose a series of snapshots of Roland's life, and assuming that each repetition of Roland's quest is at least slightly different than the prior journey, readers can also assume that the inside of the Tower changes to adapt to the new adventures Roland experiences on the road to the Dark Tower. Even though Roland cannot truly know what the Tower is because of its liveliness and its constant changes, he still moves on with the foolish hope that knowledge can be attained.

Although the genre of science fiction appears to be little more than a shrouded backdrop to *The Dark Tower* series with technological fear, robots, and travel between the worlds presented as commonplace and somewhat uninteresting when considering the larger scope of the series, the roots of science fiction are helpful for understanding the gunslinger's quest. Knowledge is needed for the gunslinger to fix the land which surrounds him, and the Dark Tower is supposed to contain and promise this knowledge, which suggests that a science fiction scenario takes place in the *Dark Tower* books. With information being the key to survival, at least within this genre, Roland's journey for the Dark Tower should not necessarily be seen as wholly ignoble or born out of pride. Yet this is not to say that neither pride nor fame are absent from the gunslinger's quest. In light of what the Dark Tower represents and what the gunslinger believes he can discover within this structure, the overwhelming question to ask is if anyone can blame Roland for trying to find the Tower and enter it, for going on a quest that he presents as one destined to save all of existence yet seems to be nothing more than a Faustian quest for knowledge at the cost of Roland's soul.

An Age of Anxiety

While it has been proposed that the ultimate goal of Roland's quest is for knowledge, despite the inherent dangers of seeking and using such knowledge, there are still questions concerning the role of the *Dark Tower* series as a lengthy volume concerned with the pursuit of knowledge within the contemporary society it was written. Although King's tale stretches across thirty years of real-time, half of Roland's tale—books V-VII, and even the revised version of volume I—is written in the 21st century, an age of information and also post-9/11 fears. This is important to consider, as "literature expresses and discusses under various shapes, as elegantly and masterly as its exponents are able, the prevailing ideas concerning the problems, material and metaphysical, of the current hour" (Summers 17). If the preceding is accepted, and if it is also accepted that the overarching aim of Roland's quest is for knowledge, what can be concluded of Stephen King's *Dark Tower* series? Can it be seen primarily as a reflection of contemporary insecurities and worries? Marleen Barr believes that this is the case as she says that "science fiction permeates reality. Science fiction permeates literary fiction" (437). Within this reality that extends beyond fiction, James Egan also observes a link between make-believe and the world at large when he says that, "beneath the mayhem which permeates King's fiction lie interrelated, troubling questions about the power, extent, and validity of science and rationalism in contemporary society" ("Technohorror" 47). As it were, perhaps King is highlighting modern-day atrocities and horrors by way of the gunslinger, a character that seeks knowledge and the progression of his quest with little consideration for who is affected, neglected, and even cast aside in the wake of ambition and a myopic world view.

Literature has often been understood as a distant window through which people can look into for a glimpse of a given society or culture, and the window into the gunslinger's world looks right back into the world in which King lives and writes, reflecting an image of not only passion but unbridled zeal aimed towards questionable goals. As Stephen King departs from his typical style of horror—typical, that is, in the eyes of those who corner King as a horror writer—and brings in many different genres to compose what some consider as his magnum opus, it must be noted that the complexity of modern living cannot be encapsulated by just one genre. One analysis of the mixing and blending of various genres, complete with their cultural stigmas of a variety of anxieties and which blurs the reader's vision of a specific fear, is the idea that ambiguity and lack of overall structure is the most prominent fear facing contemporary society. Roland's blind quest, cloaked in an array of genres, themes and styles, seems to adequately reflect the state of the average individual, one who exists in a world of complication yet endless possibility; however, this structure of multiplicity promises no structure at all. Knowledge, then, promises some sort of control and stability which Roland cannot be condemned for attempting to acquire, even though his aspirations lead to nothing but repetition. But one can still question whether or not Roland will learn what the cost of such knowledge is.

Again, if it is accepted that Roland endures the road of trials which mark the way to the Dark Tower—losing his fingers, his friends and even his humanity—for the sake of knowledge, then it is appropriate, like Roland, to return to the beginning of his quest. At first, most readers cannot decide whether or not Roland is a hero, a protagonist, or if he is an anti-hero, a despicable man who beds Allie in the town of Tull simply for information and lets a young Jake Chambers fall beneath the Cyclopean Mountains to catch the Man in Black for, above all, information. Back at this juncture of interpreting the character of Roland as one who the Constant Reader will cheer on in his adventure, or even as one that many may silently wish to fail, readers of *The Dark Tower* must also look at themselves as reflections of this ambiguous character. Tangled in a web of genres and paths to choose from, when readers are faced with decisions like Roland Deschain—whether or not to seek knowledge that may be better left alone—readers must consider that in an age of information, if he or she would make the same decision as the gunslinger: to move forward though any obstacle, no matter what sacrifices are asked to be made, and to acquire knowledge in the hope that such information delivers enlightenment, relief or solace despite the awareness that these anticipated ends are never promised or guaranteed.

As a final note on the matter of information and climax, King utilizes the ambiguous, muddled and mercurial nature of the science fiction novel, in conjunction with a strange and inventive blend of other genres, to accommodate his designs for the ending of *The Dark Tower*, an ending that is surely unexpected for most readers and does not easily fit within any particular established generic categorization of climax. Perhaps King takes this route with his writing as "expected endings function like magnetic north poles towards which the narratives always point," indicating that unsurprising or easily anticipated endings hardly make for good fiction (Stableford 1). Surely, overly aware readers rarely become immersed in a story that is too structured or notably contrived. Still, the conclusion which repeats the first line of the series is not solely a signal for a circular and repetitive continuation of the gunslinger's quest and the reader's following of this journey; it is also an appropriate continuation of King's experimentation with genre and writing within the series as a whole. Then again, the circular ending may be an escape King has sought with the conclusions of his other tales: "if we've learned anything about King by the close of this series, it's that he's terrified of endings" (Agger B14). However, with King balancing many genres and many possibilities concerning the outcome of the tale, it seems natural for the ending to truly be an original, a deviation from any previous norm that enriches the tale through its boldness and its call to re-read the story in its entirety as the circular nature of the text demands at least one subsequent reading. And while a true conclusion may be avoided by connecting the end of the *Dark Tower* tale to the beginning, the constant journey suggests that no knowledge or enlightenment is ever found, which then suggests that the gunslinger's quest does have a hint of horror to it. To discover that one's life quest is one of folly and purposelessness certainly seems to be in the mold of a Stephen King novel, which is marked by fiction that may seem to offer hope, but then pulls it away with little announcement whatsoever.

From *Inside the "Dark Tower" Series: Art, Evil, and Intertextuality in the Stephen King Novels* (2009), pp. 27-69. Copyright © 2009 Patrick McAleer. Reprinted by permission of McFarland & Company, Inc., Box 611, Jefferson, NC 28640. www.mcfarlandpub.com.

Works Cited

Agger, Michael. "Pulp Metafiction." Rev. of *The Dark Tower*, by Stephen King. *New York Times* 17 Oct. 2004: B14.

Ash, Brian. *Faces of the Future—The Lessons of Science-Fiction*. New York: Taplinger, 1975.

Badley, Linda. "The Sin Eater: Orality, Postliteracy, and the Early Stephen King." *Bloom's Modern Critical Views: Stephen King* (Updated Edition). Ed. Harold Bloom. Philadelphia: Chelsea House, 2007. 95-123.

Barr, Marleen S. "Textism—An Emancipation Proclamation." *PMLA* 119.3 (2004): 429-441.

Bayer-Berenbaun, Linda. *The Gothic Imagination: Expansion in Gothic Literature and Art*. Cranbury, NJ: Associated UP, 1982.

Browning, Robert. "Childe Roland to the Dark Tower Came." *Robert Browning's Poetry*. Ed. James F. Loucks. New York: Norton, 1979. 134-139.

Colatrella, Carol. "Science Fiction in the Information Age." *American Literary History* 11.3 (Autumn 1999): 554-65.

Collings, Michael R., and David A. Engebretson. *The Shorter Works of Stephen King*. 1985. San Bernardino, CA: Borgo, 1988.

Davis, Jonathan. *Stephen King's America*. Bowling Green, OH: Bowling Green State U Popular P, 1994.

Egan, James. "*The Dark Tower*: Stephen King's Gothic Western." *The Gothic World of Stephen King: Landscape of Nightmares*. Eds. Gary Hoppenstand and Ray B. Browne. Bowling Green, OH: Bowling Green State U Popular P, 1987. 95-106.

_____. "Technohorror: The Dystopian Vision of Stephen King." *Bloom's Modern Critical Views: Stephen King*. Ed. Harold Bloom. Philadelphia: Chelsea House, 1998. 47-58.

Freedman, Carl. *Critical Theory and Science Fiction*. Hanover, NH: Wesleyan UP, 2000.

Frye, Northrop. *Anatomy of Criticism: Four Essays*. Princeton, NJ: Princeton UP, 1957.

Greene, Thomas. "The Norms of Epic." *Comparative Literature*. 13.3 (Summer 1961): 193-207.

Gunn, James. "Toward a Definition of Science Fiction." *Speculation on Speculation*. Eds. James Gunn and Matthew Candelaria. Lanham, MD: Scarecrow P, 2005. 5-12.

Jones, Daryl. *The Dime Novel Western*. Bowling Green, OH: Bowling Green State U Popular P, 1978.

King, Stephen. *The Dark Tower*. Hampton Falls, NH: Donald M. Grant, 2004.

_____. *The Drawing of the Three*. 1987. New York: Plume, 2003.

_____. *The Gunslinger*. 1982. New York: Plume, 1988.

_____. *The Gunslinger* (Revised Edition). New York: Plume, 2003.

_____. *The Stand: The Complete & Uncut Edition*. 1990. New York: Signet, 1991.

_____. *The Waste Lands*. 1991. New York: Plume, 2003.

_____. *Wizard and Glass*. 1997. New York: Plume, 2003.

_____. *Wolves of the Calla*. 2003. New York: Scribner, 2004.

Landa, Elaine. "I Am a Hick, and This Is Where I Feel at Home." *Feast of Fear: Conversations with Stephen King*. Eds. Tim Underwood and Chuck Miller. New York: Carroll & Graf, 1989. 249-258.

Lewis, R. W. B. *Trials of the Word: Essays in American Literature and the Humanistic Tradition*. New Haven, CT: Yale UP, 1965.

Magistrale, Tony. *The Moral Voyages of Stephen King*. San Bernardino, CA: Borgo, 1989.

_____. *Stephen King: The Second Decade, Danse Macabre to The Dark Half*. New York: Twayne, 1992.

May, John R. *Toward a New Earth: Apocalypse in the American Novel*. Notre Dame, IN: U of Notre Dame P, 1972.

Miller, David A. *The Epic Hero*. Baltimore: The Johns Hopkins UP, 2002.

Moylan, Tom. *Demand the Impossible: Science Fiction and the Utopian Imagination*. New York: Methuen, 1986.

Nicholls, Richard. "Avaunt Thee, Recreant Cyborg!" Rev. of *The Waste Lands*, by Stephen King. *New York Times* 29 Sept. 1991: BR14.

Pearsall, Derek. *Arthurian Romance: A Short Introduction*. Maiden, MA: Blackwell, 2003.

Punter, David, and Glennis Byron. *The Gothic*. Malden, MA: Blackwell, 2004.

Shattuck, Roger. *Forbidden Knowledge: From Prometheus to Pornography*. New York: St. Martin's Press, 1996.

Stableford, Brian. "How Should a Science Fiction Story End?" *The New York Review of Science Fiction* 7.6 (Feb 1995): 1, 8-15.

Strengell, Heidi. *Dissecting Stephen King: From the Gothic to Literary Naturalism*. Madison, WI: U of Wisconsin P/Popular P, 2005.

Summers, Montague. *The Gothic Quest: A History of the Gothic Novel*. London: Fortune, 1938.

Westbrook, Max. "The Themes of Western Fiction." *Critical Essays on the Western American Novel*. Ed. William T. Pilkington. Boston: G.K. Hall, 1980. 34-40.

A Blind Date with Disaster:
Adolescent Revolt in the Fiction of Stephen King

Tom Newhouse

Despite his reputation as master of modern horror fiction, Stephen King has consistently shown that he is more than simply heir to a set of stock literary devices invented by Radcliffe and Maturin and subsequently employed by most writers of horror and suspense fiction. Indeed, King does more than graft elements of a traditional Gothic formula onto a familiar modern setting: beneath their archetypal trappings, King's novels evoke the troubled atmosphere of contemporary America, one harried as much by the realities of corrupt government, technology run rampant, and an uncertain domestic life as by monsters and ghosts and other mythical products of the human imagination.

In contemplation of these grim social realities, King has devoted a substantial part of his work to dramatizing the problems of growing up within circumstances of increasing complexity. King's novels and stories that depict teenage life are profoundly critical of the parental expectations, conservative values, and peer pressures which teenagers must face. In addition, King's teen protagonists come into awareness engaging the contradictions between the logical realm of routine activity and the darker regions of violent, destructive impulses. They are often outsiders who turn to violence as a response to exclusionary social environments which deny them acceptance, or who resort to destructive attitudes that they believe will advance them upward.

King's earliest writings presented tortured adolescents and violence running amuck within the sterile, orderly environment of schools. "Cain Rose Up" (1968) dramatizes a college student's tense moments before he randomly shoots passersby from his dormitory window; "Here They Be Tygers" (1968) describes a young boy witnessing his tyrannical third grade teacher being devoured by a tiger, an unlikely occupant of the boys' bathroom; and *Sword in the Darkness*, an early unpublished novel, "is a lengthy tale of a race riot at an urban high school."[1] In addition to providing a context for displaying teenage confusion, the sudden disturbance of a seemingly stable social order anticipates King's special brand of fiction—a blend of social realism and archetypal horror, exposing deficient institutional and social values and the flimsy rational biases on which they are founded. While this assault on rationality is familiar to readers of horror fiction, King eschews the customary neutrality of social environment as it generally exists in most horror fiction. Rarely an active agent of evil in the traditional horror tale, King's flawed social environments are often directly responsible for the nightmarish tragedies that proliferate in his works. King's fiction about the trials of adolescence, generally detailing a hostile social environment and value system, parallels his concerns with institutional irresponsibility that occur in his political thrillers like *The Dead Zone* (1979) and *Firestarter* (1980), or in his technological nightmares like *The Stand* (1978) and *The Mist* (1980).

Rage (1977) is King's first concrete expression of teen outrage and the first of the novels that he published pseudonymously as Richard Bachman. His most bizarre expression of teen revolt, this adolescent fantasy, remarkably, displays all of the familiar King trademarks: the colloquialism, the endless brand name references, the scatology, the perverse humor, the imaginative pacing of a tense but essentially static situation, and most importantly, the creation of a character type that would resurface in several future novels. Charlie Decker is the first in a long line of adolescent characters in King's fiction which includes Carrie White, Arnie Cunningham, Harold Lauder, and Todd Bowden. These sexually ambiguous, alienated, uniquely gifted, and destructive victim-victimizers are, despite their extreme actions, imbued with qualities, fears, and anxieties that seem typical of most modern teenagers.

In *Rage*, Charlie Decker, a student at Placerville High, fatally shoots two teachers and holds his classmates hostage. While not really a horror story, this psychological suspense thriller falls broadly within

King's own definition of the horror tale. The action signifies an "outbreak of some Dionysian madness in an Apollonian existence"[2] that is analogous to the upsetting of the romantic, infinitely less complicated world that forms the setting of the Gothic novel. At the same time, King breaks with the horror formula by indicating a deep disenchantment with the arrogant assumptions of the accepted order. Charlie is something of a berserk teen philosopher, discrediting the notion that "life is logical, life is prosaic, life is sane."[3] Speculating on life's darker mysteries, Charlie gleefully muses:

> The other side says that the universe has all the logic of a little kid in a Halloween cowboy suit with his guts and his trick-or-treat candy spread all over a mile of Interstate 95. This is the logic of napalm, paranoia, suitcase bombs carried by happy Arabs, random carcinoma. The logic eats itself. It says life grins as hysterically and irrationally as the penny you flick to see who buys lunch. (27)

But while Charlie, in his confused, murderous revolt, is a spokesman articulating the limitations of logic to make sense of the world, he is not beyond systematic, albeit perverse, calculation himself. Throughout the novel Charlie lays waste to all of his private and social demons by exposing the shallow tyrants of the established order and, in the process, shakes the foundations which they represent. School administrators and teachers are seen as hollow bullies, deluded by an authority that belies a weakness which is ultimately revealed during the tense confrontation, and parents are portrayed either as insensitive brutes or dark sexual monsters, like Charlie's Navy recruiter father.

Despite considerable distortion and stereotyping, however, King's point is clear: though Charlie's revolt has a basis in genuine madness, the causes of it are all too familiar and magnify the hostage students' similar anxieties. In fact, the day's unexpected events have a liberating effect on the students in terms of self-discovery and solidarity. If Charlie's classmates are at first repelled by the murders and understandably frightened by their hostage condition, most eventually lose the sense of danger and come to regard the experience as a valuable one. Some of the students even use their sudden freedom from artificial rules and constraints to make startling revelations of their most personal secrets, mostly having to do with parental misguidance, sexual frustration, and other sources of teen angst. Moreover, the students become quickly impatient with other students who spend the time challenging Charlie and questioning the compliance of their peers instead of engaging in purifying confessional soul-searching. As a result, Ted Jones, previously a popular student, is humiliated by his classmates, exposed as a duplicitous phony, and even physically beaten in a mass gesture intended to discredit Jones's deceptions (a trait which King clearly suggests Jones shares with his elders) and, conversely, to celebrate Charlie's and their own naked honesty.

The creation of *Carrie* (1975), King's first published novel, signals his substantial maturation as a writer.[4] While this novel deals with the familiar social milieu of cruel parents, a faceless high school, and painful rituals of conformity, King goes out of his way to achieve objectivity. A departure from the first-person confessional method of *Rage*, King employs a third-person narrator as well as the multiple points-of-view common to epistolary documentation, relating the unusual events of his tale through scientific reports, magazine articles, and a memoir. One positive result of this narrative method is a host of convincing characterizations. Administrators and teachers, previously clay pigeons for Charlie's gun blasts, are no longer defensively muttering empty platitudes. Rather, Rita Desjardins, the helpful gym teacher, and Mr. Morton, the assistant principal, are portrayed realistically, aware of the limitations of their authority and made more human by their failings. As Mr. Morton tries to remember Carrie after he is told of the shower incident, he laments, "After five years or so, they all tend to merge into one group face. You call them by their brothers' names. That type of thing. It's hard."[5]

Moreover, despite their being generally benevolent components in a system that, by its nature, engenders anonymity, the school authorities have the integrity to do the right thing in situations that require exercising fairness and responsible judgment. For instance, when the successful lawyer-father of Chris Hargensen comes to the school to legally pressure the administration to rescind punishment and permit the girls who abused Carrie to attend the prom, the principal defends Carrie and refuses to give in to his demands, even threatening to countersue.

The result of King's new objectivity is not only a meticulous realism but a shift in focus from the more abstract attack on the fragile nature of order and authority to larger problems of social organization. The primary agents of chaos here are Chris Hargensen, the snobby rich girl, upset that someone from Carrie's social caste can have an influence on her life, and Billy Nolan, the greasy, lower-class punk, who seek to punish Carrie after Mr. Hargensen's threats to the administration fail. It is especially revealing that as Chris wavers in her resolve to go through with the plot to humiliate Carrie at the prom by dousing her with pig's blood, it is Billy who insists, motivated more by a desire to assert dominance over his girlfriend, whom he resents for her superior social status, than by any hatred for Carrie. Thus, not only are clearly definable characters in verifiable relationships responsible for propelling the novel towards its end, but the final denouement has a basis in class conflict which, paradoxically, affects Carrie's fate both directly and indirectly.

While the conflict in *Carrie* is less generational than in *Rage*, King's novel is also significantly more disturbing than its predecessor because of its tragic inevitability. Despite the defense of the principal and the encouragement of Miss Desjardins and Sue Snell, Carrie's history of losing control and unleashing her dreadful powers, her impoverished home life, the demands of her religious fanatic mother, and the social realities that are so antagonistic, negate her unlikely moment of triumph at the prom with Tommy Ross. Because she is such a doomed victim, King makes Carrie's destruction of school and town seem more like an unconscious reaction than purposeful revenge, practically as impossible to prevent as the conditions which provoked it. Though not always compelling, King's narrative, with its labyrinth of explanations for the tragedy, underscores the problems of isolating simple causes based simply on personal vendetta and institutional incompetence, giving this novel a complexity and fatalistic ambivalence that his previous efforts do not display and that have little to do with horror fiction formulas.

The formidable destruction occurring at the conclusion of *'Salem's Lot* (1977) and *The Shining* (1978) also proceed directly from realistic social breakdowns. The private moral corruption of the town of 'Salem and Jack Torrance's alcoholism and history of child abuse are tragic preconditions that fuel the developing violence made certain in these two novels by the further influence of supernatural forces. Not until *The Stand* does individual will prove to be a viable element of salvation, and even then it is only accomplished through a repudiation of old established values: at the conclusion of *The Stand*, Stu Redman and Fran Goldsmith retreat from the familiar codes of civilization that have come to represent the remodeled society of the Free Zone. Perhaps not surprisingly, then, King's next examination of adolescence presented the adolescent outsider not as some doomed victim of a damaged social order but as someone whose irresponsible exploration of the dark side leads to disaster. In *Christine* (1981), the only novel so far discussed that can properly be called supernatural, the outsider figure, Arnie Cunningham, is less the victim of the demoniac powers of the car than he is a half-willing participant in the dark pleasures which the fiendish car can offer, though parental mismanagement is still a factor in the direction he takes. Indeed, Regina Cunningham's rejection of her son's impulsive gesture to buy Christine, a broken-down wreck of an automobile, illustrates a reliance on overbearing rational control which, like most forms of limited idealism presented in King's novels, does little to prevent destruction.

And through it all she had continued to smile inside because it was all working out according to plan, was all working out the way she felt her own childhood should have. Their son had warm supportive parents who cared about him. Who would give him anything (within reason), who would gladly send him to the college of his choice (as long as it was a good one), thereby finishing the game/business/vocation of parenting with a flourish.[6]

But as the tragic circumstances indicate, schemes of moderation are inadequate to deal with the flexibilities and uncertainties of growing up. That some of these uncertainties are actually overcome as the darker side begins to taint Arnie's innocence represents King's most fascinating employment of his theme of teen struggle for expression in an unstable world. Christine's evil momentarily affects Arnie for the better: it gives him the nerve to call Leigh Cabot for a date, it makes him better looking, even clearing up his acne, and it gives him sexual powers he never dreamed of possessing. But Arnie's conscious participation in his metamorphosis blurs after his initial loss of innocence, largely as a result of his increasing resemblance to the car's previous owner, the evil Roland Le Bay, and corruption ultimately overwhelms him, making his short-lived transition from outsider to social participant, like Carrie White's, a kind of dream.

Yet without the active complicity of class conflict and an extremely debilitating homelife that makes Carrie's demise so imminent, moral responsibility can no longer be excluded as a viable element in the rite of passage separating childhood from adulthood. Unfortunately, this theme is not developed and Arnie is written out of the book in the final third, removed offstage by death with his mother in a traffic accident. Flawed structure and a shifting focus often characterize the works of popular authors who write as quickly and prolifically as King does. But in King's case, narrative problems like these are perhaps more emblematic of the tension that exists in his novels between social commentary and the exigencies of the popular storyteller's obligation to his audience. In *Christine*, it is the horror story that prevails. The metaphorical elements that Christine represents as an avenue to identity implicit in the mythology of the American automobile, given thrust by, among other things, the chapter references to classic rock 'n' roll songs celebrating the subcultural fetishism of cool, are reduced in favor of plot elements that must be resolved. Once Arnie is removed from the story, Christine's more intriguing functions disappear and she becomes merely a haunted car running down everyone in sight who even remotely suggests a threat to her, and who must be stopped.

Apt Pupil (1982), King's next exploration of adolescence, is a realistic story that repeats many of the themes of *Christine*—particularly the symbiotic relationship between good and evil—but eschews the tensions between message and genre. The relationship between good and evil exists in the fascination of a "total all-American kid",[7] Todd Bowden, for a former Nazi soldier, Kurt Dussander, who lives on the boy's street. If King's other treatments of adolescent trauma dramatized alienated teens trying but failing to conform to parental or peer standards, Todd Bowden suggests just the opposite. Unlike the others, suspended between conformity and revolt, growing soft in the battle and eventually succumbing to the tenets of the nightmare, Todd creates his own hell and is not subject to the gradual moral and physical disintegration of an Arnie Cunningham or the sudden destructive outbursts of Charlie Decker or Carrie White. Recognizing evil for what it is, Todd's revolt early in the novella against the hopeless mediocrity of his unsuspecting parents, consisting of a typically weak father and a not-so-typically deferential mother, and the stifling boredom of his Southern California surroundings, comes as no surprise, and forecasts his evolution into mass killer. Though this novel, included as one of the stories in *Different Seasons* (1982), is ostensibly an attempt by King's publishers to show that he could write realistic fiction, *Apt Pupil* is scarcely a departure from King's usual obsession with horror and gore. Golden boy Todd is like a spoiled-kid version of Charlie Decker and takes King's adolescent oeuvre full circle by leaving the sunny California community strewn with bodies, the last of which is, interestingly,

Todd's high school guidance counselor. Moreover, the intrusion of chaos emerging from a calm, seemingly orderly surface, exemplified here by "the perfect kid" and by a serene California landscape, is a theme that is interchangeable with, and central to, all of King's fictional creations regardless of classification.

Without abandoning literary archetypes and often imbuing them with metaphorical purposes characterizing modern life, Stephen King eschews the easy morality that much horror fiction promotes. By exploring various avenues of escape, acceptance, and social ascension, King dramatizes the complex journey that adolescents must make. With few exceptions, adolescence is a wasteland: no love, only sex— no family life, only an irrelevant and discordant existence that, as much through its shortcomings as by the confused teen revolt against it, is reduced to ashes. Ostensibly consumed for entertainment purposes, the fiction of Stephen King has special relevance to his readers by reflecting the emptiness of the post-Watergate 70's and the dread of the nuclear 80's, decades which historically parallel his rise as a notable contemporary writer.

From *The Gothic World of Stephen King: Landscape of Nightmares*, edited by Gary Hoppenstand and Ray B. Browne (1987), pp. 49-55. Copyright © 1987 by the Board of Regents of the University of Wisconsin System. Reprinted by permission of The University of Wisconsin Press.

Notes

1. Douglas E. Winter, *Stephen King* (Washington: Starmont House, 1982), p. 28.

2. Stephen King, *Danse Macabre* (London: MacDonald Future Publishers, 1981), p. 368.

3. Stephen King, "Rage" in *The Bachman Books: Four Early Novels By Stephen King* (New York: Plume Books, 1985), p. 27.

4. In his introduction to *The Bachman Books*, King indicates that "Rage" (originally entitled "Getting It On") was begun when he was a high school senior and completed in 1971.

5. Stephen King, *Carrie* (New York: Signet, 1975), p. 19.

6. Stephen King, *Christine* (New York: Signet, 1983), p. 216.

7. Stephen King, *Different Seasons* (New York: Viking Press, 1982), p. 105.

Cotton Mather and Stephen King:
Writing/Righting the Body Politic_____

Edward J. Ingebretsen

Let us not be like a Troubled House, altho' we are so much haunted by the devils.

—Cotton Mather, *Wonders of the Invisible World* (91)

[W]ithin the framework [of a horror story] . . . we find a moral code so strong it would make a Puritan smile.

—Stephen King, *Danse Macabre* (368)

I

In "A Model of Christian Charity" John Winthrop uses a rhetoric of benevolent religious terror to create political identity (and, incidentally, to enforce social conformity). His strategy in 1630 was not new, nor since was it an isolated instance. Let us consider, for example, a particular form of Christian charity, first as it played out in the construction of New England's social polity and communal identity, and then, in these latter days, as it traces itself through a market-driven genre, the American Gothic tradition of horror and fantasy texts. I am speaking, of course, about the rite of witch-hunting (in Salem and elsewhere) and its reconstruction as perennial American myth, cultic ideology, and commodified terror. In this chapter I argue that contemporary American industries of horror (Stephen King, for particular example) are hardly "diversions" at all—or, that indeed they *are* diversions, and as such, should be paid attention. The Freddy Krueger-style dismemberings and violent fantasies indulged in the name of entertainment can hardly be considered innocuous. Or, to put it another way, the horrors dismissed as trash and consigned to the "literary basement," or, as Leslie Fiedler observes, those that we usher around to the "backdoor of culture" (54) are, as it were, the "real thing" (with apologies to the Coke ad).

By way of background, I argue that religious discourse is a narrative of considerable cultural importance; although silenced by law, it still makes itself heard, surfacing in places presumed to be dismissable—particularly in the genres of the horrific sublime, or those texts we call dark fantasy. Thus, though not about religious experience directly, this chapter is about its indirect possibilities in the civic theater. I begin with the premise that American cultic life presumes a metaphysics—perhaps one could call this the condition of interiority—that gives form to approved cultural feelings and desires. This framework is Christian in deep and pervasive ways and is, therefore, explicitly about power and implicitly about fear. Further, I argue that echoes of this discredited system—in a democracy religious discourse is rendered politically un-speakable—can be loudly heard in the fertile markets of horror and fantasy.

Horror films and texts are not merely "entertainments"—they are, as the word itself suggests, sites of erotic dalliance: "diversions," sig-nificant cultural deflections. Indeed, they embody significant political remembering. So often taboo in subject matter, their presentation is or-ganized around titillation. Consider, for example, the eroticization of the serial killer in such films as *Silence of the Lambs*. Fear and dread, once associated with the religious sublime, are now deflected into new venues; religious anxiety, marketed as commercial horror, is placed in the service of civic definition and social constraint. Thus, consumer fear may be the last vestiges, if you will, of a bankrupt religious vision. That is, they constitute cultural acts of remembering; they are politi-cally invested, civic gestures of identity and *religious* acts of alle-giance.

As an example, consider Stephen King's *Carrie*, with its distant echoes of the canonical American memory of the Salem witch trials. As Cotton Mather would use the term in *Wonders of the Invisible World*, King's "entertainment" is also an *exemplum*, a model or exam-ple. As a fiction, it employs the trope of witchery to play out an anxiety of social dis-ease; as a metaphysics it points toward a spiritual order that transcends this temporal order, while nonetheless authorizing its political arrangements and exclusions.

The year 1997 marks the 300th anniversary of the final chapter in "one of the three dark moments in New England history" (Pribek, 95-100), the Salem witch hysteria of 1692-1693.[1] On January 14, 1667, Samuel Sewall stood before his church's congregation in Salem while his pastor read Sewall's public repudiation of the part he played in the witch-trials. Salem is in so many ways the point at which American popular culture—especially its revisionist nationalism—comes of age and claims its peculiar political and economic tensions. Indeed, American "public" or even "popular" culture can be said to begin where Salem repudiated *illegal* witchery (for, of course, there were legal practitioners of the white arts, notably the clergy who first decried the presence of witches in the town). The events of 1692-1693 were to be an initial instance, following Anne Hutchinson and the Antinomian affair, of what would over time become an essential civic mechanism in the construction of normalcy. Witchery could serve as one of many excuses for invoking a rite of social expiation—a communal self-flagellation that could be invoked whenever the Body Politic was felt to need moral exercise or a gesture of self-definition and muscle toning. Yet such gestures represent a civic impulse older than the Republic, and R I. Moore traces them back through medieval Christianity's formation, as he calls it, of a "persecuting society."[2]

History books are filled with such moments of civic crisis. The emergence of the witch in medieval Christian polity, and her ubiquitous presence in subsequent uncivil/theological politics, is a case in point. Hugh Trevor-Roper argues that a Thomistic mapping of heaven and its powers and principalities prompted in turn an extensive, even obsessive, map of an inverted, although parallel, region below, complete with its attendant minions (*The European Witch-Craze of the Sixteenth and Seventeenth Centuries and Other Essays*). He charts the bizarre internal logic by which what had been initially a matter of arcane scholastic metaphysics—witch-hunting—became in time a socially necessary effect of bully politics and then, increasingly, a spectacular civic rite.[3]

As late as 1636 John Cotton and other first-generation Puritan Divines, pursuing a provisional and largely ad hoc polity to strengthen what they perceived to be a generalized spiritual and civic decline, used the language of witchery—specifically gendered—to turn back Hutchinson's religious challenge to their civil authority.[4] The Old World theologies by which they ordered Congregational polity did not—could not—admit Hutchinson's claim of religious authority; and so, with no sense of irony, the divines employed a language and ritualized civic repudiation that had by and large been abandoned in Europe. In this way, the land that was to become New England, still fluid in concept—new, yet old, royal, yet recently not, whose external boundaries lay vulnerable to all manner of political and physical enemies—turned inward. In this way the society-in-formation began systematically to map itself according to a metaphysical topography of boundaries and hierarchies, of scrutinies and surveillances, organized according to biblical precept. As John Winthrop, then governor, said in court to Anne Hutchinson, "You must keep your conscience or it will be kept for you."[5] In such an order, as Stout explains, "there was no inherent contradiction between civic loyalty and godly sanctification" (21) and "a willful rebellion against the social order was indicative of an endangered soul" (24).[6]

The Hutchinson affair anticipates Salem's witch-hysteria forty-five years later. Salem can be seen as engaged in a similar effort at righting (writing) the Body Politic. In a chaotic period of fluctuating, even nonexistent boundaries, when the Royal authorization on which the colony depended seemed in question, Salem needed a way to establish and ground itself. When demographic and economic tensions are added to the ones already mentioned, it is easy to understand why Salem turned to policing its internal boundaries. Seeking witches was, at least, a diversion that most people could agree upon. Thus, the demons Salem sought furiously to extirpate were, indeed, more visible than invisible, more human rather than less. Hutchinson, then, learned early—as did the Quakers twenty years later and still later, the unfortunate victims at Salem—that in this brave New World neither the theory of freethinking nor its practice extended inward; mental witchery must be repudiated, conventionality must be protected against the enthusiasm of the particular. Maps of heaven did, after all, shape those of earth, as metaphysics and its imperatives came to ground in the cast-off bodies of those repudiated for the civic good. For this reason John Calvin's Institutes remain important documents in social theory as well as in theology.[7]

Stephen King's many novels provide examples of how disowned theologies return, ghostlike, as moralistic social memory. King's position on the social margins participates more deeply than is sometimes recognized in an imaginative social project profoundly shaped by religious imperatives and sensibilities. In *Carrie*, for instance, he revisits a primary cultural scene played out between Hutchinson and Cotton and then later between Cotton Mather and the various women accused of witchery in Salem. In both instances at issue is the gendered, and therefore imbalanced, relationship between the single separate self's private intimacies and the metaphysical allegiances, imperatives, and repudiations of a theofederal state order. From the earliest days in New England, the rhythm of private spirituality was thought intimately to reflect its public, conventional expression. That is, private religious moments carried political import in that public confession of same was a requirement for participation in the Lord's Supper, and thus, in the public life of the community. Though theoretically the self and the *Civitas* echoed each other as metaphor, symbol, often they seemed embattled discourses whose terms divided the more they were thought to be unified. In due time theological discourse itself—the language of the public spiritual self—was, by federal law, rendered legally unspeakable. But though silenced, the discourse was not erased. Traces of its formidable presence could still be found, submerged in a nostalgic, revisionist nationalism and in the various rhetorics of normalcy, issuing from pulpits both political and secular. King's *Carrie* (1973) exploits these religious and civic tensions in a way reminiscent of Cotton Mather's *Wonders of the Invisible World* (1693). Both authors—Mather's theological fictions more obviously than King's commercial fantasy, though no less insistently—describe what might be called a rite of deviancy. This is the mechanism by which a threatened order organizes and defends its boundaries by repudiating those who fail them. Both texts reflect the instability inherent in the construction of the witch, because witch-hunting points inward toward the civic center: "The worst work of the Devil they looked for—and found—among their own kind" (Demos, 71).

But before considering King's downward revision of theology, let me turn for a moment to Cotton Mather's 1693 Miltonesque rendering of "the Fiend's descent on Salem Village" (Starkey, 242). Mather calls his account a "true History" (107), stating that he reports "matters not as an *Advocate*, but as an *Historian*" (110). At the same time, however, Mather ingenuously admits that he "was not present at any of [the trials]" (109). Mather's anxieties about how to read the whole Salem affair constantly intrude upon his narrative: "The whole business is become hereupon so *Snarled*, and the determination of the Question one way or another, so *dismal*, that . . . *We know not what to do!*" (84).[8] Mather's problem, however, was less metaphysical than practical because he makes it clear that the trials matter more as *exempla* of the moral life than as history or fiction. Or rather, they were both. That is, his theological interests—or perhaps justifications—were by necessity subsumed within the constraints of narrative, even formula, as Mather finds ready to hand the discourse of witchery derived from Old England. Staking the witch, then, was a complicated business, partly a matter of doctrine but also partly a matter of the right mix of entertainments and formulaic "spells." If staking the witch was a kind of spell by which to "right" the Body Politic, Mather concluded that "telling" the witch—"writing it"—was also a reforming action, a dis-spelling of unauthorized witchery by the authoritative "spelling" of social agents like himself. Indeed, the symbolic construction of the witch as subversive agent within a community, and her subsequent exemplary trial and condemnation, encompassed a variety of often divergent ends. For one thing, such an act of communal finger-pointing defined the abstract, ideological boundaries of a community; the violence of this scape-goating melodrama underscores, but does not discredit, routine acts of violence throughout the Body Politic. In addition, witch-hunting con-stituted an approved social gesture, in a climate generally suspicious of ritual, for maintaining religious control precisely through ritualistic means; for shaping the civic imagination; and paradoxically, for trans-gressing that imagination as well.[9] The rite was both expiatory and ex-planatory, socially clarifying as well as purgative. A habitual cry of guilt and repudiation, the Calvinistic civic cosmology of expiation was, in addition, a primary means of self-definition. But the larger point I wish to address is that, as Foucault reminds us, deviancy needs to be cultivated in order that its suppression—and its exposition—might provide an occasion for a ceremonial display of civic power.[10] Some laws, then, are meant to be broken.

In Gothic lore, monsters generally haunt the margins of society, whereas in political realities, witches emerge from within communi-ties. Observers of the dynamics of witchcraft conclude that the "bizarre mythology" leading to various resurgences of witch craze in Europe resulted from "social struggle" (Trevor-Roper, 165). Trevor-Roper notes, too, that it was a "social movement" but one that could be ex-tended "deliberately, in times of political crisis, as a political device, to destroy powerful enemies or dangerous persons" (189): "At best, the myth might be contained as in the early sixteenth century. But it did not evaporate:. It remained at the bottom of society, like a stagnant pool, easily flooded, easily stirred" (191). In *Entertaining Satan* John De-mos argues that the witch hysteria served Salem in a traditional man-ner, acting as a "social strain gauge" (276) by which one could judge not only the intersection of demographic and economic forces local to Salem's geographically divided community, but also visible fissures, where an often overlapping series of discourses and rhetorics of normalcy (religious, civil, personal, ecclesiastical, institutional) failed to hold. Witchcraft was a necessary part of communal life because it served the group by "sharpening its boundaries, reinforcing its values, and deepening the loyalty of its membership" (14).[11] Indeed, witchcraft "most often occurs where there is *both* unusual tension *and* a lack of appropriate outlets (and/or means of resolution)" (Demos, 276). But these rather dry abstractions have particular and embodied consequences; social anxiety will manifest itself in behaviors of all kinds. Symbols can kill. That is, social constructions embody metaphysical assumptions, and symbolic repudiations often shed real blood. Thus it was that metaphysics came to ground. A constellation of historical pressures native to the New England colonies came to sharp focus in the township of Salem and its local neighbors.

Sociologists and historians suggest that the civic turbulence at Salem—which emerged, in concentrated form, in the witch trials—was a way of deflecting often unrelated anxieties. In particular they note anxieties arising from the revocation of the original Bay Colonies charter in 1688. In such an unsettled social context, then, the witch hysteria at Salem and the surrounding townships can be viewed as a work of political reformation, as well as—or instead of—a theological reformation. The action was an attempt to draw lines and reform personal as well as communal boundaries in a young community whose legal definition had been, quite literally, erased by the political upheaval in Old England. In addition, however, and moving from a political map to a metaphysical one, the charge of witchcraft is rhetorically dense, a metaphor drenched with moral imperative. In the first place, although framed in conventional religious terms as *maleficium*, witchcraft in fact constituted a civil, rather than a religious, offense. Witchcraft focused social unrest within a divided community, and it was a charge tantamount to disturbing the social peace.

David Hall writes that "From the preachers' point of view, then, the lesson of the Quakers . . . and Anne Hutchinson was exactly this: they allowed Satan entrance to the self" (*Worlds of Wonder*, 146-47).[12] For residents of Salem in 1692, beleaguered by internal conflict and international confusion, the witch's body provided the same *exemplum*, and the public rending of that body ceremonially displayed the same power as did the exile (and later death) of Anne Hutchinson and the later execution of the Quakers (Boston Commons, 1656). Metaphorically, witches, Quakers, and other "freethinkers" established a wilderness site ready for settlement and domestication. The witch's body was a site of public strife—a platform on which to inscribe the authorizations of Genesis, and from which to promulgate its repudiations: Enter the land and possess it; divide, subdue, and occupy it. Confess it. Textify it. Read it in terror.[13] Clearly more was at stake at Salem than just the witch's physical person; although for that matter, even the stake was an ambiguous tool, useful for burning as well as for demarcating possession of the land.

In the witch's person—or on it in crimson letters, as in the case of Hawthorne's Hester Prynne—was written a complex grammar, a kind of palimpsest, writing over previous erasures and delineations society's exclusions and its fears.[14] For people governed by the Word, the witch embodied—and expiated—the contradiction between a law-obsessed, literal-minded people and its strongly Antinomian tendencies. Yet the witch was more than a legal marker; the stories of Susanna Martin and Bridget Bishop and other witches cobbled together by Cotton Mather also provided a sanctioned way of surreptitiously enjoying the "delights" of the immoral life while obediently repudiating them.[15] If some laws are meant to be broken for the social good, then some perverseness and demonstrations of wickedness could likewise find good social use for edification and example. And even more. For example, Increase Mather's account of Elizabeth Knapp's possession (in Groton, 1761) was described by the book-seller as "entertainment" for the "curious" (Hall, *Worlds of Wonder*, 282). Cotton Mather, likewise, recognized that witchcraft was a source of unflagging social interest. So had *news* become entertainment? Or was it the other way around? And whatever happened to theology? Mather's breathless accounts of the "Witches *Extasies*" [sic] (35), served as a diversion and distraction—a "scarlet thread" (Starkey, 239) in an otherwise mundane daily world. Whatever their theological implications, witch trials provided life and color, however perversely and voyeuristically, to an otherwise monochromatic life. As Marion Starkey notes, the "hangings were made a spectacle by intention" (208). To anticipate a later genre of tabloid political gothic, witchcraft was news. It made celebrities (not always fortunately) of those accused of witchery, while bringing fame and (or) notoriety to those sharing the spotlight. Indeed, says Demos, the "metaphor of theatre suggests itself quite naturally; every witchcraft case was, in part a public drama" (117).[16] Reconstructing such an event Demos observes:

> Meanwhile a triumphant Cotton Mather is working long and late in his study to complete a book that will soon be published under the title *Memorable Providences Relating to Witchcrafts and Possessions*. A central chapter presents some carefully selected "examples," and includes the events in which Mather himself has so recently participated. The Goodwin children will be leading characters in a local-bestseller. (9)

The charge of witchcraft offered power and individuality to witch and victim alike—who found themselves, accused and accuser, for the first time in the center of public attention and control. As Keith Thomas explains in *Religion and the Decline of Magic*, witches were "the persons whose position in society was ambiguous or insecure" (168-69). Of course, by self-definition, this could characterize an entire New England society: strangers in a strange land; outcasts, deviants by public outcry—at least to the folks left behind in Old England. Salem's example would be only one of many in which theological discourse would intersect with a normalizing rhetoric of the polite (*polis*) during periods of social unrest. Reminders of Salem echo from time to time; indeed, in contemporary formulations of the rite of deviancy, the "witch-hunt" demonstrates how ready to hand is this social corrective in times of civic distress. The language of religious terror and an appeal to the safety of the Body Politic conjoin most "naturally" in times when the *polis* is threatened, whether by actual external, historical event or by some perceived ideological threat. But thus it is that memory, in the name of nostalgia, invents the tradition it needs in order to justify its present needs, and this is as true for established cultural orders as well as individuals. Salem, then, is an early preparation for the later political melodramas and civic theater in which a socializing theology becomes normative cultic narrative of exclusion.[17]

I have briefly discussed how under pressure of a variety of social and political forces the accused witch was erased as an individual and rewritten as symbol. Like Hutchinson, the Quakers—even Hawthorne's fictional version of Hutchinson, Hester Prynne—the accused woman focused community energy for correction and vigilance, becoming at the same time a (tacitly pleasurable) religious memorial. Ironically, however, it is in her hapless role as religious memorial that the witch bears out a community's symbolic rejection of itself in the very terms by which that community defined itself. That is, the witch was feared precisely because she made explicit her unmediated relationship to the powers and principalities; she denied the efficacious mediation of the priest or minister and presumed to invoke interdicted power by virtue of her own authority. In so doing she both confirmed the Protestant principle of immediate access to the Divine while, as a woman, she challenged the male-organized civic order set in place to enforce that principle. Thus an ideology of Christian obedience—since St. Paul, a complex matter of submission to the law and an ironic freedom from it—continues to trouble American civic history. There is no place in American theological or civic history for the strong woman, of course, because that contradicts a favorite cultural narrative. As such, the witch cannot live.

We have seen how, despite Mather's attempt to moralize his accounts of Salem's witch-trials, these accounts became, however covertly, an accepted form of "entertainment." Indeed, a vestige of that function still lingers in the language of the ancient charge: a witch was brought to trial charged with "giving entertainment to Satan" (Demos, 10).[18] Let me turn next to Stephen King's *Carrie*, and see what happens when an originally theological discourse of witchcraft becomes a paradigm of civic imagination in which witches not only live for the civic good, but must, of course, die in order to be repudiated. Ideology connives in the writing of fantasy, whether deployed as civic ritual or marketed as diverting entertainment—with all that word's lethal history.[19]

II

Stephen King was not long out of college, teaching part-time and working in a laundry when he sold *Carrie* to Doubleday. Although he had written (though not yet published) other novels, *Carrie* was his first experiment in the genre of horror. Thus, King's publishing career begins with his serendipitous discovery that Cotton Mather was right: the devil—or at least deviltry—did sell. At that point, as King puts it, "Life began to move at Concorde speed" (*Danse Macabre*, 372).[20] In conversation King discounts this early novel as being the hesitant work of a "young writer," and he may not realize all the reasons for the tale's success. Carrie White is the daughter of a religious fanatic, a girl troubled by (or gifted with) telekinetic power, and King's decentered narrative is in some ways a most traditional American tale. In *Carrie* King adapts the formulas of the Captivity Narrative and Spiritual Autobiography to the ends of "horror." Captivity and possession have been metaphors with deep cultural resonance since Winthrop and the Great Migration. Jonathan Edwards probably never realized how much his terrifying sermon, "Sinners in the Hands of an Angry God" depended for *its* success upon a tradition of such images of captivity.

Even as early as 1742 Edwards's terrifying vision of the sinner captive in the hands of a relentlessly loving God offered a formulaic representation of a basic religious, and civil, fear. The possession/captivity motif has been played out since Anne Hutchinson in a variety of narratives, ranging from sermon to Indian narratives, from slave narratives to tales of domestic entrapment. King, too, reworks the formulas. Particularly, in *Carrie* King charts the dynamic, transgressive oppositions of a derivatively Calvinist cosmology, where, in Mary Douglas's terms, an insistence upon boundary, purity, and law organize and actually create the conflict they enact; and where transgression and scrutiny, rather than love, organize the community. In this social order orthodoxy and heresy create, and depend upon, each other for definition. In this respect, then, *Carrie* emerges from the same social world in which Cotton Mather struggled to define a visible world of order against an invisible world of providence and disorder. Further, King's novel can be helpfully read against the tradition of spiritual autobiography as a darkly parodic captivity narrative reminiscent of Rowlandson.

Carrie is the tale of a 16-year-old, socially-inept girl in the small New England town of Chamberlain. Her powerful and uncontrollable telekinetic powers are triggered by an abrupt and chaotic passage into menstruation, a public event that is both chaotic and humiliating for Carrie. Her subsequent destructive use of her telekinetic powers, partly in response to the visceral repudiations she experiences at the hands of various individuals, drive the plot of this fairly short (for King) novel. King's tale permits a glimpse into a moralistically Calvinistic, Lovecraftian cosmology of distance and power, where the Inscrutable Deity of Margaret White is also the Inescapable Wrath—the Great Transgressor God who is, Carrie insists, at least partly to blame for her captivity and trials. King could hardly have chosen the girl's name by accident, and he is perhaps too clever here by half. For one thing, "white" evokes a tradition in American letters in which whiteness and inscrutability are two points of a triangle, and whose third point is the futility of interpretation—a theme central to the metaphysical puzzlings of Poe, Melville, even Frost.[21] In addition, the name "Carrie" echoes in America's checkered history of social violence doled out in the name of the public good. Martha Corey was the first Salem woman cried out as a witch by Ann Putnam. The name also recalls Martha Carrier, likewise executed at Salem for witchcraft in 1692. Cotton Mather, who witnessed Carrier's execution, called her the "Queen of hell" (*Wonders*, 159). Further, White etymologically suggests witch, and both words are cognates of the word "knowledge." Like Hawthorne's revisionist Hester, Carrie's fatal difference from others is that she knows too much and disowns too little. She can not, like Sue Snell, "conform" to the socializing dictates of her community, partly because she has never been educated in the social literacy that could now help her read that text herself. Less possessed by demons than by her own dark self, her social sin is the power she refuses to cede to the girls who taunt her and the adults who ignore or misread her. Her tragedy, like the earlier social traumas in New England history, centers on the hidden, or at least disguised, center of Calvinist metaphysics—power and authority. The irony of course, is that while Carrie has power, one asks, with Yeats, has she put on the god's knowledge along with his powerful gift?

The novel's opening scene graphically portrays the social exclusionary tactics at work, although King's clumsiness in this spectacle of gender-horror reflects a larger inability to escape the trap of representing women as erotic spectacles, however debased. In this, of course, he is only following patterns set in place by, among others, Mather himself. Carrie's dark menstrual blood flowing into the school shower is meant to signal that she has come of biological child-bearing age. Carrie's body is itself the prime source of her power and mystery, and her blood flow symbolizes the various metaphysical uncertainties against which the community must arm itself. Almost in spite of King's efforts, the scene is luminous with a variety of cultural anxieties: blood, women, witchery, fear of difference. The other girls surround Carrie and respond quickly—and negatively—to her shock and embarrassment. By distancing themselves from her, they hope to secure their own "girlish" purity, although they are clearly more sexually experienced than Carrie. Their repudiation, however, also re-enacts a wider community's fear and rejection of the woman—who, biologically powerful and "ungovernable," must be rendered ideologically powerless, either by being ennobled and feminized, or debased and spectacularized. Carrie, therefore, is a convenient token for the community's intense strategies of repudiation; she embodies social self-hate. She is the foreign witch woman among the innocents, and her unchallenged presence is a powerful threat to their purity (a traditional charge against witches, of course: They prey on the children).

Carrie is a "fractured fairy tale" (Winter, 29), an Ovidian tale of implacable fate and metamorphosis. It is an apocalyptic text in which cosmic psychomachia, a war between invisible and visible worlds, is rewritten as private obsession and narcissism. In a moment of sudden stress, Carrie transforms from victim innocent of knowledge (in her ignorance Carrie thinks that tampons are for applying lipstick), into the powerful Other whose ungovernable secret threatens community stability just as literally as she threatens to deconstruct the town's sense of itself. Carrie's passage to biological maturity means, most simply, that her powers do not easily lend themselves to management, either personally or socially. Neither tampon nor the coercions of ideology effectively constrain her for very long. The speed and the thoroughness of the change from virgin to Cinderella to dark destroying Mother, and the speed with which townspeople—teachers, neighbors, fellow students—rapidly align themselves against her, indicates that here, as at Salem, witchcraft is functional rather than personal.

Throughout the novel King intersperses a variety of texts—newspapers, biographies, sensationalist accounts, scientific "explanations." The effect of these is to erase the personal, to subsume Carrie's individuality in the deceptively bland and universal rhetoric of a socially (or in some cases, biologically) determined fate. The cruelty of this fate is disguised beneath theological, communitarian sanction, as happens to the hapless women in Salem, who find themselves written *in* to Mather's text as theological justification. In *Carrie*, the reader loses sight of Carrie as she is dispersed throughout a range of rhetorics and genres. Various discourses of social defense, rituals of transgressions and victimization, merge to defend the social order of convention. In effect conformity becomes the new interiority. Carrie White, always different, writes in her school notebook a short couplet: "Everybody's guessed / that baby can't be blessed / 'til she finally sees that she's like all the rest" (37).

In *Natural Symbols: Explorations in Cosmology*, Mary Douglas argues that witch beliefs flourish under certain conditions, whose structure she metaphorically calls cosmologies. Her comments are applicable to Salem and Chamberlain; to the fictionalized history of Mather and to the historicized fiction of King. In such societies,

> the body politic tends to have a clear external boundary, and a confused internal state in which envy and favouritism flourish and continually confound the proper expectations of members. So the body of the witch, normal-seeming and apparently carrying the normal human limitations, is equipped with hidden and extraordinarily malevolent powers. The loyalty of the witch, instead of being committed firmly to his group, flies out loose. He goes alone to contend with alien personifications of lust and power. The witch himself has no firm anchorage in the social structure. In appearance he is present, but only bodily; his real inner self has escaped from social restraint. (113)

As witch, in a society governed by metaphysical mappings of proscriptions and imperatives, Carrie White is a commonplace. That is, *Carrie* embodies a formula of repudiation that was ossified long before Mather reworked its conventions. As a common ground of social contention and conflict, in her, visible and invisible worlds intersect; in other words, Carrie forms the boundary between the human and its (ill-human) sense of itself. Like the clergy in this respect, who are witches of a more legal sort, Carrie assumes a role prepared for her—one that is sacrosanct, taboo, and a matter of communal ritual. Carrie, like the witch, must exist, if only as type and scapegoat of what the society fears and must repudiate. Obligingly, her community reads her—interprets and confirms her—in the role, if only to prevent themselves from occupying it. She embodies, in quite literal fashion, a social order's habitual need to establish, above all else, and authorizing all else, a sacred hierarchy of pain and victims, one made holy—and horrible—in the name and suffering authority of Jesus.

Carrie is not only the story of an isolated case of repressed telekinesis. It is also the story of a culture's ghosts, chief of which is its Calvinistic idealizations, a suppression of the body in favor of the spirit. *Carrie* is apocalypse rendered as personal metaphor, shattering not only the ill-fated individual life but also the larger town and the discourses designed to contain its extravagances. What is socially discredited is often symbolically central; thus, a culture that privileges the spirit, by inverse necessity, repudiates the body—displaces it into a rhetoric of moralizing concern over its place and functions. In *Carrie* this is reflected in the pattern of anxieties about the body, and, obliquely, about the place of women in the larger Body Politic.[22] As metaphor, the body provides a convenient site on which a culture can imagine and protect its vulnerabilities; as such the body is the object of managerial control. Women's bodies, especially, are considered both extraordinary in their dangerous appeal and remarkable in their weakness; traditionally they are the objects of social regulation, and the occasion, too, for much noble-sounding rhetoric. But this, of course, is simply discourse reworked as a kind of policing. Theologies are not dissimilar from political myth in this respect, and, as the Inquisition knew well, the body is the soul's guarantor, and control of the body is tantamount to domesticating the soul.[23]

Carrie, then, is a social cipher. Her presence highlights, and energizes, a socially authorized politics of interpretation and its powers of coercion. In the semiotic exercises of gossipy Chamberlain, she occupies the center of an interpretive storm, a "gaping, whistling hole" (41). She is an emptiness, vulnerable to the powers of society in whose interests she will be "read" and violently interpreted—first as the "frog among swans," then as society's "butt," and then, as a Dark Cinderella. Finally, as "Typhoid Mary," empowered by her telekinetic strength, she is "capable of destroying almost at will" (102). Carrie, however, is not the problem; rather, she is the victim, structured to articulate an otherwise unspeakable town dynamic of exclusion. She enables the classist and misogynist community to function—its demonstrable acts of violence expended on her deflect away from the casual and daily violences by which it defines itself. More broadly speaking, Carrie functions as a buttress and demonstration; she calls into play the metaphysics of repudiation by which certain exclusions are authorized as socially necessary, approved as they are by a presumptive "right" reading of Revelation. As a witch, then, like Martha Carrier (Starkey, 146ff.) Carrie White is both victim and expiation; transgressor and exemplary subject of the law; witch and messenger of a dark god. As a witch, Carrie inscribes a society's long memories in her own blood. She symbolizes the social order's need to repudiate at all costs that which it can neither understand nor manage, its fears of radical instability and boundarylessness—anxieties as old as Winthrop and Mather.

In her final conflict with the religiously paranoid Margaret White, Carrie offers her a present: "What you always wanted. Darkness. And whatever God lives there" (211). For theologies, no less than fantasies, are constrained by the urgent need of the human imagination, to which no scrap of usable memory, pain, or pleasure, goes wasted. Yet Carrie's unsophisticated although nonetheless astute reflections emphasize the real experience behind theological abstraction. However heretical it might be as doctrine, the thought is comforting that somewhere the All-powerful God of love has his All-horrorful equal—or as Whitman suggested, is Himself such an equal, the Square Deific. Carrie "did not know if her gift had come from the lord of light or of darkness" (98). For the community, for her mother, it didn't matter. There had long ceased to be any difference between either of the two inscrutable lords, and a community order that posed terror as the proof of the Divine could no longer understand love or the Divine except as a variety of fear. For this reason Margaret White can find no distinction to be made between Carrie's "devil-spawn, demon-power" and the "kind, vengeful hand" (55) of the deity whose portrait she keeps locked in the closet. If Carrie on occasion needs to be locked away, her power suppressed by fear and silence, so, too, does the God she fears. Ironically, then, she locks "Derrault's conception of Jonathan Edwards's famous sermon, *Sinners in the Hands of an Angry God*" in the closet with Carrie, and both languish "below a hideous blue bulb that was always lit" (54). Both need vigilance; both need to be watched. Alone and locked in the closet with the shadow of Jonathan Edwards, Carrie bears the repudiations of "Momma's angry God" (57), which are played out in the secrets and in the silences of a closet-happy society. If the apocalyptic mind gets what it imagines, Carrie becomes for her society the apocalypse uncovered, the closeted God of terror uncloseted, its love revealed as something quite awful to behold. She is one point of an unholy trinity, whose other "twin shadows" are the "crucified Jesus and Momma" (52). Carrie is the pig-bloody sacrifice, the "angel with a sword" countering the sentimentality of the "savior jesus meek and mild" (22).

"To deny King's worth . . . is to deny the society in which we live" (Magistrale, xiv). Indeed, in Carrie's possession by inscrutable forces, in her subsequent isolation and expiatory death, King's tale "enact[s] the recurrent American nightmare" (Winter, 2). She embodies, in the most literally unspeakable way, the Jeremiad—a communal self-narrative drenched with an obsessive sense of responsibility and denial. Though doctrine might be debased over time, religious metaphors remain constant, though shifting, centers of symbolic energy. There will always be a victim, sentimentally divinized even as repudiated. No wonder the cross in their home had "given Carrie endless nightmares in which the mutilated Christ chased her through dream corridors, holding a mallet and nails, begging her to take up her cross and follow Him" (39). Carrie is the new Jesus, as there will be, in time, others after her. In her final moments of agony, praying in the Congregational Church before her final destructive walk home, Carrie understands the emptiness at the center of religious practice. In her misery she becomes Jesus in the

Garden, praying to the dark: "No one was there—or if there was, He/It was cowering from her" (200). And, she wonders, why not? This "horror was as much His doing as hers" (200). Mather harbored similar suspicions, and in classic dysfunctional fashion, turned his doubts not upon God, who deserved them, but onto his fellow citizens in Salem, who did not.

Mary Douglas writes, "The reasons for any particular way of defining the sacred are embedded in the social consensus which it protects" (*Implicit Meanings*, viii-ix).[24] Carrie is important for what she suggests about the role of the demonic in a social order; that is, what sort of "social consensus" is created by means of the ritual communal gestures of cleansing and purging that gather around her? To her mother, Carrie signifies that "the devil has come home" (210). To Mr. Quillan, her presence likewise signals that "the Devil came to Chamberlain" (181). For the demonic is less object or agent than a necessary and tacitly agreed-upon civic mechanism in which Carrie exists in order to facilitate, even justify, a process of exclusion. She is the prohibition, the taboo, the ritualized effacement by which the community, however haltingly and imperfectly, comes to self-knowledge. As happened in Salem, community needs—social cleansing, role clarification, boundary vigilance—connive to isolate Carrie, first as agent of the demonic, and then, as the Demonic itself. When she attends the Prom in her deep red dress, and stands before the assembled community, she is similarly attired as Hester Prynne, who similarly is the meaning behind a communal convocation. Carrie's humiliation in and exclusion from the social fabric is a social event; the carnivalesque moment in the shower is repeated at the Prom, where the threat of change, social upheaval, is made visible and its agent effaced. Carrie intends the meaning her community needs for itself, but which it cannot read or interpret clearly. She is the ritual speech by which the society says what it cannot understand. By erasing Carrie, by placing her as the central icon at the center of a community ritual, the townspeople draw a line between her and themselves, and thus, at least temporarily, they escape the same fate.

It is in this respect, then, that the novel *Carrie* is deeply respectful, if also unaware, of its own religious roots. In the inscrutable universe of spiritual determinism, a hunger for victims seems a divine logic, and anxieties of communal annihilation and personal expiation go hand in hand. *Carrie*, then, as the tale of one chosen for this role, is a narrative of vocation and exceptionality. She is the one chosen of the gods as *Monstrum*, the ambiguous and unspeakable sign of human complicity in the responsibility for evil. Thus, the final irony: Carrie is not only witch, not only a feminized Jesus, but silenced woman and hero— etymologically, the powerful one offered to the goddess Hera. She is, then, the saving sacrifice of the people.

III

Salem's abjection of its witches establishes the crucial beginnings of an Anglo-American religious community, a "People of the Word" governed almost obsessively, however obliquely, by rituals and by texts.[25] In such a civic order, allegory is privileged meaning, and revelations are the chief currency of exchange. Accordingly, Carrie dies as expiation only to be resurrected in the symbolic order. She signifies the meaning of transcendence that gives her society its shape. She is what transcendence means, an inevitable distortion, even denial of the self, in favor of its "unselfing" and effacement. Carrie is *Monstrous* in the word's original meaning: revelatory of Divine intent, a sign revealing the order and purpose of the cosmos—at least as that order is humanly construed for social and political purposes. Stephen King, then, like Cotton Mather, could agree that the history of human pain can be read as a trace of religious iconographies. Even debased religion can be peculiarly, sometimes brilliantly revelatory, as it is here. Despite the rhetorical, even nostalgic commitment to love in the sentimental American practice of religion, transgression is religious clarification; pain is privilege and grace; expiation is justification and final triumph.

So, despite the contrivance of so much contemporary horror, the real horror of King's fiction, or of Blatty's *The Exorcist*, or, further back, of Mather's witch narrative, is the evidence these pose of how a religious society "reads" and interprets itself in terms of its metaphysics. Carrie's dark powers—arbitrary, vengeful, inscrutable—terrify the people of Chamberlain (and, vicariously, the reader?) because in them can be seen inscribed the metaphysics of contradiction and opposition against which, historically, the American private and most intimate self has been defined. The social order that makes Stephen King possible is one in which the marginal monsters speak directly to the gods in the center. Those gods continue to be supported, as Douglas notes, because they permit, even secure, a way of life and means of power. We are invested in our religious practices for the same reason Mather is; in our vigilance (hear the religious echo in the word) keeps ever secure the fluctuating boundaries between the human and ill-human, between human and the unhuman. And, as tradition teaches, the Deity, whether Blake's "Nobodaddy" or Margaret White's "Three-lobbed Eye," is the most unhuman of all—and especially so, thank you, Mr. Jonathan Edwards—when dreadfully provoked and holding us over the fire, he manifests his unconditional love. Thus, no wonder that this derivatively Calvinistic social order, badly parodied as it is in Mrs. White, keeps the threatening deity in the closets of fantasy. A society of transgression learns its way from the gods it chooses to worship; whereas that same society defines the "real" of its social order by the fantasies and horrors it feels it must repudiate.

To end where we began. Lastly, the charge of witchcraft in the Massachusetts Code represents a specific civil violation, a rending of the social fabric. Nonetheless, in important ways, "entertaining Satan" was a weaving together of the fabric, a construction of the Body Politic on the dismembered bodies of its victims. Whereas Weisman argues that "secular and ecclesiastical concerns were synthesized in the social regulation of witchcraft" (10), so, too, were less tangible concerns of the imagination. Dismembering is a remembering, after all. The social fabric continues this somewhat schizoid process of rending/mending itself through its well-oiled machineries of terror. The great Silenced Text of religious discourse continues to be written, evident most clearly in the ephemera and entertainments that are, after all, "diversions." Indeed, and diversions from what, one wonders? After all, the writer of horror fiction is, says Stephen King, an "agent of the norm" (*Danse Macabre*, 58), someone who, in King's pithy expression, "watches for the mutant."

So our horrific entertainments are the formulaic diversions by which we divert ourselves from other lies. They are, in effect, religious rituals, by which we encounter the sacred and the cultically taboo.[26] Back to a question hinted at earlier: Why *did* William Blatty find it necessary, in *The Exorcist*, to exchange the real-life young boy with a fictionalized adolescent girl? Many reasons come to mind, not all of them salutary. This is a question we may not be able to answer at the moment, except to draw a backward line to Salem. The dispossessed Regan is the Body Politic, sanitized—the little house on Prospect Street, domesticated, swept, and cleaned. Regan, demonless, domesticated as well, sounds rather like a character from a different kind of text, *Little Women*. Securely domesticated by a society's repressions, she is, of course, safe—as indeed, was Ann Putnam years later, as she confessed to the crowded church the error of her earlier witchlike ways. Conversion—of the body, of the soul—is an important civic motif, and it is, finally, about control. That is why possessed boys, in real life, become girls in fiction. It is also why King, ignorant finally of all irony, can say that *Carrie* is "largely about how women find their own channels of power, and what men fear about women and women's sexuality" (*Dance Macabre*, 170). Indeed. If Carrie is the powerfully sexual woman men fear, she has still not escaped the narrow confines of the patriarchal imagination.

Notes

1. The other two "shames" were the 1656 persecution of the Quakers and the 1721 campaign for smallpox inoculation.

2. See R. I. Moore, *The Formation of a Persecuting Society.* The connection between the articulation of the soul (theology) and the description of the *polis* (politics) thus makes itself still heard. See, for example, Sacvan Bercovitch, *The Puritan Origins of the American Self,* and Garry Wills, *Under God: Religion and American Politics.*

3. Norman Cohn traces remnants of this process in a recent review of Elaine Pagels's *Satan;* speaking of the expiatory quality of the Judeo-Christian metaphysical tradition, Cohn writes, "for all the differences between [the gospel accounts], they embody a characteristic world view, and one which has remained potent down to the present day" (18). Further, "[Pagels] has demonstrated, more fully and convincingly than has been done before, how ancient the demonizing tradition in Christianity is" (20).

4. The text of Excommunication reads as follows:

> Forasmuch as you, Mrs. Huchison [*sic*], have highly transgressed and offended and forasmuch as you have soe many ways troubled the Church with your erors and have drawen away many a poor soule and have upheld your Revelations: and forasmuch as you have made a Lye, etc. Therefore in the name of our Lord Jesus Christ and in the name of the Church I doe not only pronounce you worthy to be cast out, but I doe cast you out and in the name of Christ I doe deliver you up to Sathan that you may learne no more to blaspheme to seduce and to lye. And I doe account you from this time forth to be a Hethen and a Publican and soe to be held of all the Bretheren and Sisters of this Congregation, and of others. Therefor I command you in the name of Christ Jesus and of this Church as a Leper to withdraw your self out of the Congregation; that as formerly you have dispised and contemned the Holy Ordinances of God and turned your Backe on them, soe you may now have no part in them nor benefit by them. (Hall, *The Antinomian Controversy,* 388)

5. Winthrop to Hutchinson.

6. Richard Bushman draws a portrait of this society some years later:

> The whole society suffered from a painful confusion of identity. People were taught to work at their earthly callings and to seek wealth; but one's business had to remain subservient to religion and to function within the bounds of seventeenth-century institutions. The opportunities constantly prompted people to overstep both boundaries, thereby evoking the wrath of the powerful men who ruled society. Even relations with neighbors deteriorated as expansion multiplied the occasions for hard feelings. (15-46)

7. See *Puritanism in America: New Culture in a New World* by Larzer Ziff, *Puritan Influences in American Literature* edited by Emory Elliott; and *Saints and Revolu-*

---

tionaries: Essays on Early American History, edited by David D. Hall, John M. Murrin, and Thad W. White.

8. Mather comments on the ambiguities that had prompted his essayistic justification of the trials: "If the Evil One have obtained a permission to Appear, in the Figure of such as we have cause to think, have hitherto Abstained, even from the Appearance of Evil: It is in Truth, such an Invasion upon Mankind, as may wee Raise an Horror in us all" (101).

9. Mather shows the degree to which boundaries and borders possess him, if I may use the word: "but indeed, all the Unreformed among us, may justly be cry'd out upon, as having too much of an hand in letting of the Devils into our Borders" (95). Throughout my argument I am indebted to Peter Stallybrass and Allon White's discussion of boundaries in *The Politics and Poetics of Transgression*.

10. See Weisman, especially his introductory chapter.

11. Kai Erickson and Weisman extend Demos's observation by arguing that witchcraft fulfills a crucial social function. It is, says Weisman, a ritual by which a society oversees the "creation of social meanings" (10)—specifically the exclusionary politics encoded around social deviancy. In addition, other functions can be discerned. As D. H. Lawrence observes, America has been "the land of Thou shalt not" (5). So from the very first days of the Republic the trials served as a socialized rhythm by which a community defined the parameters of the acceptable by repudiating the unacceptable.

12. See Carol F. Karlsen, *The Devil in the Shape of a Woman: Witchcraft in Colonial New England*.

13. See Michael Clark, "Witches and Wall Street: Possession Is Nine-Tenths of the Law." Clark argues that in the witchcraft trials "authority performs the same hermeneutic function that interpretation performs for Mather. In the trials that knowledge ['right interpretation' of often contradictory evidence] was constituted not by providence, but by power, the very channels of social hierarchy through which evidence emerged" (133). In *Witch-Hunting in Seventeenth Century New England: A Documentary History, 1638-1692*, David D. Hall similarly observes that "Witch-hunting was thus a process of interpretation that began at the village level before moving to the courts" (10).

14. For a provocative discussion of the Body-as-Text see Robert Detweiler's *Breaking the Fall: Religious Readings of Contemporary Fiction*, especially "Sacred Texts/Sacred Space."

15. Demos writes, "the qualities of witchcraft are at the heart of the story. In one broad aspect they are everywhere similar: they express a tendency to 'project,' to 'scapegoat,' to extrude and expel that which individuals (or groups) define as bad. . . . Diversity is the rule in the fantasies, the generative circumstances, the contingent values, the interpersonal structures—which support and reflect any given 'system' of witchcraft belief" (13).

16. Marion Starkey likewise comments that the "possession" of Margaret Rule, in which Mather had a hand, was the "major theatrical attraction in Boston" that season (243).

17. Indeed, the popular reclamation, as national memory, of Salem's disowned and repudiated politics, provides us still a ready-made vocabulary and model for policing

---

the Body Politic—a point made pellucidly clear when Clarence Thomas, in Senate hearings, deftly recontextualized a charge of sexual harassment into a racially tinged "witchhunt"—it will be recalled that the diversion had its desired effect.

18. Further, the word itself speaks more than a little history, in its evident erasures and the slippage of discourse: Is Satan entertaining? Are we entertaining Satan? Who is at dalliance with whom? In the language of Rosemary Jackson and Terry Heller, societies strengthen themselves by "reenacting repression." That is, they channel threatening energy into sanctioned forms of deviancy that can then be safely abjected, [dis]spoken, silenced. See Rosemary Jackson, *Fantasy: The Literature of Subversion* and Terry Heller, *The Delights of Horror: An Aesthetics of the Tale of Terror.*

19. To cite one example, important thematic, social, and even literary links can be made between Elizabeth Knapp, the "'demoniac'-girl" of Groton (Demos, 111), and Regan, William Blatty's demon-girl of *The Exorcist.*

20. It was on the heels of the rejection of one novel that Doubleday published *Carrie.* Four of King's previously unpublished novels were subsequently published under the pseudonym of Richard Bachman. See Bill Thompson, "A Girl Named Carrie" (especially pages 29-34), as well as King's *Danse Macabre* (372).

21. See Harry Levin, *The Power of Blackness: Hawthorne, Poe, Melville.*

22. King is accurate in his assessment that horror American-style is constructed around cultural anxieties about the power and place of women—especially power as it is wrested back from an inscrutable God and, often, less scrutable social systems in service of that God. Nonetheless, despite Tabitha King's introduction to the text, "explaining" it, King's *Carrie* is not the book "of woman's power" that King would like it to be.

23. In *The European Witch-Craze* Hugh Trevor-Roper suggests that a debased language of religion and prescribed (unmanaged) sexuality are commonly found linked in the ritual symbologies of the witch-hunt.

24. This is even more clear in a culture that still is, in many respects, a sectarian culture, organized around the specific revelation of an Unspeakable [Unspeaking] metaphysic. Bryan Wilson makes the point that in a sectarian society "worship of God is worship of the community" (cited in Douglas, *Natural Symbols*, 115).

25. See Julia Kristeva, *Powers of Horror: An Essay on Abjection.*

26. For a discussion of New England and ritualism, see *Worlds of Wonder, Days of Judgment: Popular Religious Belief in Early New England* by David D. Hall (especially Chapter 4, pages 166-212); *Puritan Influences in American Literature*, edited by Emory Elliott; *Saints and Revolutionaries: Essays on Early American History*, edited by David D. Hall, John M. Murrin, and Thad W. White.

Works Cited

Bercovitch, Sacvan. *The Puritan Origins of the American Self.* New Haven: Yale University Press, 1975.

Bushman, Richard. "Jonathan Edwards as Great Man: Identity, Conversion, and Leadership in the Great Awakening." *Soundings* 52 (1969): 15-46.

Clark, Michael. "Witches and Wall Street: Possession Is Nine-Tenths of the Law." *Herman Melville's Billy Budd, Benito Cereno, Bartleby the Scrivener, and Other Tales*. Edited by Harold Bloom. New York: Chelsea, 1987, 127-47.

Cohn, Norman. "Le Diable au Coeur." Review of *The Origin of Satan*, by Elaine Pagels. *The New York Review of Books*, 21 September 1995, 18-20.

Demos, John. *Entertaining Satan: Witchcraft and the Culture of Early New England*. Oxford: Oxford University Press, 1982.

Detweiler, Robert. *Breaking the Fall: Religious Readings of Contemporary Fiction*. San Francisco: Harper and Row, 1987.

Douglas, Mary. *Implicit Meanings: Essays in Anthropology*. Boston: Routledge & Paul, 1975.

_____. *Natural Symbols: Explorations in Cosmology*. New York: Random House, 1970.

Elliott, Emory, ed. *Puritan Influences in American Literature*. Urbana: University of Illinois Press, 1979.

Erickson, Kai T. *Wayward Puritans: A Study in the Sociology of Deviance*. New York: Wiley, 1966.

Fiedler, Leslie. "Fantasy as Commodity and Myth." *Kingdom of Fear: The World of Stephen King*. Edited by Tim Underwood and Chuck Miller. New York: Signet, 1986, 47-52.

Hall, David D., ed *The Antinomian Controversy, 1636-1638: A Documentary History*. Boston: Northeastern University Press, 1991.

_____. *Witch-Hunting in Seventeenth Century New England: A Documentary History, 1638-1692*. Boston: Northeastern University Press, 1991.

_____. *Worlds of Wonder, Days of Judgment: Popular Religious Belief in Early New England*. New York: Knopf, 1989.

Hall, David, John M. Murrin, and Thad W. White, eds. *Saints and Revolutionaries: Essays on Early American History*. New York: Norton, 1984.

Heller, Terry. *The Delights of Horror: An Aesthetics of the Tale of Terror*. Urbana: University of Illinois Press, 1987.

Jackson, Rosemary. *Fantasy: The Literature of Subversion*. New York: Methuen, 1981.

Karlsen, Carol F. *The Devil in the Shape of a Woman: Witchcraft in Colonial New England*. New York: Random House, 1987.

King, Stephen. *Carrie*. New York: Signet, 1974.

_____. *Danse Macabre*. New York: Everest, 1981.

Kristeva, Julia. *Powers of Horror: An Essay on Abjection*. Translated by Leon S. Roudiez. New York: Columbia University Press, 1982.

Lawrence, D. H. *Studies in Classic American Literature*. New York: Viking, 1964.

Levin, Harry. *The Power of Blackness: Hawthorne, Poe, Melville*. New York: Knopf, 1964.

Magistrale, Tony, ed. *The Dark Descent: Essays Defining Stephen King's Horrorscape*. Westport, CT: Greenwood, 1992.

Mather, Cotton. *Wonders of the Invisible World*. Boston, 1693; reprint, John Russell Smith, 1862.

Moore, R. I. *The Formation of a Persecuting Society: Power and Deviance in Western Europe, 950-1250*. New York: Basil Blackwell, 1987.

Pribek, Thomas. "Witchcraft in 'Lady Eleanor's Mantle.'" *Studies in American Fiction* 15 (1987): 95-100.

Stallybrass, Peter, and Allon White. *The Politics and Poetics of Transgression*. London: Methuen, 1986.

Starkey, Marion. *The Devil in Massachusetts: A Modern Enquiry into the Salem Witch Trials*. New York: Knopf, 1949.

Stout, Harry S. *The New England Soul: Preaching and Religious Culture in Colonial New England*. New York: Oxford University Press, 1986.

Thomas, Keith. *Religion and the Decline of Magic*. New York: Scribner's, 1976.

Thompson, Bill. "A Girl Named Carrie." *Kingdom of Fear: The World of Stephen King*. Edited by Tim Underwood and Chuck Miller. New York: New American, 1986, 29-34.

Trevor-Roper, Hugh. *The European Witch-Craze of the Sixteenth and Seventeenth Centuries and Other Essays*. New York: Harper, 1969.

Weisman, Richard. *Witchcraft, Magic, and Religion in Seventeenth-Century Massachusetts*. Amherst: University of Massachusetts Press, 1984.

Wills, Garry. *Under God: Religion and American Politics*. New York: Simon and Schuster, 1990.

Winter, Douglas E. *Stephen King: The Art of Darkness*. New York: New American, 1986.

Ziff, Larzer. *Puritanism in America: New Culture in a New World*. New York: Viking, 1973.

The Prisoner, the Pen, and the Number One Fan:
Misery as a Prison Film_____

Mary Findley

> There is a justice higher than that of man. I will be judged by him.
>
> —*Misery*, 1990

While much has been written about *The Shawshank Redemption* (1994) and *The Green Mile* (1999), two prison films that stick out as anomalies in Stephen King's cinematic landscape and often garner shocked responses such as, "*That's* a King film?" or "Stephen King wrote that?" from self-professed antihorror fans, no critical analysis currently exists that posits the film *Misery* in it's rightful place: as one of King's prison movies. Although set in a semi-comfortable rural farmhouse in Colorado, a far cry from the stagnant walls of Shawshank Prison or cell block E on Death Row with the infamous green mile, *Misery*'s main character, novelist Paul Sheldon, is an innocent man unjustly sentenced to a life of solitary confinement with no one to rely on but his cruel and irrational jailer, Annie Wilkes. Like Andy Dufresne of *The Shawshank Redemption* and John Coffey of *The Green Mile*, Paul Sheldon must somehow find redemption in the face of extraordinarily cruel circumstances and seemingly insurmountable obstacles. These circumstances and obstacles, along with his inner resolve to free himself from his unjust imprisonment and his eventual personal growth as a result of this experience, place *Misery* as the first of King's prison film trilogy.

The critical analysis that does exist on what might easily be considered King's own personal nightmare, being held captive by a deranged fan hell-bent on controlling his creative power, focuses mostly on gender issues, as is evidenced by Kathleen Lant's article "The Rape of Constant Reader: Stephen King's Construction of the Female Reader and Violation of the Female Body in *Misery*," sexual symbolism, as discussed in Natalie Schroeder's article "Stephen King's *Misery*: Freudian Sexual Symbolism and the Battle of the Sexes," and the reader/writer relationship. *Misery* has even been touted as "a thinly veiled self-examination of his fans, his writing, and his genre work" by Gary Hoppenstand and Ray Browne (13). In addition, criticism has largely focused on the novel, with only Tony Magistrale's *Hollywood's Stephen King* undertaking a critical analysis of Rob Reiner's phenomenal film adaptation for which Kathy Bates won the 1990 Best Actress Oscar.

What is even more interesting, however, is the fact that nearly all of the existing criticism uses specific language that warrants a closer examination of *Misery* within the context of a prison narrative or prison film. For example, in the article "Stephen King's *Misery*: Freudian Sexual Symbolism and the Battle of the Sexes," Natalie Schroeder states, "At the beginning of *Misery*, Paul Sheldon regains consciousness to learn gradually that he is the victim of a car wreck and that he has been saved and *imprisoned* by Annie Wilkes" ("Stephen King's *Misery*," 137; emphasis in the original). In "The Rape of Constant Reader," Kathleen Margaret Lant states that Paul Sheldon is "the *prisoner* of Annie Wilkes" (94), clearly creating the idea of Paul as prisoner and Annie as his jailer. Hoppenstand and Browne contend that "King's novel chronicles Annie's continued *imprisonment* and torture of Paul as she forces him to revise his despised character, Misery, and write a new adventure for her" (14), and Magistrale states, "Without his craft, Paul Sheldon could not have survived his *sentence as a prisoner* in Annie Wilkes's haunted farmhouse" (*Hollywood's Stephen King*, 70; emphasis mine). While following their own scholarly discourse in relationship to the novel or film, one thing clearly emerges here: the language and subtext of this scholarship indicates that, perhaps, *Misery* should really be examined through a different critical lens.

Much like Andy Dufresne in *The Shawshank Redemption*, who foolishly positioned himself outside of the house of his adulterous wife and her lover who were later found murdered, and John Coffey in *The Green Mile*, who chose to cradle two dead girls and cry that he "tried to take it back" as search teams approached, Paul Sheldon also makes a critical error that sets his life in a downward spiral. His decision to drive his ill-equipped '65 Ford Mustang in the Colorado mountains during a snowstorm proves to be a fatal mistake whose implications alter the course of his life. His inability to handle the slippery snow-laden roads result in a devastating accident that sentences him to the enslavement of his physical injuries and to a life imprisoned by Annie Wilkes. The latter is his crazed number one fan who pulls him from his cold metal coffin, breathes life back into him (much like a Death Row inmate nursed back to health in order to live out his or her sentence), and takes him back to her farmhouse where, unbeknownst to him, his prison sentence begins.

From the start, Reiner visually sets up the idea that Sheldon is housed in a veritable prison. Wilkes's spare bedroom, which doubles as Sheldon's makeshift hospital room, is devoid of anything remotely comforting and homey. There are no pictures on the walls, there is no carpeting, no furniture other than an end table or two and the single hospital-like bed, no television, no radio, no computer, no color present anywhere in the room; there is nothing but the bare necessities and an inlaid shelf that, curiously enough, holds extra rolls of toilet paper and other stock items typically found in a prison cell. Aligning the audience with Sheldon's point of view, Reiner continues creating a visual prison for the audience. Pulled into Sheldon's mental state of haze and drug-induced confusion, a strange blurred image slowly pulls into focus as he wakes from a state of unconsciousness. The image, the audience realizes, is that of a shadow cast on a sterile white wall by light coming through a window; a shadow that, curiously enough, resembles a barred window, an obscure and symbolic prison looming in both the cinematic foreground and in Paul Sheldon's future. A booming voice, that of Annie Wilkes proclaiming that she is his number one fan, pulls Sheldon from his unconscious stupor and into the reality of his situation: he is bedridden, helpless, confined, and at the mercy of this total stranger who also happens to be a registered nurse. At first, he is grateful for what appears to be a sincere effort to save his life, but his vociferous gratefulness quickly turns to silent fear as he soon discovers the mental instability of his nurse who later acts as his jailer.

This concern escalates, and his true predicament, that of a prisoner sentenced to solitary confinement with only a mentally and emotionally unstable, Jekyll-and-Hyde personality to rely on, becomes extremely clear to both Sheldon and the audience when Wilkes enters Sheldon's bedroom, her face half framed in the dark shadows of the night (visually creating the Jekyll-and-Hyde dichotomy), and subjects him to a raging tirade after finishing the recently released *Misery's Child*, the last of the Misery books. Distraught, out of control, and gripped by fury because Sheldon has killed off her favorite character, Wilkes unleashes her vehemence, smashing objects around the room in a tirade before she verbally hands down his sentence, asserting her merciless control over his life. This scene is perhaps one of the most visually symbolic and important scenes in the entire film. Judge Wilkes dictates his sentence and closes the door while the innocent and stunned Paul Sheldon feels the weight of his sentence pressing down upon him. Once the door closes, the camera angle shifts to a long side-shot of Sheldon in bed. He is illuminated by moonlight drifting through the window and this time the image and the picture are clear. Shadowy bars cast by the windowpanes envelop him and illuminate his dire situation. In the next shot the audience is again aligned with Sheldon's point of view as he looks out, this time through what appears to be a barred window, as Annie's vehicle pulls out of the driveway. In contemplation over what to do next, he glances at the door. The camera angle reveals vertical slats, once again resembling prison bars, then the shot switches back to Sheldon in bed, this time framed in front of vertical bars that make up the headboard behind him. The consistent use of prison imagery here shows that he is symbolically barred in, and his desperate attempt to escape, by falling to the floor and pulling himself along by one arm, results in excruciating pain as would be the result of any prisoner's desperate and unplanned attempt at escape. As he slinks closer to the door, the audience is once again positioned with his point of view and the looming door, pinstriped wallpaper, and vertical slats on the nearby shelf further confirm the feeling of entrapment and imprisonment. As he reaches up for the doorknob, he confirms what the audience already suspects. The door is locked. The symbolic prison has clanked shut around him and he is left with only the echo of his thoughts to fulfill the long, lonely hours in his cell.

Up until this point in the film, Annie's power over Paul has been felt and alluded to, but not visibly or physically forced. Her declaration that she has not told anyone about him, however, changes the power dynamic and puts Sheldon in a precarious position. With all personal power stripped, he will now have no choice but to bend to the will of his jailer, even when it compromises his sense of personal integrity and his belief in what is right and wrong. Much like Andy Dufresne, an innocent man who previously walked the straight and narrow and is forced to keep corrupt accounting books in prison, something that clearly goes against his personal sense of integrity and truth, Sheldon, who knows his latest manuscript is a true representation of his personal truth as a writer, is forced to burn it and engage in resurrecting Misery, the character he had finally put behind him. This goes completely against his sense of personal truth, integrity, and the authentic voice of his writing, but, like Dufresne, he cannot move forward and cannot move on, until he first surrenders his will and engages his own personal suffering. A similar activity is paralleled in *The Green Mile* when John Coffey is taken from Death Row in the middle of the night and asked to heal the brain tumor of the warden's wife. Although Coffey's childish innocence makes him eager to go for a ride and causes him to delight in seeing the stars in the night sky, he is still given little choice in the matter. He is forced to use his gift, possibly to his own detriment, in order to help someone else. Sheldon, Dufresne, and Coffey all sacrifice their own needs and want to satisfy the needs and wants of someone else;

they do so, not willingly, but because they have to. Their lives depend on it.

All three of King's prison films–*The Shawshank Redemption*, *The Green Mile*, and *Misery*—share an important theme: personal redemption. All three characters must redeem or win back their freedom and come to terms with their definition of truth. Andy must find a way to manipulate the very system and people that put him in prison in order to free himself, both physically and spiritually. John Coffey must find a way, jailed and sitting on Death Row, to free himself from the constant torment, pain, and responsibility that comes with his gift to heal others, a gift that causes him great anguish because he feels and experiences the pain of others. Paul Sheldon must find a way to use his writing, the very thing that ultimately attracted Annie and caused her to imprison him, in order to free himself both physically and spiritually. It is this theme of redemption, of freeing oneself both physically and spiritually despite the mounting odds, that links these three films together as cinematic siblings. To understand *Misery*'s proper place in the King film canon, it is necessary to consider it in context with these other films.

While other interpretations of *Misery*, both the novel and the film, certainly hold merit, they tend to focus on isolated aspects, microcosms within the story, and not on the story as a whole. Lant asserts that "the true horror . . . resides in King's own view of the creative process and, primarily, in the sexual roles he imposes upon that process," with creativity being a male prerogative and readership being a female prerogative that can "usurp the creative process" and "threaten the artist's autonomy and his masculinity" ("The Rape," 90). Although her essay touches on the prison theme, its true direction is in pursuing the microcosm of male/female sexual roles, even though the article has been set up to beg the question of whether King himself is entrapped and imprisoned by his own celebrity. She states, "He is a victim of his own celebrity status. King is a household name, a contemporary figure of popular culture. . . . King can no longer attend conventions or book fairs; he is so heavily in demand that he finds himself threatened physically by the affection of his fans" ("The Rape," 90). By positing Paul Sheldon as a shadow double for King himself, and focusing on Sheldon's imprisonment as a result of his celebrity status, the theme of imprisonment enters into the forefront of her argument.

Additionally, King positions Paul Sheldon as a prisoner when discussing where the idea for the novel originated. In his book *On Writing*, he states,

> In the early 1980s, my wife and I went to London on a combined business/ pleasure trip. I fell asleep on the plane and had a dream about a popular writer (it may or may not have been me, but it sure to God wasn't James Caan) who fell into the clutches of a psychotic fan living on a farm somewhere out in the back of the beyond. The fan was a woman isolated by her growing paranoia. She kept some livestock in the barn, including her pet pig, Misery. The pig was named after the continuing main character in the writer's best-selling bodice-rippers. My dearest memory of this dream upon waking was something the woman said to the writer, who had a broken leg and was being kept *prisoner* in the back bedroom. I wrote it on an American Airlines cocktail napkin so I wouldn't forget it, then put it in my pocket. (165; emphasis in the original)

King, again, refers to Sheldon as a prisoner a little further on: "By the time I had finished that fast Brown's Hotel session, in which Paul Sheldon wakes up to find himself Annie Wilkes's *prisoner*, I thought I knew what was going to happen" (167). He also uses this opportunity to discuss the idea of redemption that, I assert, ties *Misery* thematically to *The Shawshank Redemption* and *The Green Mile*: "Paul Sheldon turned out to be a good deal more resourceful than I initially thought, and his efforts to play Scheherazade and save his life gave me a chance to say some things about the redemptive power of writing that I had long felt but never articulated" (168).

As previously mentioned, all three protagonists—Sheldon,

Dufresne, and Coffey—have gifts that are exploited by their jailers. Dufresne's gift is with accounting and bookkeeping, Coffey's gift surrounds the act of healing, and Paul's ability to write all, in one way or another, keep them alive. Coffey's gift keeps him alive in a figurative sense, maintaining his hope and belief in that which is good, alive despite being faced with daily evidence to the contrary, such as the irrational and cruel behavior displayed by Percy. Andy's and Paul's gifts, however, keep them alive in a literal sense. As long as they are both useful to their respective jailers and continue to provide them with some sense of emotional or financial fulfillment, their security remains intact. Their usefulness and their ability to prostitute their individual gifts buy them time, time to live and time to hatch an escape plan. Paul realizes quickly, however, that any attempt at physical escape is out of the question for two reasons: his body, though on the mend, is still incapacitated, and Annie, whose physical strength and bulk far outweigh Paul's, will either directly or indirectly foil any attempt he makes to escape. His plan to drug Annie with an overdose of Novril, either to kill her off or to buy him time to escape, for example, is foiled by her clumsiness at an impromptu dinner in her dining room to celebrate *Misery's Return*. His second plan, to stab her with a butcher knife hidden in his sling, is also foiled when she realizes he has been out of his bedroom-cell. As punishment for his rebellion, and to insure his physical compliance with his imprisonment, she ties him to the bed and smashes both of his ankles with a sledgehammer, an act she calls "hobbling," all the while proclaiming her love for him. The prevalence of Annie's use of violence against Paul mirrors the violence experienced or seen by both Dufresne and Coffey. Dufresne experiences violence from other inmates and also from the warden, who hands out stints in solitary confinement as a way to break Dufresne's spirit; Coffey is forever tormented by the violent behavior of his jailer, Percy, towards others on the cellblock.

The passage of time in this film, as is common with prison films, is noted by the changing of seasons that occurs outside of Paul's window.

Deep winter melts slowly into spring, spring blooms into summer. Paul, busily trying to ward off Annie's sporadic propensity toward violence, undertakes the task of bringing Misery back to life at her demand. Annie's meticulous attention to detail and insistence on perfection, however, reminds him that he cannot cheat. He cannot get his characters (or himself) out of their predicaments dishonestly. He must stay true to the story and find a way to bring Misery back from the dead. As a parallel, he soon realizes he must also stay true to the larger game that has become his life. Like Andy, he must defy his own personal integrity in order to play by the rules created and dictated by his jailer. Paul's challenge, much like Andy's, is to intellectually outsmart his jailer opponent by using the very thing she is forcing him to do (write) to defeat her in the end. Though both were innocent men when they entered into confinement, Paul and Andy have no choice but to turn to criminal activities in order to free themselves from the injustice imposed upon them. The environment in which they are forced to perform, an environment of criminal activity, is the only playing field they have.

Gaining physical strength by lifting the old Royal typewriter he is forced to write with, and gaining mental and emotional strength by figuring out a way to outsmart Annie at her own game, Sheldon quietly acquiesces to his sentence and goes along with the daily routine laid out before him. Everything is structured and repetitive: his conversations with Annie, his writing schedule, his meals (which arrive on cafeteria trays with equally divided portions), his sleep schedule, and even his bodily functions. He urinates on cue into a plastic jug while Annie waits, a further testament to the fact that, like a prisoner, he has lost any sense of privacy. Even Paul's thoughts are open for review as Annie reads each chapter of *Misery's Return*. It is through this act of writing, however, that Paul regains the strength and spiritual resolve to win back his freedom. She can control his physical activity, his schedule, his food, his work, even his bodily functions, but she cannot control his imagination. Though she believes she can control his writing, she merely dictates that it occurs. His mind, the wellspring that feeds his writing, can be played with, but never controlled. She can make him act out in defiance of whom and what he knows himself to be, but she cannot make him accept this as his personal truth. Just as Andy and Coffey are controlled and forced into actions that compromise their personal choice and integrity, their minds and their hearts, those areas wherein exists the essence of who they really are, remain indomitable. Andy commits fraud and becomes a criminal in order to secure his freedom, but not because he *is* a criminal. It is because he was *not* a criminal that he could secure his freedom and be redeemed from the rotten hand life had dealt him. Because John Coffey was not a murderer, he willingly goes to his death with the assurance that his pain will finally be over and he will be at peace in a better place. It is because Paul Sheldon was *not* the murderer Annie contended he was for killing Misery, that he could murder Wilkes with the very instrument she forced upon him, and later tell his agent, "In some way, Annie Wilkes, that whole experience helped me." Having lived through their own personal hells, having everything stripped from them, having no foreseeable way out of their cruel predicaments, Paul Sheldon, Andy Dufresne, and John Coffey all found redemption and emerged stronger than the circumstances that once imprisoned them.

The parallels between *The Shawshank Redemption* and *The Green Mile*, both of which were directed by Frank Darabont, are more obvious than any parallels that include *Misery*, but this is largely because of Darabont's creative consistency in both films. For example, both of Darabont's films are narrated and told as flashbacks. *The Shawshank Redemption* is narrated by Red, played by Morgan Freeman, and *The Green Mile* is narrated by Paul Edgecomb, played by Tom Hanks. Both films also posit the main characters as easily identifiable victims, almost childlike in their behavior at times. These characters are lovable, likeable, and seem almost sweetly innocent. The audience sides with them immediately and wants them to emerge victorious in the end. King even refers to *The Green Mile* as "the first R-rated Hallmark Hall of Fame production," and goes on to say that "for a story that is set on death row, it has a really feel good, praise-the-human-condition sentiment to it" (Magistrale, *Hollywood's Stephen King*, 13). It is this same "feel good, praise-the-human-condition sentiment" that audiences have come to expect from King's prison films and it is also what makes both *Shawshank* and *The Green Mile* stick out as anomalies on Stephen King's cinematic landscape. This sentiment of good feeling is clearly missing from *Misery* and is a key reason why it has not been looked at in the same scholarly light. Whether the audience even likes Paul Sheldon at the beginning of the film is up for debate. A successful, popular novelist disgruntled with the very writing that has brought him fame, fortune, and opportunity is a far cry from the likes of Andy Dufresne or John Coffey, making it difficult for the audience, at first, to understand or side with Sheldon. An audience can perhaps sympathize with his physical predicament and with the extent of his injuries, but his personality does not have the obvious innocence, likability, or redeeming qualities necessary to win it over. As a matter of fact, Annie Wilkes is the more likable character at the start of the film, and it isn't until her mental instability and violence position her as the antagonistic monster that the audience's allegiance begins to align with Sheldon. Even at that point, however, the audience is pulled into feeling sorry for Annie at times as "she may be viewed as an unfortunate victim of her own mental illness, as she exhibits nearly textbook symptoms of a manic depressive personality" (Magistrale, *Hollywood's Stephen King*, 65). This is not the case with Warden Norton, who forces Andy into his criminal bookkeeping activity, or Percy Wetmore, the cruel jailer in *The Green Mile*. These characters have no logical or physical excuse for their erratic and cruel behavior and the audience's disgust at their behavior is established from the start. Andy Dufresne and John Coffey are clearly victims and pawns in the hands of these monsters, and the audience wants justice. In *Misery*, the audience wonders whether, perhaps, Paul Sheldon deserves a bit of what he gets at the start. Perhaps his smugness at the very living that brought him fame and fortune will turn to humbleness when he realizes how quickly it can all be taken away.

Another reason *Misery* is overlooked as a prison film is the absence of the feel-good sentiment at the film's end. In *The Shawshank Redemption* the audience rejoices with Andy's freedom and Red's ability to join him for a blissful future at the ocean's edge. The sunny beach, the blue water, the ocean breeze all wash over the audience and cleanse any residual feelings of angst leftover from Dufresne's prison days. In *The Green Mile* John Coffey's death, though difficult and heart wrenching to watch, means that he is finally at rest, while Paul Edgecomb, the last of the green mile wardens to survive, carries part of Coffey's gift into the future, living years beyond his normal life span. Though it is possible to view Edgecomb's seeming immortality in a negative fight, he is nevertheless the bearer of Coffey's love and light into the future. At the end of *Misery*, however, there is little to rejoice about. Even though Paul Sheldon has regained his freedom and reclaimed his literary career with a novel that is not part of the Misery series, the ghost of Annie Wilkes still lingers near. This ghost, it seems, or the memory of what happened to him during his imprisonment, is not a positive influence over Paul, but a threatening cloud of doom that lingers dangerously near. The last scene in the film is a testament to Annie's haunting presence. Sheldon, peacefully sitting with his agent, starts to squirm and move forward in his chair when he believes he sees the threatening likeness of Annie Wilkes wheeling a cart to the table. Though he remains calm, a trick he mastered to survive his time in Annie's imprisonment, his body language clearly shows his discomfort, even after the apparition transforms into a harmless waitress who professes that she is his "number one fans It is a chilling reminder that Paul may still not be completely safe from Annie's grasp. Even though she is dead, her influence lingers.

Thanks in part to Frank Darabont's creative style and narrative referencing, King's film audience has come to expect a certain formulaic structure and emotional sentiment from his prison films. *Misery* does not operate within such a recognizable structure. Nonetheless, although Rob Reiner's film adaptation of Stephen King's novel *Misery* was released in 1990, four years before the release of *The Shawshank Redemption* and nine years before the release of *The Green Mile*, his film is the first of King's prison movies.

Works Cited

The Green Mile. Dir. Frank Darabont. Screenplay by Frank Darabont. Perf. Tom Hanks, Michael Clarke Duncan, and David Morse. CR Films, Castle Rock Entertainment, 1999.

Hoppenstand, Gary, and Ray Browne. "The Horror of It All: Stephen King and the Landscape of the American Nightmare." *The Gothic World of Stephen King*. Edited by Gary Hoppenstand and Ray Browne. Bowling Green, OH: The Popular Press, 1987. 1-19.

King, Stephen. *On Writing: A Memoir of the Craft*. New York: Scribner, 2000.

Lant, Kathleen Margaret. "The Rape of Constant Reader: Stephen King's Construction of the Female Reader and Violation of the Female Body in *Misery*." *Journal of Popular Culture* 30 (1997): 89-114.

Magistrale, Tony. *Hollywood's Stephen King*. New York: Palgrave Macmillan, 2003.

Misery. Dir. Rob Reiner. Screenplay by William Goldman. Perf. Kathy Bates and James Caan. Castle Rock Entertainment, Columbia Pictures, 1990.

Schroeder, Natalie. "Stephen King's *Misery*: Freudian Sexual Symbolism and the Battle of the Sexes." *Journal of Popular Culture* 30 (1990): 137-148.

The Shawshank Redemption. Dir. Frank Darabont. Screenplay by Frank Darabont. Perf. Tim Robbins, Morgan Freeman, and Bob Gunton. Castle Rock Entertainment, 1994.

RESOURCES

1947	Stephen Edwin King is born on September 21 to Donald Edwin King and Nellie Ruth Pillsbury King in Portland, Maine.
1949	Donald King leaves the family.
1950-1957	Nellie moves Stephen and his brother, David, around the Northeast and Midwest as she seeks work and family support. During this time, they live in Maine, Massachusetts, Illinois, Wisconsin, and Indiana before settling in Stratford, Connecticut, where they live for six years.
1958	The King family moves to Durham, Maine, to be near Nellie's parents.
1965	King's first published short story, "I Was a Teenage Grave Robber," appears in *Comics Review.*
1966	King begins writing *Rage* and graduates from Lisbon Falls High School. He enrolls as an English major at the University of Maine in Orono, where he writes a column for the student newspaper. During his freshman year, he also completes his first novel, *The Long Walk*, and submits it to Random House, which rejects it.
1967	King makes his first sale with "The Glass Floor," which is published by *Startling Mystery Stories.*
1970	King finishes a draft of the first *Dark Tower* novel. He graduates from the University of Maine.
1971	King marries Tabitha Spruce, who was also a student at the University of Maine, and begins teaching at Hampden Academy. He writes in the evenings and works in an industrial laundry during the summers. A daughter, Naomi, is born. *The Running Man* is rejected for publication.
1972	King begins writing *Carrie*. A son, Joseph, is born.

1973	King begins work on *'Salem's Lot*. Doubleday buys *Carrie* and then sells the paperback rights for $400,000. King quits his teaching job to write full-time. Nellie Ruth King dies in December.
1974	*Carrie* is published and becomes a paperback best seller. King travels to Colorado with Tabitha and begins work on *The Shining*.
1975	*'Salem's Lot* is published.
1976	The film adaptation of *Carrie* is released.
1977	A son, Owen, is born in February. *The Shining* is published and becomes a hardback best seller. King creates the Richard Bachman pseudonym and publishes *Rage* under it. The Kings leave for England in the fall, planning to live there for one year, but return before the new year. King begins work on *Cujo* and meets Peter Straub while in England.
1978	King begins work on *The Stand*, which is published later in the year.
1979	A made-for-television movie of *'Salem's Lot* airs. *The Dead Zone* is published, and *The Long Walk* is published under Bachman's name.
1980	*Firestarter* is published. The film adaptation of *The Shining*, directed by Stanley Kubrick, is released. King buys a home in Bangor, Maine.
1981	*Cujo* and *Danse Macabre* are published under King's name. *Roadwork* is published under Bachman's name.
1982	*Different Seasons*, a collection of novellas, is published, as is *The Gunslinger*, the first book in the *Dark Tower* series. *The Running Man* is published under Bachman's name. The film *Creepshow*, for which King writes his first original screenplay and in which he acts, is released. King starts his own publishing house, Philtrum Press, to print high-quality, limited editions of a small number of his works.
1983	*Christine* and *Pet Sematary* are published. King begins writing *The Eyes of the Dragon* for his daughter.

1984	A limited edition of *The Eyes of the Dragon* is published by Philtrum Press; *Thinner* is published under Bachman's name. King collaborates with Peter Straub to write *The Talisman*, which is published later in the year.
1985	King is revealed to be Richard Bachman in January. A collection of the four Bachman books, *The Bachman Books: Four Early Novels by Stephen King*, is published later in the year, and Bachman's "death" is announced in a press release. *Skeleton Crew* is published.
1986	*Maximum Overdrive*, King's directorial debut and an adaptation of his short story "Trucks," is released. *Stand by Me*, Rob Reiner's film adaptation of King's short story "The Body," is also released. *It* is published. King speaks at a Banned Books Week event about censorship.
1987	A mass-market and revised edition of *The Eyes of the Dragon* is published; *The Tommyknockers* and *Misery* are published along with *The Drawing of the Three*, the second *Dark Tower* novel. The film adaptation of *The Running Man* is released.
1988	The film adaptation of *Pet Sematary* is released. Concerned about King's accelerating substance-abuse problems, Tabitha stages an intervention, and King gives up alcohol and drugs. "Head Down," an essay about baseball, appears in *The New Yorker*. The film *Misery* is released.
1989	*The Dark Half* is published.
1990	An unabridged edition of *The Stand* and a collection of novellas, *Four Past Midnight,* are published.
1991	*The Waste Lands*, the third *Dark Tower* novel, and *Needful Things* are published.
1992	King forms the Rock Bottom Remainders, a rock cover band, with Barbara Kingsolver, Amy Tan, Dave Barry, Garrison Keillor, Matt Groening, Robert Fulghum, and other writers. *Gerald's Game* is published. A mentally unbalanced fan breaks into the Kings' home.

1993	*Dolores Claiborne* is published.
1994	The short story "The Man in the Black Suit" appears in *The New Yorker*. *The Shawshank Redemption*, a film adaptation of the short story "Rita Hayworth and Shawshank Redemption," is released. *Insomnia* is published, and King embarks on a cross-country motorcycle trip to promote it and independent bookstores.
1995	*Rose Madder* is published.
1996	"The Man in the Black Suit" wins the O. Henry Award. *The Green Mile* is published as a six-part serial. *Desperation* and *The Regulators* are published in a single volume, with *Desperation* attributed to Stephen King and *The Regulators* attributed to Richard Bachman.
1997	*Wizard and Glass*, the fourth of the *Dark Tower* novels, is published. *Six Stories* is published by Philtrum Press.
1998	*Bag of Bones* is published.
1999	*The Girl Who Loved Tom Gordon*, *Storm of the Century*, and *Hearts in Atlantis* are published. In June, while out for his daily walk, King is struck by a van and seriously injured. The film adaptation of *The Green Mile* is released in December.
2000	*On Writing: A Memoir of the Craft* is published. King ventures into online publishing by offering "Riding the Bullet," a short story, and segments of *The Plant*, an as-yet unfinished novel, as downloads.
2001	*Black House*, another collaboration with Peter Straub, is published, as is *Dreamcatcher*.
2002	*From a Buick Eight* and *Everything's Eventual: Fourteen Dark Tales* are published. King announces that he will retire from writing.
2003	*Wolves of the Calla*, the fifth *Dark Tower* novel, is published. King wins the National Book Foundation's Medal for Distinguished Contribution to American Letters.

2004	*The Journals of Eleanor Druse: My Investigation of the Kingdom Hospital Incident* and *Song of Susannah*, the sixth of the *Dark Tower* novels, are published in June; *The Dark Tower,* the seventh novel in the *Dark Tower* series, is published in September. A collaboration with Stewart O'Nan, *Faithful: Two Diehard Red Sox Fans Chronicle the Historic 2004 Season*, is published.
2005	*The Colorado Kid* is published.
2006	*Cell* and *Lisey's Story* are published.
2007	*Blaze* is published under Richard Bachman's name.
2008	*Duma Key* and *Just After Sunset*, a short-story collection, are published.
2009	*Under the Dome* and *Stephen King Goes to the Movies* are published. King announces that he is planning a new novel in the *Dark Tower* series, tentatively titled *The Wind Through the Keyhole*.

Long Fiction

Carrie, 1974

'Salem's Lot, 1975

The Shining, 1977

The Stand, 1978 (unabridged edition, 1990)

The Dead Zone, 1979

Firestarter, 1980

Cujo, 1981

Pet Sematary, 1983

Christine, 1983

Cycle of the Werewolf, 1983 (novella; illustrated by Berni Wrightson)

The Eyes of the Dragon, 1984

The Talisman, 1984 (with Peter Straub)

The Bachman Books: Four Early Novels by Stephen King, 1985 (includes *Rage*, *The Long Walk*, *Roadwork*, and *The Running Man*)

It, 1986

Misery, 1987

The Tommyknockers, 1987

The Dark Half, 1989

Needful Things, 1991

Gerald's Game, 1992

Dolores Claiborne, 1993

Insomnia, 1994

Rose Madder, 1995

Desperation, 1996

The Green Mile, 1996 (six-part serialized novel)

Bag of Bones, 1998

The Girl Who Loved Tom Gordon, 1999

Storm of the Century, 1999

Black House, 2001 (with Peter Straub)

Dreamcatcher, 2001

From a Buick Eight, 2002

The Journals of Eleanor Druse: My Investigation of the Kingdom Hospital Incident, 2004 (as Eleanor Druse)

The Colorado Kid, 2005

Cell, 2006

Lisey's Story, 2006

Duma Key, 2008
Under the Dome, 2009

Long Fiction (*Dark Tower* series)

The Gunslinger, 1982 (illustrated by Michael Whelan; revised 2003)
The Drawing of the Three, 1987 (illustrated by Phil Hale)
The Waste Lands, 1991 (illustrated by Ned Dameron)
Wizard and Glass, 1997 (illustrated by Dave McKean)
Wolves of the Calla, 2003 (illustrated by Bernie Wrightson)
Song of Susannah, 2004 (illustrated by Darrel Anderson)
The Dark Tower, 2004 (illustrated by Michael Whelan)

Long Fiction (as Richard Bachman)

Rage, 1977
The Long Walk, 1979
Roadwork, 1981
The Running Man, 1982
Thinner, 1984
The Regulators, 1996
Blaze, 2007

Short Fiction

Night Shift, 1978
Different Seasons, 1982
Skeleton Crew, 1985
Dark Visions, 1988 (with Dan Simmons and George R. R. Martin)
Four Past Midnight, 1990
Nightmares and Dreamscapes, 1993
Six Stories, 1997
Hearts in Atlantis, 1999
Everything's Eventual: Fourteen Dark Tales, 2002
Just After Sunset, 2008

Nonfiction

Danse Macabre, 1981
Black Magic and Music: A Novelist's Perspective on Bangor, 1983
Bare Bones: Conversations on Terror with Stephen King, 1988 (Tim Underwood and Chuck Miller, editors)
On Writing: A Memoir of the Craft, 2000

Faithful: Two Diehard Red Sox Fans Chronicle the Historic 2004 Season, 2004 (with Stewart O'Nan)
Stephen King Goes to the Movies, 2009

Screenplays
Creepshow, 1982 (with George Romero)
Cat's Eye, 1984
Silver Bullet, 1985
Maximum Overdrive, 1986
Pet Sematary, 1989
Sleepwalkers, 1992

Teleplays
The Stand, 1994
Storm of the Century, 1999
Rose Red, 2002

Children's Literature
The Girl Who Loved Tom Gordon: A Pop-Up Book, 2004 (text adaptation by Peter Abrahams, illustrated by Alan Dingman)

Edited Text
The Best American Short Stories 2007, 2007

Miscellaneous
Nightmares in the Sky, 1988

Bibliography

Badley, Linda. *Writing Horror and the Body: The Fiction of Stephen King, Clive Barker, and Anne Rice*. Westport, CT: Greenwood Press, 1996.

Beahm, George. *Stephen King: America's Best Loved Boogeyman*. Kansas City, MO: Andrews McMeel, 1998.

_____. *Stephen King from A to Z: An Encyclopedia of His Life and Work*. Kansas City, MO: Andrews McMeel, 1998.

_____. *The Stephen King Story: A Literary Profile*. 1991. Boston: Little, Brown, 1993.

Bloom, Harold, ed. *Stephen King*. Bloom's BioCritiques. Philadelphia: Chelsea House, 2002.

_____, ed. *Stephen King*. Modern Critical Views. Philadelphia: Chelsea House, 1998.

Blue, Tyson. *The Unseen King*. Mercer Island, WA: Starmont House, 1989.

Coddon, Karin, ed. *Readings on Stephen King*. San Diego, CA: Greenhaven Press, 2004.

Collings, Michael R. *The Annotated Guide to Stephen King: A Primary and Secondary Bibliography of the Works of America's Premier Horror Writer*. Mercer Island, WA: Starmont House, 1986.

_____. *The Films of Stephen King*. Mercer Island, WA: Starmont House, 1986.

_____. *The Many Facets of Stephen King*. Mercer Island, WA: Starmont House, 1985.

_____. *Scaring Us to Death: The Impact of Stephen King on Popular Culture*. 2nd ed. San Bernardino, CA: Borgo Press, 1997.

_____. *Stephen King as Richard Bachman*. Mercer Island, WA: Starmont House, 1985.

_____. *The Stephen King Concordance*. Mercer Island, WA: Starmont House, 1985.

_____. *The Stephen King Phenomenon*. Mercer Island, WA: Starmont House, 1987.

_____. *The Work of Stephen King: An Annotated Bibliography and Guide*. San Bernardino, CA: Borgo Press, 1996.

Collings, Michael R., and David Engebretson. *The Shorter Works of Stephen King*. Mercer Island, WA: Starmont House, 1985.

Davis, Jonathan P. *Stephen King's America*. Bowling Green, OH: Bowling Green State University Popular Press, 1994.

Docherty, Brian, ed. *American Horror Fiction: From Brockden Brown to Stephen King*. New York: St. Martin's Press, 1990.

Furth, Robin. *Stephen King's "The Dark Tower": The Complete Concordance*. New York: Charles Scribner's Sons, 2006.

Herron, Don, ed. *Reign of Fear: Fiction and Film of Stephen King*. Los Angeles: Underwood-Miller, 1988.

Hohne, Karen A. "The Power of the Spoken Word in the Works of Stephen King." *Journal of Popular Culture* 28 (Fall 1994): 93-103.

Hoppenstand, Gary, and Ray B. Browne, eds. *The Gothic World of Stephen King: Landscape of Nightmare*. Bowling Green, OH: Bowling Green State University Popular Press, 1987.

King, Stephen. *Bare Bones: Conversations on Terror with Stephen King*. Ed. Tim Underwood and Chuck Miller. New York: McGraw-Hill, 1988.

Lant, Kathleen Margaret, and Theresa Thompson, eds. *Imagining the Worst: Stephen King and the Representation of Women*. Westport, CT: Greenwood Press, 1998.

McAleer, Patrick. *Inside the "Dark Tower" Series: Art, Evil, and Intertextuality in the Stephen King Novels*. Jefferson, NC: McFarland, 2009.

Magistrale, Tony. *Hollywood's Stephen King*. New York: Palgrave Macmillan, 2003.

_____. *The Moral Voyages of Stephen King*. Mercer Island, WA: Starmont House, 1989.

_____. *Stephen King: The Second Decade, "Danse Macabre" to "The Dark Half."* New York: Twayne, 1992.

_____, ed. *A Casebook on "The Stand."* Mercer Island, WA: Starmont House, 1992.

_____, ed. *The Dark Descent: Essays Defining Stephen King's Horrorscape*. Westport, CT: Greenwood Press, 1992.

_____, ed. *Discovering Stephen King's "The Shining."* San Bernardino, CA: Borgo Press, 1998.

_____, ed. *The Films of Stephen King: From "Carrie" to "Secret Window."* New York: Palgrave Macmillan, 2008.

_____, ed. *Landscape of Fear: Stephen King's American Gothic*. Bowling Green, OH: Bowling Green State University Popular Press, 1988.

_____, ed. *"The Shining" Reader*. Mercer Island, WA: Starmont House, 1990.

Power, Brenda Miller, Jeffrey D. Wilhelm, and Kelly Chandler, eds. *Reading Stephen King: Issues of Censorship, Student Choice, and Popular Literature*. Urbana, IL: National Council of Teachers of English, 1997.

Reino, Joseph. *Stephen King: The First Decade, from "Carrie" to "Pet Sematary."* Boston: Twayne, 1988.

Rogak, Lisa. *Haunted Heart: The Life and Times of Stephen King*. New York: Thomas Dunne Books, 2008.

Russell, Sharon. *Revisiting Stephen King*. Westport, CT: Greenwood Press, 2002.

Schweitzer, Darrell, ed. *Discovering Stephen King*. Mercer Island, WA: Starmont House, 1985.

Spignesi, Stephen J. *The Complete Stephen King Encyclopedia: The Definitive Guide to the Works of America's Master of Horror*. Chicago: Contemporary Books, 1991.

_____. *The Essential Stephen King: The Greatest Novels, Short Stories, Movies, and Other Creations of the World's Most Popular Writer*. Franklin Lakes, NJ: New Page, 2001.

_____. *The Lost Work of Stephen King: A Guide to Unpublished Manuscripts, Story Fragments, Alternative Versions, and Oddities*. Secaucus, NJ: Birch Lane Press, 1998.

_____. *The Shape Under the Sheet: The Stephen King Encyclopedia*. Ann Arbor, MI: Popular Culture Ink, 1991.

Strengell, Heidi. *Dissecting Stephen King: From the Gothic to Literary Naturalism*. Madison: University of Wisconsin Press, 2005.

Terrell, Carroll F. *Stephen King: Man and Artist*. Orono, ME: Northern Lights, 1990.

Underwood, Tim, and Chuck Miller, eds. *Fear Itself: The Horror Fiction of Stephen King, 1976-1982*. 1982. New York: New American Library, 1985.

_____, eds. *Feast of Fear: Conversations with Stephen King*. 1989. New York: Carroll & Graf, 1992.

_____, eds. *Kingdom of Fear: The World of Stephen King*. New York: New American Library, 1986.

Van Hise, James. *Stephen King and Clive Barker: The Illustrated Masters of the Macabre*. Las Vegas: Pioneer Books, 1990.

Vincent, Bev. *The Road to the Dark Tower: Exploring Stephen King's Magnum Opus*. New York: NAL Trade, 2004.

Wiater, Stanley, Christopher Golden, and Hank Wagner. *The Stephen King Universe: A Guide to the Worlds of the King of Horror*. Los Angeles: Renaissance Books, 2001.

Winter, Douglas E. *The Art of Darkness: The Life and Fiction of the Master of the Macabre, Stephen King*. Rev. ed. New York: New American Library, 1989.

_____. *Stephen King*. Mercer Island, WA: Starmont House, 1982.

CRITICAL INSIGHTS

About the Editor

Gary Hoppenstand is Professor in the Department of English at Michigan State University. He has published thirteen books, seven scholarly reprint editions of classic novels for Signet Classics and Penguin Classics, and more than fifty scholarly articles on topics ranging from popular culture studies to literary studies and media studies. He is currently writing a book-length study titled *Popular Culture: The Basics* for Routledge. His work as editor of the periodical *Midnight Sun* has been twice nominated for the World Fantasy Award, one of the top literary awards in the United States, and his *Popular Fiction: An Anthology* (1998) won the Popular Culture Association's Ray and Pat Browne Award in the textbook/reference category for 1997. As the series editor of the six-volume *Greenwood World Encyclopedia of Popular Culture*, he was again the recipient of the Ray and Pat Browne Award for 2007 for a reference/primary source work. He is a former Area Chair, Vice President, and President of the national Popular Culture Association, and for the past seven years he has served as the editor of *The Journal of Popular Culture,* the most widely read and respected peer-reviewed scholarly journal in its field in the world. He won the top scholarly honor of the national Popular Culture Association—the Governing Board Award—in 2008 ("for his contributions to popular culture studies and the Popular Culture Association"). At Michigan State University, he has won the College of Arts & Letters 2008 Paul Varg Award for Faculty ("in recognition of outstanding teaching and scholarly achievement"), and Michigan State University's 2008 Distinguished Faculty Award ("in recognition of outstanding contributions to the intellectual development of the University").

About *The Paris Review*

The Paris Review is America's preeminent literary quarterly, dedicated to discovering and publishing the best new voices in fiction, nonfiction, and poetry. The magazine was founded in Paris in 1953 by the young American writers Peter Matthiessen and Doc Humes, and edited there and in New York for its first fifty years by George Plimpton. Over the decades, the *Review* has introduced readers to the earliest writings of Jack Kerouac, Philip Roth, T. C. Boyle, V. S. Naipaul, Ha Jin, Ann Patchett, Jay McInerney, Mona Simpson, and Edward P. Jones, and published numerous now classic works, including Roth's *Goodbye, Columbus*, Donald Barthelme's *Alice*, Jim Carroll's *Basketball Diaries*, and selections from Samuel Beckett's *Molloy* (his first publication in English). The first chapter of Jeffrey Eugenides's *The Virgin Suicides* appeared in the *Review*'s pages, as well as stories by Rick Moody, David Foster Wallace, Denis Johnson, Jim Crace, Lorrie Moore, and Jeanette Winterson.

The Paris Review's renowned Writers at Work series of interviews, whose early installments include legendary conversations with E. M. Forster, William Faulkner, and Ernest Hemingway, is one of the landmarks of world literature. The interviews received a George Polk Award and were nominated for a Pulitzer Prize. Among the more than three hundred interviewees are Robert Frost, Marianne Moore, W. H. Auden, Elizabeth Bishop, Susan Sontag, and Toni Morrison. Recent issues feature conversations with Salman Rushdie, Joan Didion, Norman Mailer, Kazuo Ishiguro, Marilynne Robinson, Umberto Eco, Annie Proulx, and Gay Talese. In November 2009, Picador published the final volume of a four-volume series of anthologies of *Paris Review* interviews. *The New York Times* called the Writers at Work series "the most remarkable and extensive interviewing project we possess."

The Paris Review is edited by Philip Gourevitch, who was named to the post in 2005, following the death of George Plimpton two years earlier. A new editorial team has published fiction by André Aciman, Colum McCann, Damon Galgut, Mohsin Hamid, Uzodinma Iweala, Gish Jen, Stephen King, James Lasdun, Padgett Powell, Richard Price, and Sam Shepard. Poetry editors Charles Simic, Meghan O'Rourke, and Dan Chiasson have selected works by John Ashbery, Kay Ryan, Billy Collins, Tomaž Šalamun, Mary Jo Bang, Sharon Olds, Charles Wright, and Mary Karr. Writing published in the magazine has been anthologized in *Best American Short Stories* (2006, 2007, and 2008), *Best American Poetry, Best Creative Non-Fiction*, the Pushcart Prize anthology, and *O. Henry Prize Stories*.

The magazine presents two annual awards. The Hadada Award for lifelong contribution to literature has recently been given to Joan Didion, Norman Mailer, Peter Matthiessen, and, in 2009, John Ashbery. The Plimpton Prize for Fiction, awarded to a debut or emerging writer brought to national attention in the pages of *The Paris Review*, was presented in 2007 to Benjamin Percy, to Jesse Ball in 2008, and to Alistair Morgan in 2009.

The Paris Review was a finalist for the 2008 and 2009 National Magazine Awards in fiction, and it won the 2007 National Magazine Award in photojournalism. The *Los Angeles Times* recently called *The Paris Review* "an American treasure with true international reach."

Since 1999 *The Paris Review* has been published by The Paris Review Foundation, Inc., a not-for-profit 501(c)(3) organization.

The Paris Review is available in digital form to libraries worldwide in selected academic databases exclusively from EBSCO Publishing. Libraries can contact EBSCO at 1-800-653-2726 for details. For more information on *The Paris Review* or to subscribe, please visit: www.theparisreview.org.

Gary Hoppenstand is Professor in the Department of English at Michigan State University. He has published thirteen books and more than fifty scholarly articles on topics ranging from popular culture studies to literary studies and media studies. He is currently the editor of *The Journal of Popular Culture*, the most widely read and respected peer-reviewed scholarly journal in its field in the world. He won the top scholarly honor of the national Popular Culture Association—the Governing Board Award—in 2008 and also received Michigan State University's 2008 Distinguished Faculty Award ("in recognition of outstanding contributions to the intellectual development of the University").

Thomas B. Frazier is Professor and Chairman of English and Modern Foreign Languages at University of the Cumberlands in Williamsburg, Kentucky.

Nathaniel Rich, an editor at *The Paris Review*, is the author of *The Mayor's Tongue*, a novel.

Amy Palko received her doctorate from the University of Sterling in 2009 and continues to teach English literature at the university. Her thesis is titled "Charting Habitus: Stephen King, the Author Protagonist and the Field of Literary Production."

Philip L. Simpson received his doctorate in American literature from Southern Illinois University in 1996. He serves as Associate Provost at the Palm Bay campus of Brevard Community College in Florida. Before that, he was Professor of Communications and Humanities at the Palm Bay campus of Brevard Community College for eight years and Department Chair of Liberal Arts for five years. He also served as President of the Popular Culture Association and Area Chair of Horror for the Association. He received the Association's Felicia Campbell Area Chair Award in 2006. He sits on the editorial board of *The Journal of Popular Culture*. His first book, *Psycho Paths: Tracking the Serial Killer Through Contemporary American Film and Fiction*, was published in 2000, and his second, *Making Murder: The Fiction of Thomas Harris*, was published in 2009. He is the author of numerous essays on film, literature, popular culture, and horror.

Dominick Grace is Associate Professor of English and Chair of the Arts and Humanities Division of Brescia University College. His research interests are eclectic; his publications range from work on Geoffrey Chaucer and William Shakespeare to work on contemporary literature and popular culture.

Matthew J. Bolton is Professor of English at Loyola School in New York City, where he also serves as Dean of Students. He received his doctor of philosophy degree in English from the Graduate Center of the City University of New York (CUNY) in 2005. His dissertation at the university was titled "Transcending the Self in Robert Browning and T. S. Eliot." Prior to attaining his Ph.D. at CUNY, he also earned a master of philosophy degree in English (2004) and a master of science degree in English education (2001). His undergraduate work was done at the State University of New York at Binghamton, where he studied English literature.

Clive Barker is an English author and film director specializing in fantasy and horror fiction. He has written many short stories and novels belonging to the horror genre, some of which have been adapted into films, most remarkably the *Hellraiser* series. His latest novels are *Absolute Midnight* (2010) and *The Scarlet Gospels* (2011).

Michael R. Collings is an author, poet, literary critic, and former Professor of Creative Writing and Literature at Pepperdine University. Known for his bibliographies of the works of Stephen King and Orson Scott Card, he also centers much of his poetry and literary critiques on the topics of science fiction and horror. He is the author of *Stephen King Is Richard Bachman* (2008), *In the Image of God: Theme, Characterization, and Landscape in the Fiction of Orson Scott Card* (1990), and *The Many Facets of Stephen King* (1985).

Douglas E. Winter is an American lawyer, critic, and writer. His practice in Washington, D.C., deals primarily with trial and appellate litigation, entertainment law, and products liability. Passionate about horror stories, he has published eleven books, including *Revelations* (1997), *Prime Evil* (1989), and *The Art of Darkness* (1984). He has also contributed to many literary and legal magazines and newspapers, such as *Harper's Bazaar*, *Gallery*, and the *Atlanta Journal-Constitution*.

Heidi Strengell is Director of the Language Center at the University of Lapland, Finland. She is the author of *Dissecting Stephen King: From the Gothic to Literary Naturalism* (2005), a popular study of Stephen King's treatment of gender and sexuality, gothic tropes, and mythological influences.

Samuel Schuman is Chancellor Emeritus at the University of Minnesota and Professor of Language and Literature at the University of North Carolina. He is the author of *Vladimir Nabokov: A Reference Guide* (1979) and several books about various colleges and universities in the United States. He is currently working on a book titled *Seeing the Light: Religious Colleges in Twentieth-Century America*.

Jonathan P. Davis is an author, freelance writer, and musician. In addition to ghostwriting a teenage horror novel, he also published his own original novel, *Life, Inc.: A Parafable* (2006). In 1994 he released *Stephen King's America*, which was authorized by Stephen King; this work examines the American themes used in King's fiction.

Tony Magistrale is Professor of English and Associate Chair of the Department of English at the University of Vermont, where he has taught for more than twenty-five years. His publications include *Hollywood's Stephen King* (2003), *Poe's Children: Connections of the Horror and Detective Genres* (1999), and *The Poe Encyclopedia* (1997).

James Egan is Professor of English at the University of Akron. He has been the associate editor of *Seventeenth-Century News* since 1975 and is actively involved in such scholarly associations as Milton Studies and Prose Studies. He has an interest in the fantasy, horror, and science-fiction genres, and he has published numerous articles and essays on the works of such authors as Ray Bradbury, Stephen King, and Joe Haldeman.

Patrick McAleer is a Ph.D. candidate at the Indiana University of Pennsylvania. He is the author of *Inside the "Dark Tower" Series: Art, Evil, and Intertextuality in the Stephen King Novels* (2009) and cochair of the Stephen King area of the annual National Popular Culture Association Conference.

Tom Newhouse is a lecturer in the English Department at State University of New York at Buffalo. His first book, *The Beat Generation and the Popular Novel in the United States, 1945-1970* (2000), is a scholarly study that explores the subgenres of the beat generation: the gay novel, the drug novel, new journalism, and the novel of identity.

Edward J. Ingebretsen is Associate Professor in the Department of English and Director of the American Studies Program at Georgetown University. His lectures focus on American cultural studies, specifically gay and lesbian studies and gothic and popular culture. He is currently working on his book *Sanctuary as Torture: Ecclesiology and the Diminishment of Human Rights*.

Mary Findley is Assistant Professor of English, Humanities, and Social Science at Vermont Technical College. She serves as chair of two positions at the Popular Culture Association: The Vampire in Literature, Culture, and Film; and Stephen King. She is currently researching and writing her forthcoming book *Stephen King: Into the Millennium*, a collection of scholarly essays on the popular horror author.

Acknowledgments

"Stephen King" by Thomas B. Frazier (updated by Gary Hoppenstand). From *Dictionary of World Biography: The 20th Century*. Copyright © 1999 by Salem Press, Inc. Reprinted by permission of Salem Press.

"The *Paris Review* Perspective" by Nathaniel Rich. Copyright © 2011 by Nathaniel Rich. Special appreciation goes to Christopher Cox, Nathaniel Rich, and David Wallace-Wells, editors at *The Paris Review*.

"Surviving the Ride" by Clive Barker. From *Kingdom of Fear: The World of Stephen King*, edited by Tim Underwood and Chuck Miller (1986), pp. 55-63. Copyright © 1986 by Underwood-Miller Publishers. Reprinted by permission of the author.

"King and the Critics" by Michael R. Collings. From *The Stephen King Phenomenon* (1987), pp. 60-81. Copyright © 1987 by Wildside Press. Reprinted by permission of Wildside Press.

"Do the Dead Sing?" by Douglas E. Winter. From *Stephen King: The Art of Darkness* (1984), pp. 1-11. Copyright © 1984 by New American Library. Reprinted by permission of the author.

"King, His World, and Its Characters" by Heidi Strengell. From *Dissecting Stephen King: From the Gothic to Literary Naturalism* (2005), pp. 7-17. Copyright © 2005 by the Board of Regents of the University of Wisconsin System. Reprinted by permission of The University of Wisconsin Press.

"Taking Stephen King Seriously: Reflections on a Decade of Best-Sellers" by Samuel Schuman. From *The Gothic World of Stephen King: Landscape of Nightmares*, edited by Gary Hoppenstand and Ray B. Browne (1987), pp. 107-114. Copyright © 1987 by the Board of Regents of the University of Wisconsin System. Reprinted by permission of The University of Wisconsin Press.

"The Struggle for Personal Morality in America" by Jonathan P. Davis. From *Stephen King's America* (1994), pp. 36-47. Copyright © 1994 by the Board of Regents of the University of Wisconsin System. Reprinted by permission of The University of Wisconsin Press.

"Toward Defining an American Gothic: Stephen King and the Romantic Tradition" by Tony Magistrale. From *Landscape of Fear: Stephen King's American Gothic* (1988), pp. 11-22. Copyright © 1988 by the Board of Regents of the University of Wisconsin System. Reprinted by permission of The University of Wisconsin Press.

"Technohorror: The Dystopian Vision of Stephen King" by James Egan. From *Extrapolation* 29, no. 2 (Summer 1988): 140-152. Copyright © 1988 by The Kent State University Press. Reprinted by permission of The Kent State University Press, Kent, OH 44242. All rights reserved.

"The Ending Is Only the Beginning: Genre and Its Influence on Climax" by Patrick McAleer. From *Inside the "Dark Tower" Series: Art, Evil, and Intertextuality in the*

Stephen King Novels (2009), pp. 27-69. Copyright © 2009 by Patrick McAleer. Reprinted by permission of McFarland & Company, Inc., Box 611, Jefferson, NC 28640. www.mcfarlandpub.com.

"A Blind Date with Disaster: Adolescent Revolt in the Fiction of Stephen King" by Tom Newhouse. From *The Gothic World of Stephen King: Landscape of Nightmares*, edited by Gary Hoppenstand and Ray B. Browne (1987), pp. 49-55. Copyright © 1987 by the Board of Regents of the University of Wisconsin System. Reprinted by permission of The University of Wisconsin Press.

"Cotton Mather and Stephen King: Writing/Righting the Body Politic" by Edward J. Ingebretsen. From *Imagining the Worst: Stephen King and the Representation of Women*, edited by Kathleen Margaret Lant and Theresa Thompson (1998), pp. 11-30. Copyright © 1998 by Greenwood Press. Reprinted by permission of Greenwood Press.

"The Prisoner, the Pen, and the Number One Fan: *Misery* as a Prison Film" by Mary Findley. From *The Films of Stephen King: From "Carrie" to "Secret Window,"* edited by Tony Magistrale (2008), pp. 91-100. Copyright © 2008 by Palgrave Macmillan Ltd. Reprinted by permission of Palgrave Macmillan Ltd.

Index

Pillsbury, Nellie Ruth. *See* King, Nellie Ruth

Podhoretz, John, 116

Poe, Edgar Allan, 24, 46, 48, 99, 145, 190-191, 195

Puritanism, 142, 192, 279

Racism, 47

Rage (King), 12, 268, 275

Rainey, Mort (*Secret Window, Secret Garden*), 63, 74

Randall Flagg. *See* Flagg, Randall

Ratliff, Larry, 109

"Reach, The" (King), 126, 129

Reed, Rex, 111

Reesman, Jeanne Campbell, 148

Reiner, Rob, 111, 306

Reino, Joseph, 55

Rogak, Lisa, 51

Roland Deschain. *See* Deschain, Roland

Rose Madder (King), 48

Rosenbaum, Mary H., 158

Russell, Sharon A., 56

Sage, Victor, 143

'Salem's Lot (King), 4, 29, 102, 115, 139, 142, 149, 181, 211-212, 272

Schroeder, Natalie, 305

Schuman, Samuel, 172

Schweitzer, Darrell, 52

Science fiction, 123, 199, 219, 252, 260

Secret Window, Secret Garden (King), 61, 66, 74

Senf, Carol, 151

Sexism, 47, 53, 150

Shakespeare, William, 44, 158

Shapiro, Susin, 109

Shattuck, Roger, 257-258, 260

Shawshank Redemption, The (film), 304, 313

Sheldon, Paul (*Misery*), 63, 304

Shining, The (King), 4, 10, 32, 103, 115, 136, 187, 191, 272; film adaptation, 11, 32

Shooter, John (*Secret Window, Secret Garden*), 63

Skeleton Crew (King), 26

Smith, Greg, 54

Smith, Johnny (*The Dead Zone*), 130, 149, 152

Spignesi, Stephen J., 49, 148

Spruce, Christopher, 125

Spruce, Tabitha. *See* King, Tabitha

Stableford, Brian, 252

Stand, The (King), 5, 92, 103, 129, 173, 195, 206-208, 232, 268, 272

Stand by Me (film), 11, 108, 111-112, 157

Stark, George (*The Dark Half*), 63, 70

Starkey, Marion, 143, 285, 300

Stella Flanders. *See* Flanders, Stella

Stern, Philip Van Doren, 138

Straub, Peter, 40, 52, 109, 130

Strengell, Heidi, 56, 219-220, 227-228, 232, 234, 241, 245, 248

Sullivan, Jack, 132

Sun Dog, The (King), 176

Talisman, The (King and Straub), 109, 129, 146

Technohorror, 138, 199, 212, 219, 261

Terrell, Carroll F., 55

Thad Beaumont. *See* Beaumont, Thad

Themes, 137, 148; adolescent revolt, 267; apocalypse, 244; childhood, 136, 138, 146, 150; journeys, 82, 129, 195, 216, 226; moral, 168, 186, 196, 203; outsiders, 149, 267, 272; redemption, 304, 309; religious, 144, 248, 293; writers and writing, 61

Thomas, Keith, 285

Thompson, Theresa, 53